What Are the Results of the Establishment of Secular Humanism? (Serial Antidisestablishmentarianism Part Four)

by

Michael J. and Mary C. Findley

Published by Findley Family Video

What Are the Results of the Establishment of Secular Humanism? (Serial Antidisestablishmentarianism Part Four)

by Michael J. and Mary C. Findley

copyright 2010 Findley Family Video Smashwords Edition

"Speaking the truth in love."

Fighting against the tidal wave of profanity, obscenity and vulgarity that assails Christian senses every day may seem hopeless but there was a time when we still fought, and frequently won. We used to fight for ourselves, too, not just our children. Now we just think, "I wish you wouldn't do that," and wonder why people spew garbage at us all day, every day, from bad language to bad philosophy to bad education to bad science. Well, perhaps it's because we let them and only think about objecting. We've been told to be tolerant, so we've become way too tolerant. We think it's being nice. But it's kind of like mental food poisoning. You can tolerate some. Maybe you'll just get a mental "tummy ache." Maybe your organs will fail one by one and you'll die horribly. But at least you were tolerant.

Remember that one vital Secular Humanist tenet is that people should focus on unity rather than being divisive. Nowhere is that philosophy more obvious than in politics. The cry of the liberals is that conservatives are divisive and that nothing can be accomplished because they won't come to the table ready to compromise for the good of the people. If there are politicians who really haven't compromised some principles to get elected they've hidden themselves well from those of us who would love to support them. No one is perfect. Everyone fails. But a candidate who deliberately says, "I have to keep silent on this, this and this because getting elected and doing some good is more important than those things" had better be really, really sure where the line should be drawn. He or she can't step backward from serious compromise.

Table of Contents

1. What Is Darwinism?

2. What Happens When Civilizations Practice Secular Humanism?

3. What Has Secular Humanism Done to the Church?

4. What Happens to Those Who Practice Secular Humanism?

5. What Can We Do About Secular Humanism?

Preface: Disestablishmentarianism

... When they knew God, they glorified him not as God, neither were thankful; but became vain in their imaginations, and their foolish heart was darkened. Professing themselves to be wise, they became fools...
Romans 1:21, 22

The most religious people on earth are those who claim not to have any religion. Dogmatic, intolerant, and bigoted, they refuse to allow anyone to so much as speak their opposition. Yet these same people demand political power and tax support. The mildest opposition, such as the mere mention of Intelligent Design (not God), has blacklisted tenured professors. Just two parents in a middle school in Texas made the national news by objecting to Gideon Bibles placed, without comment, on a table outside the school office.[1] Such people dishonestly claim that they are not religious and "religion" is a group of mythologies. The truth is that they are the ones promoting mythology. In every aspect of life they promote this mythology with unproven dogmatic assertions under the guise of "Science" vocabulary. After hijacking the word "Science," they use the courts to elevate their misuse of the term to an established religion.

Science is the study of the world around us, the use of the experimental method and the improvement of our lives through the application of technology. It is divided into various academic disciplines such as Chemistry, Physics, Mathematics and Biology. However, what the federal courts, the Academic community and the mainstream Western media mean by science is uniformitarianism. It is the cosmological foundation of the religion of Secular Humanism. "Since the fathers fell asleep, all things continue as they were from the beginning of the creation" (II Peter 3:4). This concise description of Uniformitarianism clearly shows that it is completely and entirely a religious belief in antiscientific myths.

Secular Humanists use words which have been in the English language for hundreds of years but give them "new" meanings. However, "there is no new thing under the sun" (Ecclesiastes 1:9, KJV). The words believe, faith and trust are all historic judicial terms and they also form the foundation of the true scientific method. What Secular Humanists promote as their version of the scientific method consists of preconceptions, presuppositions and assumptions. It is the opposite of an open mind.

A true open mind is founded in belief, faith and trust. The historic meaning of believe is to perceive or understand with the mind and then make an informed decision.[2] The most basic use of the word believe which the average American would understand is that of a juror in court. Which witness do you believe? Which piece of evidence is believable? A synonym would be the word credible. When we believe something or someone and then act on that belief, that is faith. The active part of belief is faith. The passive part of belief is trust. Suppose your brother says that he will drive you to the doctor. If you believe him, then you understand what he says and you make a decision to get ready. If you get in the vehicle with him, that is faith. You act on your belief. When you sit in the vehicle as he drives, that is trust, a passive reliance on what you have proven true. You trust in his driving skills. You trust in the vehicle. You trust the roads, etc. Everything we do is a combination of belief, faith or trust. By restoring their historic definitions, belief, faith and trust re-emerge as the clear language of true experimental science. These terms were deliberately segregated from science to deceive people into believing Secular Humanism.

Liberals, Secular Humanists and materialists, however, use the word "belief" as a synonym for a philosophical position, just an opinion. Faith and trust to them are metaphysical words which mean different things to different people. And this is just the tip of an enormous iceberg. Secular Humanists have redefined hundreds of words to support their religion, such as sin, judgment and anthropology. A conversation with them can be very difficult since they use historical English words but mean something entirely different.

The traditional role of religion is to place priesthood as intermediary between God and man. The traditional role of an establishment of religion places the government in that intermediary role between God and man. In the Middle Ages the Roman Catholic Church put itself between man and God, as other religions have in the past. Johann Tetzel, a "professional pardoner," sold

x

indulgences representing forgiveness for sins in Germany. Indulgences were based on the "storehouse" of good works believed to exist because of the sacrifice of Christ and the good deeds and prayers of past saints. Tetzel was said to promise that, "As soon as a coin in the coffer rings, a soul from purgatory springs."3

Selling indulgences was the final act of many which brought on the Reformation. People wouldn't have bought them if they hadn't believed the Catholic Church alone could placate God on their behalf. Martin Luther convinced the princes of Germany that they did not need to send their money to Rome because they could go to God directly. Rome sent armies to collect the money. Even Modern Roman Catholics who do not believe that their church today claims to stand between them and God have to admit that the medieval Roman Catholic Church did.

The combined power of Church and State restricted personal worship, scientific study and access to historical truth. Today Secular Humanism has done the same by removing foundational truths from education. It excludes study and discovery that contradicts uniformitarianism. It rewrites history to undermine morality and freedom of expression.

The union between the medieval Romanist church and the state came to an end in two ways. In Southern Europe during the Renaissance, art, architecture, literature, and learning opened up to all men, not just those who were part of the church and state system. The Renaissance left the power intact, however. In Northern Europe, the Reformation abolished the need for a church like

Rome through the great affirmations of the Reformation: The Scriptures are the absolute authority; Justification is by faith alone apart from works; and every believer is his own priest with direct access to God. The Reformation made a special priesthood class unnecessary because men could pray directly to God and read His Word on their own.

The medieval Roman Catholic Church kept the Scriptures almost exclusively in Latin to prevent ordinary people from studying them, forcing people to come to the priest. The priest would not only tell them what the Scriptures said, but he also mingled that with the church's interpretation. In order for ordinary people who did not know Latin to read the Bible for themselves, the Scriptures had to be translated into the language of the ordinary people. Translation work by Reformers was essential to enable ordinary men to read the Scriptures for themselves, even though it was punishable by death under the Church-State system. The Renaissance and the Reformation worked together in the development of moveable type to make printing and distribution of translations of the Scriptures easier. Renaissance scholars revived interest in studying forgotten manuscripts and making translations into the vernacular. Erasmus's Greek New Testament provided a basis for more accurate translations of the Scriptures.

The Medieval Romanist Church-State system took away freedom by forcing man to rely on and accept its teachings. The Renaissance and the Reformation restored freedom by returning art, science, and all forms of learning to ordinary people. In particular the people were able to worship God as the Scriptures taught, without Church-State control. Modern western culture, and American culture in particular, was founded on this religious freedom. American culture is more Christian than European cultures, but neither of these cultures can survive if the foundation of religious freedom is destroyed.

It is this Christian foundation of religious freedom which is the real target of Secular Humanists. These Secular Humanists have taken outrageous liberties in their unrelenting quest to replace religious freedom with their established religion of Secular Humanism, which they incorrectly call science or Natural Law. Their major tool is the US court system. Sympathetic US courts have consistently supported Secular Humanism by using every possible opportunity to replace the word religion with the ancient concept of Natural Law. However, since Natural Law has been used so many different ways, the courts had to standardize the term Natural Law. Their version of Natural Law goes back to Plato's *Republic*. Though Plato never used the phrase "natural law" in his *Republic,* translator Benjamin Jowett's notes state that, "Plato among the Greeks, like Bacon among the moderns, was the first who conceived a method of knowledge... "[4] Plato's *Republic* is at least the foundation of modern Natural Law, if not the detailed finished product. Together with Aristotle, Plato is supposed by secularists to have laid the foundation for learning and development of the Sciences. This is really is essence of Natural Law.

Jowett goes on to say that Plato provided for a means to spread his method of acquiring knowledge. "In the ideal State which is constructed by Socrates, the first care of the rulers is to be education."[4] Jowett makes it clear that Socrates meant to impart much more than mere academic knowledge, just as Natural Law means to teach more than mere Science. Socrates promoted "the conception of a higher State, in which 'no man calls anything his own,' and in which there is neither 'marrying nor giving in marriage,' and 'kings are philosophers' and 'philosophers are kings;' and there is another and higher education, intellectual as well as moral and religious, of science as well as of art, and not of youth only but of the whole of life."[4]

Many know that Plato in his *Republic* based his state on a philosopher/king. Few, however, are aware that he believed in communism and free love and that these two "natural" principles were to be foundational principles of the state.

Though the preceding condensation by Benjamin Jowett is an excellent job, as you can read for yourself, the actual words of Socrates, as quoted by Plato, are much longer and more difficult to understand. "None of them will have anything specially his or her own." "... Their legislator, having selected the men, will now select the women and give them to them [the legislator gives selected women to selected men]... they must live in common houses and meet at common meals ... they will be together ... And so they will be drawn by a necessity of their natures to have intercourse with each other..." "... Until philosophers are kings, or the kings and princes ... have the spirit and

xiv

power of philosophy, and political greatness and wisdom meet in one ... cities will never have rest from their evils."5

The philosopher/king, according to Socrates, was to lay these foundational ideas through education. Though he did not use the phrase "establishment of religion," Plato clearly advocated an established religion. It was to be put in place by a philosopher/king through education based on a state where "no man calls anything his own" and where there is neither "marrying nor giving in marriage." Though this education would begin with children, it would continue throughout a person's entire life. This is the Natural Law which the US Court system has imposed.

The US needs to disestablish its Establishment of Religion and reestablish religious freedom. In the 1800's churches which tried to break away from the Church of England were called disestablishmentarians. The people who fought against the disestablishment of those churches within the Church of England in the 1800s were called Antidisestablishmentarians. Today, the mainstream media, liberal politicians, the academic community, the liberal courts and all others who file lawsuits, blacklist, fire, refuse to hire, tax, legislate against, libel, slander and do whatever is necessary to maintain their positions of privilege and power are modern Antidisestablishmentarians.

---

1 (No author) "Parents Fuming as Texas Schools Let Gideons Provide Bibles to Students," Tuesday, May 19, 2009, *Fox News.com.* "A spokeswoman

for the school district said that a number of materials are made available to students this way, including newspapers, camp brochures and tutoring pamphlets. College and military recruitment information is available all year long. The Gideon Bibles were made available for just one day. 'We have to handle this request in the same manner as other requests to distribute non-school literature — in a view-point neutral manner,' Shana Wortham, director of communications for the district, wrote in an e-mail to *FoxNews.com*.

2 Alexander Hamilton, in an 1802 letter to James Bayard. "I have carefully examined the evidences of the Christian religion, and if I was sitting as a juror upon its authenticity I would un-hesitatingly give my verdict in its favor. I can prove its truth as clearly as any proposition ever submitted to the mind of man."

3 Philip Schaff, *History of the Christian Church,* Volume 7, "The Reformation," Charles Scribner's Sons, 1910.

4 Plato, *The Republic* (c. 360 B.C.), translated by Benjamin Jowett over a period of 30 years until his death in 1893, completed posthumously by Lewis Campbell. (Introductory material (in double quotes) and paraphrases of Plato's ideas (in single quotes) were written by Jowett.)

5 Plato, *The Republic*, Book Five Dialogue excerpts among Socrates, Adeimantus, Glaucon and Thrasymachus have been placed in parentheses within Jowett's introductory material.

Introduction

Facts are stubborn things; and whatever may be our wishes, our inclinations, or the dictates of our passion, they cannot alter the state of facts and evidence.[1]
John Adams

Sometime in the early twentieth century, Secular Humanist indoctrination convinced almost everyone in the United States that "an establishment of religion" in the first phrase of the first amendment of the United States Constitution is vague and can mean just about anything. "The state of the facts and evidence," as John Adams so eloquently put it, is the exact opposite.

Section One of this work documents what the founders meant by the phrase "an establishment of religion." The Founding Fathers made as clear a statement as the English language permitted. The Constitution of the United States is founded on English law and to a lesser extent, various European laws, especially German and Dutch. In each of these countries, an Establishment of Religion was the collection of taxes to support education, welfare and public worship. The various governments appointed the teachers, welfare workers and pastors and expected these people to support the government in turn.

The original state constitutions not only permitted, but openly encouraged establishments of religion, especially in the areas of welfare and education. The foundation of the US Constitution is the fact that federal government was to have no control whatsoever in these areas. Their concept of a separation of Church and State was the exact opposite of what the courts have rammed down our throats for the past hundred years. The church should have the right to pray and teach without any federal intervention whatsoever. Judges should have the right to post any Scriptures they want. The courts should have no authority whatsoever to comment. Removing a state judge from office for posting the Ten Commandments is not merely an Establishment of Religion. It is the Inquisition.

Section Two documents the foundations of Secular Humanism and how it grew to become America's Establishment of Religion. The words "Secular Humanism" come from various groups in the 1950's. The phrase "Secular Humanist" is found in court documents to describe this set of beliefs. Secular Humanism is as old as civilization, but the primary foundation of twenty first century Secular Humanism is Plato's *Republic*. In America, Secular Humanism can be said to have originated with Thomas Paine. Secular Humanism has specific beliefs which are written down in various manifestos. Like Christianity, Islam and Judaism, Secular Humanism has many variations. Though Secular Humanists do not like the term, the most accurate words to describe these variants are "sects" or "denominations." Like Christians, Muslims and Jews, many Secular Humanist denominations do not get along with one another.

Therefore, we have attempted to point out the beliefs which have the greatest agreement.

Section Three defines science, since Secular Humanists claim that science separates them from all other religions. Since true science is founded in the belief, faith and trust of the Bible, all of these words are defined carefully and in detail. In the Bible, belief, faith and trust are legal terms. Believe means to examine the evidence and come to a reasoned conclusion. Action taken on that belief is faith. Trust is the passive version of faith.

The Scientific Method is the biblical version of belief, faith and trust applied to the material world which God created for us. In the Bible, the Scientific Method recognizes that God is the creator, that we are required to be responsible managers of the material world God has given us, and that there is a final judgment after death which will include how well we managed the gifts God allowed us to use.

Our book concludes with Section Four, the results of having Secular Humanism as an Establishment of Religion. With the exception of America's founding documents and the ancient documents such as Plato, Plutarch and Genesis, hundreds of other quotes could easily be substituted for the quotes that appear here. There is nothing new or unique in this book. It is a combination of what used to be common knowledge in America before Secular Humanism took over and destroyed the education system and current events. If we were to start over today, we would pull different stories from the daily news. Though the individual stories would be different, the points would be the same. "There is nothing new under the sun" (Ecclesiastes

1:9). Or to state the same thing another way, the more things change, the more they stay the same.

America's Established Religion is Secular Humanism. This work is dedicated to exposing, defining and disestablishing it.

---

1 John Adams, "Argument in defence of the [English] soldiers in the Boston Massacre trial," December 1770.

2 "Alabama's Judicial Ethics Panel removed Chief Justice Roy Moore from office Thursday for defying a Federal judge's order to move a ten commandments monument from the State Supreme Court building." Friday, November 14, 2003. Posted 6:56 AM Eastern time. *CNN.com*

1. What is Darwinism?

"... To establish atheism on the ruins of Christianity [is] to deprive mankind of its best consolations and most animating hopes and to make a gloomy desert of the universe."[1]
Alexander Hamilton

The purpose of this work is not to refute evolution. It is especially not to bring up endless examples of "evidences" of evolution and to prove them false. The purpose is to unmask the religious doctrine of Secular Humanism, to break its stranglehold on America, and to dethrone it from its current status as our country's Established Religion. Antonin Scalia's opinion in the case of *Edwards v. Aguilar* makes Secular Humanism's position clear. "The United States Supreme Court has held that secular humanism is a religion. ... Belief in evolution is a central tenet of that religion."[2] Unfortunately, since secularism relies upon evolution to replace God and true science, it is necessary to deal with one of modern evolution's foundational "believers," Charles Darwin.

Darwin's teachings support secularist teaching. This teaching includes progression from primitive to advanced, barbaric to civilized, inferior to superior, everything getting better and better. Faith in the perfectibility of the biological universe is essential to acceptance of man's perfectibility.

Perfectible man doesn't need a Creator God to remind him that he will always be inferior in some measure. To be treated as a fallen sinner is intolerable. He most certainly does not need an atoning Savior. He must be able to confidently reject future judgment.

Charles Darwin said that he thought the only reason men refused to believe they were descended from some form of ape was because they were arrogant. "That man is descended from some lowly organised form, will, I regret to think, be highly distasteful to many."[3] In order to support his conclusion that such a descent did indeed occur, he resorts to a form of rationalism. "There can hardly be a doubt that we are descended from barbarians." He brings up his sighting of a party of savages on the Chilean archipelago at the southernmost tip of South America, *Tierra del Fuego*. "The reflection at once rushed into my mind - such were our ancestors."

> *"These men were absolutely naked and bedaubed with paint, their long hair was tangled, their mouths frothed with excitement, and their expression was wild, startled and distrustful. They possessed hardly any arts, and like wild animals lived on what they could catch; they had no government and were merciless to every one not of their own small tribe."*[3]

Anthropologists might be able to make many objections to these people having no "arts," government, or mercy. Darwin did not give a lifetime to their study but barely a passing glance. Yet even if we acknowledge their hopeless savagery, doing so does not make them an example of what our ancestors were like. The conclusion is drawn from no evidence, no study, and complete presupposition.

Here's the line of reasoning. Today there are men in the world who are savages, exemplified by a man whom Darwin says "delights to torture his enemies, offers up bloody sacrifices, practices infanticide without remorse, treats his wives like slaves, knows no decency and is haunted by the grossest superstitions."[3] We know that there are also men who are skilled in the arts, in government, and in showing mercy, in which category Darwin, no doubt humbly, places himself. Unfortunately for Darwin's reasoning, "savages" and civilized men can be archaeologically demonstrated to have lived side by side for centuries. If his premise had any validity why would there still be savages? Why wouldn't savages have died out by now and the entire world be filled with civilized men?

The other and even more troubling side of the coin is that these characteristics of "savagery" he has listed all exist in civilized societies as well as in "savage." Nero of Rome delighted in setting his enemies afire as torches in his gardens. Cultures of high civilization such as Sumer, the Aztecs, the Chinese, all engaged in blood sacrifices, human and animal. Infanticide was practiced to root out inferior types in exalted Greece. With a few exceptions in parts of Greece and Egypt, every civilized culture has treated its women as property, as being discardable, as being devious and untrustworthy. Granting that decency is a broad term, the Roman Emperor Caligula may serve for a "civilized" man who seems to have had none whatsoever.

When Darwin reaches the point in his list where he insists that to be savage is "to be haunted by the grossest superstitions,"[3] we begin to see where he is going with his argument. Clearly civilized men have been haunted by gross superstitions. A pantheon of debauched and deceitful gods fills the heavens of India, Central America and the Mediterranean. So it is that we unmask Darwin's claim to be a scientific observer of natural phenomena. He seriously claims that he is talking about bloodlines and heredity but he is merely attributing social behavior to physical causes without any evidence to back it up.

Since Darwin brings up *Tierra del Fuego,* it is worth pointing out that those savages were indisputably humans, not some primitive ancestor. Five of sets of remains were recently returned to Chile for burial. These "savages" were kidnapped and exhibited in Europe in the late 19th century by the "civilized" proprietor of a "human zoo." This phenomenon developed in part because of Darwin's theories and people's acceptance of social Darwinism as a natural consequence. *Der Spiegel,* a German newspaper, reported on January 13, 2010, that "The remains of five members of the Kawesqar Indian tribe, abducted by a German explorer 130 years ago for display in 'human zoos,' found their way back home to *Tierra del Fuego* on Tuesday ... Chilean filmmaker Hans Mülchi ... found evidence that the Chilean government had cooperated with Hagenbeck [the man who took the people to exhibit]."[4]

So civilized governments and explorers conspired to kidnap and display supposed savages for the entertainment of other civilized people. And Darwin thinks that people who don't believe his theories are too arrogant to accept that they are descended from lower forms. How much arrogance does it take to acknowledge that there is savagery in all of us because we are all fallen creatures and that it is a sin nature that determines behavior and not evolution? Is it not rather arrogance to despise and think of as inferior men who make a more obvious display of their rejection of the true God? Is it not outrageous to attempt to dismiss God from the picture and say that man has gotten better and better on his own, that animals are more "noble" as potential ancestors? What has nobility got to do with anything if it's all bloodlines and natural selection?

> *"He who has seen a savage in his native land will not feel much shame, if forced to acknowledge that the blood of some more humble creature flows in his veins. For my own part I would as soon be descended from that heroic little monkey...as from a savage..."*[3]

Rudyard Kipling, in the *Jungle Book* story "Kaa's Hunting," expresses a very different opinion of "that heroic little monkey," and of the responsibility of Mowgli, as a "man-cub," to be different from the "Bandar-Log." Baloo the bear warns him sternly against his new "friends" who he thinks are like him because "they walk on two feet" as he does.

> *"... the Monkey-Folk... have no law. They ... use the stolen words which they*

*overhear when they listen, and peep, and
wait up above ... They are without
leaders. They have no remembrance.
They boast and chatter and pretend that
they are a great people about to do great
affairs in the jungle, but the falling of a
nut turns their minds to laughter and all
is forgotten. We ... do not drink where the
monkeys drink; we do not go where the
monkeys go; we do not hunt where they
hunt; we do not die where they die.
...They are very many, evil, dirty,
shameless, and they desire, if they have
any fixed desire, to be noticed by the
Jungle People. But we do not notice
them..."*[5]

Kipling had no delusions about man's flawed
nature but he certainly did not believe man could
make himself better by discarding God and
declaring he shared bloodlines with this kind of
"people."

In 1971 the world was introduced to the Tasaday, a
group living in the rainforests of Mindanau in the
Philippines. At the time the small group was
presented as a stone-age tribe, subsisting nearly
naked in caves in a hunter-gatherer style and
possessing a unique language. Subsequent studies
have caused some to doubt whether these people
were "real," or a hoax manufactured for political
purposes by the Marcos government. Clearly they
were widely publicized in a day when people were
looking for unspoiled, peaceful people living in
harmony with nature against the backdrop of war
in Vietnam. Some believe their reality was falsely
discredited when political conditions turned

against Marcos and it became "necessary" to claim that everything Marcos touched was corrupt.

This tribe may have been real or a hoax. Some even believe the truth lay somewhere in between, that they were in fact "corrupted" by their contact with the outside world and their pristine culture "spoiled" by metal tools and tee shirts. What matters is that an important philosophy came out of the incident, something akin to the TV series *Star Trek's* "Prime Directive," the order not to interfere with a developing culture or species. When the BBC denounced the Tasaday as a hoax, at the close of the article was included this statement.

> "The Tasaday Hoax led many anthropologists to reconsider how they deal with indigenous tribes. It is a situation full of dilemmas. Anthropologists are often faced with situations where members of the tribe they are studying die on a regular basis from easily curable diseases. But administering medicine may be the first step toward the loss of a culture. Many tribes actually express desire to become more technological. Anthropologists usually pressure them not to do so. One Brazilian indigenous tribal chief, after hearing such a recommendation, is quoted saying, 'Do they think we like not having any clothes? It may be the way of our ancestors, but the bugs bother us...' Should tribes like these be exposed to the modern world? There are no easy answers."[6]

It seems as if "civilized" man has not changed much from Darwin's day. He prefers to stand back and stare in awe at primitive man, whether to be horrified or to be mesmerized, rather than realize primitive man is just man, not a link with a simpler species or a better culture. People used to think the Australian Aborigines or African blacks were a link in the evolutionary chain and used this to justify outrageous bigotry. Now they just believe "primitive" is better. Perhaps it is better, if these "savages" know enough to want to learn about medicines to help them live and to wear clothes to protect them. How is it civilized to deny lifesaving technology and basic comfort for the sake of preserving what the people themselves don't like and don't want to preserve? And even more reprehensible, this philosophy justifies denying people the right to hear of Christ and the Scriptures.

Our civilized modern culture has grasped this lesson very clearly and seeks to impart it to those of us who might not yet have understood it. One episode of Star Trek the Next Generation shows the "correct" handling of such a situation. Scientists had a technological "duck blind" enabling them to study a "Proto-Vulcan" race without being seen. The "cloaking" device failed and in such a way that a native man not only saw the scientists but also was critically injured. The Enterprise crew saved his life and tried to erase his memories of the incidents to avoid "contamination" The memory wipe failed and he conceived from his fragmented recollections that a god called "The Picard" (The captain of the Next Generation Enterprise is named Picard) had brought him back from the dead and needed to be worshiped. He led some of his people into a fanatical, violent cult based on this belief.

The catch was that these people had already "evolved" beyond belief in gods, according to the people studying them. The point of the episode was that this belief in a god had to be disproved, because it was based on a misunderstanding of the "fact" that miracles were only the acts of ordinary mortal beings with greater skills and technology. Once this was made clear to the Proto-Vulcans they were able to go back to their atheism with the warm glow of knowing that they could become just like the people they had been foolish enough to mistake for gods.

The message is unmistakable. The woman who leads the tribe and has already stated all the steps in the process of her people's "evolution" from primitive to civilized, cave dwelling to hut-dwelling, pagan to atheist. She is the one chosen as "advanced" enough to understand the message and she gets it right away. We get it too. Man evolves from primitive to advanced and part of being advanced is giving up the "need" for gods which must be fictitious anyway. Anyone who believes in gods is a wild-eyed, fanatic who has to shoot somebody with a bow and arrow before he can be straightened out.[7]

Charles Darwin would have been proud of this realization of his *Descent of Man*. No wonder some people objected to the title and wanted it to be called the "Ascent of Man." The Professor of Geology at Cambridge, Adam Sedgwick, a colleague of Darwin's, expressed a very different opinion of Darwin's work, however.

"Tis the crown & glory of organic science that it does thro' final cause, link material to moral; ... You [Charles Darwin] have ... done your best ... to break it. Were it possible (which thank God it is not) to break it, humanity in my mind, would suffer a damage that might brutalize it -- & sink the human race into a lower grade of degradation than any into which it has fallen since its written records tell us of its history."[8]

Sedgwick saw that the promotion of Secular Humanism's dogma that science must separate itself from God would result in man's loss of moral integrity. We must get our moral standards from God. What the professor did not understand was that while it may not be possible to truly break the link between the material and the moral, secularists since Darwin have so weakened it that humans have indeed sunk themselves into degradation. The effects can be seen in civilizations throughout the modern world as they demand the secularization of their governments and all their institutions.

---

1 *The Papers of Alexander Hamilton,* Harold C. Syrett, editor, (NY: Columbia University Press, 1979), Vol. XXI, pp. 402-404,"The Stand No. III", New York, April 7, 1798.

2 *Edwards v. Aguillard, U.S. Supreme Court,* 1987 "The United States Supreme Court has held that secular humanism is a religion. ..." Id., at E-36 (Sen. Keith) (referring to Torcaso v. Watkins, 367 U.S. 488, 495, n. 11 (1961)); 1 App. E-418 (Sen.

Keith); 2 id., at E-499 (Sen. Keith). "Belief in evolution is a central tenet of that religion." 1 id., at E-282 (Sen. Keith); id., at E-312 -- E-313 (Sen. Keith); id., at E-317 (Sen. Keith); id., at E-418 (Sen. Keith); 2 id., at E-499 (Sen. Keith).

3 Charles Darwin, *The Descent of Man,* Princeton University.

Press, Princeton NJ, 1981.4 Gerald Traufetter, *International: Zeitgeist Archive* "Europe's 'Human Zoos' -- Remains of Indigenous Abductees Back Home after 130 Years," *Der Spiegel,* 1/13/2010.

5 Rudyard Kipling, *The Jungle Book,* written 1893-1894, originally published serially.

6 *BBC online*, updated April 10, 2002.

7 Richard Manning & Hans Beimler, writers, Director: Robert Wiemer, Executive Producer: Rick Berman, created by Gene Roddenberry, "Who Watches the Watchers?" *Star Trek the Next Generation,* Season Three, Episode Four, first aired October 16, 1989.

8 Adam Sedgwick (Woodwardian Professor of Geology at Cambridge) in a Letter to Charles Darwin, November 24, 1859.

2. What Happens when Civilizations Practice Secular Humanism?

"Citizen Doctor ...ask no more. If the Republic demands sacrifices from you, without doubt you as a good patriot will be happy to make them. The Republic goes before all. The People is supreme."
... There could have been no such Revolution, if all laws, forms, and ceremonies, had not first been so monstrously abused, that the suicidal vengeance of the Revolution was to scatter them all to the winds.[1]
A Tale of Two Cities
Charles Dickens

Secular Humanism can be most accurately described as the push to take power from God and give it to man, to create an atmosphere of indifference at best or hostility at worst toward God and His worshippers. In Genesis Chapter Four Cain, son of Adam and Eve, spoke one on one to God yet managed to disregard what God directly told him what was necessary: obedience and self-control. "Why are you angry? Why is your face downcast?" God essentially told him, "I am the Creator. I know how it has to work. There is no other way." "If you do what is right, will you not be accepted? But if you do not do what is right, sin is crouching at your door; it desires to have you, but you must master it."

Cain also disregarded the value of his own brother's life. He decided somehow that if obedient Abel was out of the picture Cain's life would be better. Instead, God said that because of the murder of Abel, Cain would never be able to do what he had chosen to do before. "When you work the ground, it will no longer yield its crops for you. You will be a restless wanderer on the earth." Instead of anything remotely like repentance or even sorrow, Cain replied, "My punishment is more than I can bear. Today you are driving me from the land, and I will be hidden from your presence; I will be a restless wanderer on the earth, and whoever finds me will kill me." It is also interesting that Cain assumed God would cut him off, yet the Scriptures don't say that.

Who actually left? "So Cain went out from the LORD's presence and lived in the land of Nod, east of Eden." Some seek to dismiss God because of the "bloody bully" theory of His dealings with His people in the Old Testament. They believe the "Mark of Cain" was part of the curse, but it was actually an evidence of God's mercy. It protected Cain from being killed, rather than mark him as an evildoer. "Then the LORD put a mark on Cain so that no one who found him would kill him." God didn't curse him. Cain did that himself and made it necessary to find a new occupation. Once again, in spite of God's warning, Cain tried to take the opposite course from "becoming a wanderer." "Cain was then building a city, and he named it after his son Enoch." (Genesis 4, various, NIV.)

City-building is not in itself evil, but anything in direct defiance of God's clear statement of the facts is evil. God commanded Adam, and later Noah, to fill the earth. He also told Cain that he would be a wanderer. This city of Cain represented man trying to ignore the restless emptiness of defying God in favor of consolidating his power and his self-worship. Nimrod, builder of many cities, may have wanted the Tower of Babel to be so high that it would be a permanent rallying point, a place everyone could see and always return to. Noah, the preacher of righteousness, was almost certainly still living at this time. Nimrod had no doubt heard him say that God had told them to "Be fruitful and increase in number and fill the earth." (Genesis 9:1, NIV.) But like Eve in the Garden, having heard the clear words of God, he was still a skeptic who preferred to make his own decisions about what to believe.

Like Cain, these people under Nimrod meant to stick together after God had told them to fill the earth. Sticking together and filling the earth are not mutually compatible goals. So, in ignoring the command to fill the earth, they set themselves up as the authority. The tower may very well have been a straightforward attempt to set Nimrod up as a god. It unified the people and it gave them an illusion of power and control. Some of the seeds of future secularist thinking began to germinate here. Rabbinical scholars wrote about the callous disregard for a man falling to his death off the construction scaffolding, neglect of the weak and sick, and forbidding even women in labor from leaving the work. This was juxtaposed with grief over a broken dropped brick, since, after the building had continued forty-eight years,

34

construction materials took a year to transport from bottom to top.[2]

Examples like this from as far back as written records go demonstrate that in some form this rule by man and dismissal of God coupled with violence toward dissenters has existed since the Fall of Man. Emperor worship is an ancient form of secularism that spans the globe in historical governments. The appalling indifference to human life in ancient cultures parallels the attempt to disregard God, who made man in His image. The targeting of anyone who does not worship man, and particularly believers, for violence, is necessary because they are the enemy of secularist supremacy. Accusing Christians of being the violent ones, like Nero did when he set Rome ablaze, marginalizes them and their God most effectively.

Gradually this secularism has felt less and less of a need to cloak itself in religious trappings but the worship of man known as Secular Humanism is still a religion and it still seeks dogmatic control. Power includes political power, social control and the indoctrination of future generations to keep the worship going. Frequently the appeal is to the "common people," as was the case in the French Revolution. Governments and the established religions which draw power from them have genuinely oppressed people. These people who think they are obtaining "Liberty, Equality, and Brotherhood" end up repeating the same cycle of disdaining God and seeking to exalt self while attacking violently any who oppose that exaltation.

When the French Revolution occurred, one of the first acts of the new government of the people (besides the endless, merciless executions) was to seize and sell off the wealth of the aristocrats and their brothers-in-arms, the Established State Religion of the Roman Catholic Church, with the stated purpose of easing the poverty of the common people in France. Priests were ordered to swear loyalty to France above the Pope or be killed. After the French Revolution collapsed, a compromise allowed religion to exist again in France. Subsequent legislation closed religious schools and modern France is moving to suppress all outward religious expression. Ever since France crowned the goddess of Liberty and danced the *Carmagnole,* the world has known what secularist government will mean to the people who live under it.

France provided the model for later revolutionaries. The bloody history of people murdered by the hundreds of millions following this secularist religion to its natural conclusion includes Karl Marx, Vladimir Lenin, Joseph Stalin, Adolph Hitler, Mao Tse-Tung, Ho Chi Minh, Fidel Castro and hundreds of lesser known but equally evil men. Different places, different languages, different cultures, but the same attack on belief in God and exaltation of the "people," meaning the state, which are the few elites in charge, along with the setting up of a worship of self. The People's Republic of wherever means a totalitarian regime of absolute obedience to the state. Anyone in any of these People's Republic paradises who refuses absolute obedience to the state is kidnapped to a "reeducation" camp. The term reeducation is quite accurate.

If all men are equal, why was Lenin's body placed in a glass coffin with crowds passing by to idolize him? Why were men sentenced to ten years in prison simply because they were the first to stop clapping during a Stalin tribute at which Stalin was not even present?[3] Why do modern journalists exalt murdering dictators who pretend to have elections and then club their people down in the streets when they protest the predetermined outcome? Kim Jong Il, North Korean dictator and mass murderer, is the subject of a somewhat lighthearted *BBC* profile that depicts him as vain, heavy-drinking, obsessed with celebrities. He is pictured as altogether mysteriously fascinating, even though the article admits that "As head of North Korea's special forces for much of the 70s and 80s, he has been linked by defectors to international terrorist activities, including the 1986 bombing of a Korean Airlines jet in which 115 people died."[3] Kim Jong Il is a near perfect picture of the secularist, self-exalting destroyer of opposition and he should not fascinate anyone.

Individual modern secularists claim they are not monsters, not murderers. Unitarian minister A. Powell Davies once defined democracy as "the social and political expression of the religious principle that all men are brothers and mankind a family."[4] They point to events like the Crusades and Islamic terrorism as proof that theists uniformly are monsters and murderers. Yet the past and present secularist totalitarian regimes have routinely imprisoned, tortured and murdered opponents by the millions if they couldn't convert them to the religion of Secular Humanism.

Two far more famous (and honest) secularists provide the truth about how democracy can be a tool toward an undesirable end. "Even in fighting the proletariat the peasantry stands in need of democracy, for only a democratic system is capable of giving exact expression to its interests and of ensuring its predominance as the mass, as the majority,"[5] Vladimir Lenin said. And Karl Marx made the point even more clearly. "The rule of the bourgeois democrats, from the very first, will carry within it the seeds of its own destruction, and its subsequent displacement by the proletariat will be made considerably easier."[6] Democratic Secular Humanism emerged in the 1980's to combat, according to editor Paul Kurtz, a supposed "reappearance of dogmatic authoritarian religions; fundamentalist, literalist, and doctrinaire Christianity"[7] and a list of other religions. This brand of secularism has taken much of its game plan to attack Theism from the socialist handbook, though it claims to oppose totalitarianism. The influence of the philosophy of secularism has spread far beyond the overt totalitarian governments of today. Many governments around the world once thought to be tolerant now seek legal restrictions on non-secular behavior and expression.

Pastor David Jones and his wife Mary, who live in San Diego County in California, held a Bible study at their home. "April 10, 2009, Good Friday, a ... county employee appeared in the front yard and proceeded to take pictures." The Western Center for Law and Policy sent a demand letter to county officials detailing this disturbing event. "... She did not provide any paper work or identification ... 'Do you have a regular weekly meeting in your home?'"

This question was strange enough, but there was more to come. "'Do you sing? Do you say "amen"? Do you say, "Praise the Lord"?'" This interrogation apparently had a "legal" purpose, as incredible as it may seem. "The pastor's wife ... was then told ... she must stop holding 'religious assemblies' until she and her husband obtain a Major Use Permit."[8]

The law firm went on to explain what such a permit would involve." ... Traffic and environmental studies, compliance with parking and sidewalk regulations and costs that top tens of thousands of dollars. If they fail to pay for the MUP, ... the couple would be charged escalating fines beginning at $100, ... $1000, 'and then it will get ugly.'"[9]

Eventually this action was withdrawn after an avalanche of public protest but the county still had the option of imposing parking restrictions on the Bible study.

The U.S. Equal Employment Opportunity Commission publishes guidelines for conduct in the American workplace. "Once ...an employee objects to religious conduct ... the employer should take steps to end the conduct ..." One would suppose that they would be concerned with protecting religious freedom in the workplace but apparently equality and freedom are mutually exclusive. "... Even conduct that the employer does not regard as abusive can ... affect the conditions of employment if allowed to persist in the face of the employee's objection."[9] This "conduct" has already been shown to include keeping a Bible on one's desk or reading it while on break, wearing a pin that quotes the Pledge of Allegiance phrase "One nation under God," or objecting to special work-related events consistently occurring on Sundays.

Some protest the dismantling of religious liberty in the name of "diversity," "unity," or, in plain language, secularism. They are shocked to discover a government ready with legislation to hand over their financial powers to secular control and lawsuits if they complain. "... Bill 1098 ... singled out Catholic parishes forced them to reorganize contrary to church law and the First Amendment," Diocese Bishop William E. Lori reported. He referred to Connecticut's effort to force Catholic diocese to turn over control of their finances to the laity. "Our diocese responded in the most natural, spontaneous, and frankly, American, of ways."[10]

"We alerted our membership ... we encouraged them to exercise their free speech by contacting their elected representatives; and we organized a rally at the State Capitol." Their pro-test effort resulted in a lawsuit being filed trying to force the Diocese to register as a lobbyist. "How can this possibly be called lobbying?"[10] In the government's mind, an attempt to control private sector finances is a natural extension of its power. And it must fight to suppress any opposition by that private entity with all the power at its disposal. Accusing a church of lobbying is just another form of secularism's old tactic of redefining words for its own purpose. The state must find ways to control everyone's money.

The greatest tool used by Plato's guardians in Western societies to achieve the Secular Humanist ideal was debt. Unscrupulous politicians use debt to buy votes and every favor creates obligations, debts monetary and moral. Any kind of sinful indulgence is available on credit. And when the individual is in debt, he must spend his time doing nothing except paying off this debt. He has no time to serve God, help his neighbor or take care of his family. He certainly has no time for ministry.

Zoning laws make housing unaffordable near a job. To travel to a job from affordable housing requires enormous additional transportation debt. Time spent working, on education, and in traveling back and forth to work increases food and clothing costs. Government "help" usually means more debt. This is not just "part of life" but a well thought-out secularist agenda to enslave Americans. Finally, when all else fails, the guardians add oppressive taxation. As Thomas Jefferson warned:

> *"I believe that banking institutions are more dangerous to our liberties than standing armies. ... First by inflation, then by deflation, the banks and corporations that will grow ... will deprive the people of all property until their children wake up homeless on the continent their fathers conquered."*[11]

Since Secular Humanists want people enslaved to them, and not enough people are willing to put themselves into this kind of debt slavery, secularists must force them into debt. Jobs are unobtainable without an education. The education costs more than the job is worth. The education neither adequately prepares for the job or for life. It simply increases debt. Education is also the tool secularists use to indoctrinate into Secular Humanism. Education in modern industrialized countries, including the United States of America, exists to indoctrinate, not to teach information. The major goals of education to a secularist are, as Plato wrote in his *Republic*, socialization (getting along with other secularists), isolating students (from traditional values and those who believe those values) and self-indulgence in Secular Humanist values. Lies are not only acceptable, but encouraged, if they help you get what you want. The ultimate goal is a happy group of slaves controlled by elites under the guise of equality.

The secularist ideal of education is not to educate at all. It is simply to build loyal citizens of the state. But in order to do that, secularists redefined education. Muriel Sparks, British novelist and poet, said, "... Education is a leading out of what is already there in the pupil's soul. ... Putting in of something that is not there ... is not what I call education, I call it intrusion."[12] Since what is naturally in the soul of man is his sin nature, secularist education will produce people content with ignoring God, worshiping self, and exalting reason just like their educators do. America, however, is not as effective at this kind of education yet as some other countries.

German laws declared homeschooling illegal under the Nazis and those laws have never changed. A fifteen-year-old girl who had fallen behind in some classes and was being tutored at home. "Local Youth Welfare Office arrived at the family home with about 15 uniformed police officers ...They had in hand a court order allowing them to take her into custody, 'if necessary by force.'" She was taken "to a psychiatric ward after a social worker and judge determined she had a 'school phobia.'" Other families reported "fines equal to thousands of dollars, frozen bank accounts ... threat of the sale of the family home."[13]

"The minister of education does not share your attitudes toward so-called homeschooling," says an official letter. "... You complain about the forced school escort of primary school children ..." Police have been sent to non-compliant homes to take children to public school. "... In order to avoid this ...the education authority is in conversation with the affected family ... to ... bring the religious convictions of the family into line with the unalterable school attendance requirement."[13]

The German government "has a legitimate interest in countering the rise of parallel societies that are based on religion," explained Wolfgang Drautz, consul general for the Federal Republic of Germany. "... School teaches not only knowledge but also social conduct ... and helps students to become responsible citizens." Lutz Gorgens, German consul general for the southeast U.S., further said, "For reasons deeply rooted in ... our belief that only schools ... ensure the desired level of excellent education, we (Germany) go a little bit beyond that path which other countries have chosen."[13]

"When an opponent declares, 'I will not come over to your side, and you will not get me on your side,' I calmly say, 'Your child belongs to me already.'"[13] That "deeply rooted history" goes all the way back to the words of Adolph Hitler himself. "A people lives forever. What are you? You will pass on. Your descendants however now stand in the new camp. In a short time they will know nothing else but this new community."[14]

In England, Members of Parliament have asked why "a government inquiry into home education ... calls for tougher rules on parents who teach their children at home. ... Former education director Graham Badman recommended that all home educators register with their local authority." This recommendation also "called for parents to be asked for a 12-month plan detailing what they would be teaching their children... Parents who [homeschool] say they have been stigmatised as more likely to be child abusers."[15] That would explain why they are "known" to social services.

Badman responded that,"...We should know that the risk factor is proportionately double. ... the percentage of home-educated children who are not in employment, education or training is higher than in the national population." Diana Johnson, the schools minister, was asked by MPs "whether the review had focused too much on the potential dangers of home education." The response from Johnson was an insistence that "a lot of the recommendations are about creating a positive relationship ... We don't know the number of children, we don't know their educational outcomes."[15] If they don't know the number of children or the "outcomes," how do they arrive at these doubled risk factors and higher unemployment percentages?

Fiona Nicholson, representing the support group Education Otherwise, has said that a registration scheme would "completely shift the balance of power. The state is coming into family life and trying to regulate it. It is an extraordinary invasion of the family."[15]

Jacob G. Hornberger, former Texas attorney and law and economics professor, visited Cuba and observed government functions, schools and ordinary people. His observations there should surprise no one, but he draws a comparison with our own country that should give us pause.

> ... Cubans on the street ... despise (and quietly ridicule) the socialist economic system under which they suffer. But significantly, Cubans fully understand that such government programs as public schooling and national health care (and occupational licensure and economic regulations) are socialist programs.
>
> Contrast this with the American people. Expressing outrage over the suggestion that children are the property of the state, Americans honestly believe that public schooling is a feature of free enterprise or capitalism. They block out of their minds that through public schooling, children are effectively made the property of the state right here at home.[16]

Well, that's not America, the response might be. And yet a work of fiction written in 1962 takes note of the philosophy of education already in place in America. " ... She discovered that I was literate and looked at me with more than faint distaste." Harper Lee's *To Kill a Mockingbird* details Scout's [Jean Louise Finch] first day at school. "Miss Caroline told me to tell my father not to teach me any more, it would interfere with my reading." In spite of Scout's protests that her father couldn't possibly have taught her how to read, the teacher is adamant. "'It's best to begin reading with a fresh mind. You tell him I'll take over from here and try to undo the damage.'" Miss Caroline wishes to nip any thought of parent-educated children in the bud. "'Ma'am?' 'Your father does not know how to teach.' I mumbled that I was sorry and retired meditating upon my crime."[17]

In case this example is dismissed as a work of fiction, and from the sixties, today any casual internet search turns up hundreds of articles encouraging parental involvement in children's public school education. "Parental involvement is a combination of commitment and active participation on the part of the parent to the school and to the student."[18] This sounds like a complete reversal from the attitude of the teacher in Jean Louise Finch's school, but a perusal of similar articles leads to puzzlement about exactly how a parent is to participate.

"Parents feel unwelcomed at school, lack knowledge and education, and may not feel that education is important."[18] This statement implies that a majority of parents are going to be inferior to the teacher because they are ignorant and probably uneducated. "... Encouraging the student, being sympathetic, reassuring, and understanding,"[18] sounds like good advice to parents but it may just mean to encourage the student to accept whatever secularist indoctrination occurs without questioning. "Another source of embarrassment is memories of the parent's failure in school."[18] If he/she won't participate, the parent probably has bad memories about his own schooling. This reinforces the parent's inferiority. "Ultimate responsibility for creating harmony between the school and the home rests with the principal."[18] In most people's minds the principal is a disciplinarian or a liaison with the state, not between the parents and the teacher. Is this intended to intimidate or distance the parents? Or does it just turn the principal into a PR specialist whose job is to help everyone get along?

On the subject of communication, one theme seems to recur with alarming frequency. Parents should participate when the schools "sponsor a parent/student fund raising."[18] As parents of public school students, the authors attended "meet the teachers nights" and PTA meetings but discovered they were both merely pushes for more fundraising. "Alumni events have been shown to be an excellent way to improve parent/community involvement and a way to raise needed money."[18] Considering the crushing weight of taxes already collected from parents for public education, leading to the inability to participate in school activities due to working to pay those taxes, this constant push for more money is clearly another tactic to cripple with more obligations, otherwise known as debt.

"Many parents are more than willing to share their knowledge of occupations, foreign travel, special skills and hobbies."[18] Parents may be qualified to "share" in areas educators call "enrichment," which means kids don't really have to pay attention to it or are free to treat it as entertainment. Having parents provide "enrichment" learning actually breeds a degree of contempt for the parents because they are not presenting "real" knowledge like the teacher is. Meanwhile the parent's active participation is seen as support for the whole education system and its secularist indoctrination. Parents who think they are going to prevent this indoctrination by getting involved are deceiving themselves.

Thomas A. Boweden reports on a decision by the court system which defines how secularist educators look at parents. " ... Los Angeles County court ... declared homeschooling illegal in California ... Justice H. Walter Croskey's Feb. 28 decree ... ordered the parents of 'Rachel L.' to ... get a 'legal education'."

Bowden rightly points out that this is nothing less than a demand that parents surrender their children to the state or be treated as "outlaws." "California legislators ... feared ... social disorder ... from 'allowing every person to make his own standards on matters of conduct in which society as a whole has important interests'."[19] It is outrageous to contemplate that legislators believe the State has an "interest" in our children. Bowden's nutrition analogy may be more appropriate than he realizes, considering that the federal School Lunch Program is a welfare program for schools.

> "... Education, like nutrition, should be recognized as the exclusive domain of a child's parents ... the fact that some parents may serve better food than others does not permit government to seize control of nutrition, outlaw home-cooked meals, and order all children to report for daily force-feeding at government-licensed cafeterias."[19]

Bowden tells us what we should already know. The whole education system is tied into the economic survival of Secular Humanism's control of the state and the state's control of the people depends on controlling the education. "... Apologists for government education--teachers' unions, educational bureaucrats, and politicians ... financial survival depends on a policy that treats children as, in effect, state property--but only rarely is the undiluted collectivism of that policy trumpeted so publicly."[19] Bowden wants to know if we are going to stand for this kind of government abuse of power. "... Are parents mere drudges whose social duty is to feed and house their spawn between mandatory indoctrination sessions at government-approved schools? Or are they sovereign individuals whose right to guide their children's development the state may not infringe?"[19] Secularists sincerely hope you don't come to understand this and interfere with their plan.

"Institutions and associations ... exist only with the permission of the state and to exist lawfully, they must abide the dictates or norms of the state,"[20] lamented Cardinal George Pell. He insisted that "... Believers should not be treated by government and the courts as a tolerated and divisive minority whose rights must always yield to the minority secular agenda..."[20] The Cardinal may believe that Christians are in the majority, but an examination of the "beliefs" of modern-day professors to this majority position reveals a pathetic path of appeasement, compromise and toleration. It may be worthwhile to ask whether Christianity has not brought upon itself the state the Cardinal describes.

[Author's Note: Readers wishing to know more about the inroads Secular Humanism has made on America's culture and education should read Allan Bloom's excellent book, *The Closing of the American Mind,* copyright 1987 by the author, Touchstone edition by Simon and Schuster, New York, NY, 1988.]

---

1 Charles Dickens, *A Tale of Two Cities,* 1859.

2 *Greek Apocalypse of Baruch* iii. English translations were published from the Slavonic by W. R. Morfill (Apocrpyha Anecdota II, ed. M. R. James [T&S 5.1] Cambridge: CUP, 1987. Pp. 95-102) and from the Slavonic and Greek by H. M. Hughes (APOT 2. Pp. 533-41). The pseudepigraphon was composed in the beginning of the second century A.D., but it is difficult to discover whether it was written in Greek, Hebrew, or Aramaic. (Background note from Charlesworth, James H. The Pseudepigrapha and Modern Research: with a Supplement. SBLSCS 7. Chico, Ca.: Scholars Press, 1981.)M. R. James's publication of the Greek text, until then entirely unknown, in "Texts and Studies: Contributions to Biblical and Patristic Literature," edited by J. Armitage Robinson, v., No. i., pp. 84-94, Cambridge, 1897.

3 Mike Bates,"Aleksandr Solzhenitsyn: The Power of One," *The National Ledger, an Eclectic Mix,* August 7, 2008. The article quotes from Aleksandr Solzhenitsyn's *The Gulag Archipelago,* Volume 1:

> *"Aware of all the falsity and all the impossibility of the situation, he still kept on applauding! Nine minutes! Ten! In*

anguish he watched the secretary of the District Party Committee, but the latter dared not stop. Insanity! To the last man! With make-believe enthusiasm on their faces, looking at each other with faint hope, the district leaders were just going to go on and on applauding till they fell where they stood, till they were carried out of the hall on stretchers! And even then those who were left would not falter. . . . Then, after eleven minutes, the director of the paper factory assumed a businesslike expression and sat down in his seat. And, oh, a miracle took place! Where had the universal, uninhibited, indescribable enthusiasm gone? To a man, everyone else stopped dead and sat down. They had been saved! The squirrel had been smart enough to jump off his revolving wheel. That, however, was how they discovered who the independent people were. And that was how they went about eliminating them. That same night the factory director was arrested. They easily pasted ten years on him on the pretext of something quite different. But after he had signed Form 206, the final document of the interrogation, his interrogator reminded him: "Don't ever be the first to stop applauding!"

Bates' article goes on to report on how Solzhenitsyn came to America and found that he had not entirely escaped secular persecution and cruelty.

The author then lived in Vermont for almost 20 years. The Solzhenitsyn family learned that liberals here have their own forms of political exile. In 2004, one of Solzhenitsyn's sons told the New York Times of what happened to him and his brothers in a private school the day after Ronald Reagan was elected president.

The school placed its flag at half-staff and held an assembly. There the headmaster lamented "what America would become once the dark night of fascism descended under the B-movie actor." Asking the student body if it concurred, only three boys expressed dissent, the sons of Solzhenitsyn. On that November day, they were sent outside without coats for an hour to reflect on the error of their ways.

3 "Asia/Pacific Profile: Kim Jong Il," *BBC news online*, page last updated at 11:14 GMT, Friday, 16 January 2009.

4 A. Powell Davies, *America's Real Religion*, Beacon Press, Boston, MA, 1965.

5 Vladimir Ilyich Lenin, "Will the Sweep of the Democratic Revolution be Diminished if the Bourgeoisie Recoils from it?" *Two Tactics of Social-Democracy in the Democratic Revolution*, 1905. Written June-July 1905, first published as a pamphlet in Geneva, July 1905, translated by Abraham Fineburg and Julius Katzer, published in Lenin's Collected Works, Volume 9, 1962, Moscow. Taken from Marxist Internet archive.

6 Karl Marx, "Address of the Central Committee to the Communist League," written with Friedrich Engles, London, 1850.

7 Paul Kurtz, Editor, *A Secular Humanist Declaration,* issued in 1980 by The Council for Democratic and Secular Humanism (now the Council for Secular Humanism). Published in *Free Inquiry Magazine.*

8 Drew Zahn, "Pastor waits for final word in Bible study citation: Couple ordered to get permit to host friends not out of woods yet." *WorldNetDaily* Posted: June 01, 2009 10:07 pm Eastern.

9 "Disparate Treatment Based on Religion," *Best Practices for Eradicating Religious Discrimination in the Workplace,* The U.S. Equal Employment Opportunity Commission, last modified on July 23, 2008.

10 Drew Zahn, "State moves to restrict Catholics in politics. Official contends church must register as 'lobbyist' to speak out." *Faith Under Fire,* Posted: June 01, 2009 9:30 pm Eastern, *World Net Daily.*

11 Thomas Jefferson, Letter to the Secretary of the Treasury, Albert Gallatin, 1802.

12 Muriel Sparks, *The Prime of Miss Jean Brodie,* Harper Collins, New York, NY, 1961.

13 Bob Unruh, "Homeschooler flees state custody: Melissa Busekros surprises parents at 3 a.m." Posted: April 23, 2007 12:33 pm Eastern, and "Homeschoolers on run win U.S. asylum Judge: Teaching children 'basic right no country has right to violate.'" *World Net Daily,* January 26, 2010 11:02 pm Eastern.

14 Adolph Hitler, in a speech given at Elbing, Germany, November 6, 1939.

15 Jessica Shepherd, "Children educated at home twice as likely to be known to social services, select committee told," and "Home pupils more likely to be known by social services and be out of work, education or training." *guardian.co.uk,* Tuesday 13 October 2009.

16 Jacob G. Hornberger, "Your Children Are the Property of the State," *The Future of Freedom Foundation Website,* April 2000.

17 Harper Lee, *To Kill a Mocking-Bird,* Harper and Row, New York, NY, 1961 (copyright 1960 by the author, renewed 1988).

18 Jeri LaBahn, "Education and Parental Involvement in Secondary Schools: Problems, Solutions, and Effects," *Educational Psychology Interactive.* Valdosta, GA: Valdosta State University, 1995.

19 Thomas A. Bowden, "Your Child Is Not State Property," *FrontPage Magazine,* April 4, 2008, reproduced at *Ayn Rand Center for Individual Rights Website.* (Thomas A. Bowden is an analyst at the Ayn Rand Institute, focusing on legal issues.)

20 Cardinal George Pell, "Varieties of Intolerance: Religious and Secular," *Thomas More Lecture on Religion in the Public Square,* hosted by the Oxford University Newman Society, *LifesiteNews,* published March 12, 2009.

3. What has Secular Humanism Done to the Church?

"Standing aloof may produce ostracism and persecution; but it will maintain power and influence...The reason why men do not look to the Church today is that she has destroyed her own influence by compromise."[1]
G. Campbell Morgan

Recently the authors visited at a medium-sized church with an evident love for the Lord and His Word. In the Sunday school class, however, the teacher commented that there are more people alive today than the combined total who have ever lived in the history of the Earth, a seemingly innocent statement. Consider, however, that Jewish tradition puts the number of Adam and Eve's children at fifty-six. People before the flood lived hundreds of years and frequently had scores of children. Very large families have been the norm for centuries but especially in antediluvian times. Simple mathematics indicates that it is likely that more people were alive at the time of the flood than are now.[2]

Thus Secular Humanism creeps into good churches and people never realize they are giving it their unintentional support. Population is just one area where secularism seeks control, and fear of overpopulation is one of the mechanisms for control. This is just one example of small infiltrations secularism can make into churches, eroding the purity of God's work with few people realizing how far the erosion has progressed.

Sometimes the infiltrations are not so small. Sometimes years of deliberate compromise allows secularists easy access to and control of a church. One easy inroad is the understandable desire of churches to attract and keep youth. Though it is wrong to say that the primary focus of a church is to train young people to serve Christ, if it fails to undertake that task it will soon have no members. This demands far more than just winning them to Christ. They must be edified, built up in the Scriptures, but the evangelical community has stopped emphasizing the authority of the Scriptures and frequently stopped teaching the Bible altogether.

Evangelism is a catchall phrase which allows lazy preachers to preach similar messages over and over again. While this technique brings in many new church members, it also drives away many faithful members. People of all ages need to be instructed in the Word. Failing to properly ground believers in the faith makes them shallow at best, eventually confused and frustrated when all the church does is teach salvation week after week, or at worst hardened in heresy and lost to the service of Christ.

Surprisingly enough, the teaching of Creation as a literal and scientific reality may be the key to retaining young Christians and an essential part of edifying believers. "What does the age of the Earth have to do with the exodus of young people from

American churches? Ken Ham [of] ... Answers in Genesis ... says a major study [reveals] ... in a scientific fashion ... two-thirds of young people in evangelical churches will leave ...[in] their 20s..."3

Young people in their twenties leaving the church happens across denominations, especially in liberal churches that aren't teaching anything or in those families who attend infrequently or have parents who don't walk the walk. "'Sunday School syndrome,' ... children who faithfully attend Bible classes in their church over the years actually are more likely to question the authority of Scripture."3 But this is a frightening admission. The more a child is "churched" the less he believes the Bible is true? How can this be? And why is it so? All of the following disheartening realities seem to be borne out by this survey.

> *"Regular participants in Sunday School are more likely to: Leave the church, Believe that the Bible is less true, Defend the legality of abortion and same-sex marriage, Defend premarital sex."3*

What has gone wrong? What heresy is the evangelical church teaching that causes young people to abandon it and the clear teachings of Scriptures? "...The church opened a door for the exodus of youth, beginning in the 19th Century, when it began teaching that 'the age of the Earth is not an issue as long as you trust in Jesus and believe in the resurrection and the Gospel accounts.'"3 Remember Plato's admonition that the young must be taught fictional stories as moral examples? The Secular Humanist education system has allowed the church to teach young people its stories while reinforcing the idea that they are fictional morality tales. " ... Teens come to believe 'that what they are taught in school is reality, but the church teaches stories and morality and relationship."[3]

It's the "Bible as Literature" approach, but the school doesn't bother to teach the literature, because the church is already doing a satisfactory job of undermining the Scriptures by failing to reinforce their literal truth. "'Bible teaching is not real in the sense of real history.' ... Parents or leaders tell youth they can 'continue to believe in evolution, millions of years,' ... 'Well, I can then believe what I'm taught at school – but school has nothing to do with God.'"[3] That much is certainly true. "... Doubt about the Bible's account of origins causes youth to doubt the authority of Scripture." The schools have smugly sat back and watched churches bow down to "true education" and pervert the Scriptures. Ken Ham doesn't mince words about what results. Maybe salvation doesn't depend on the age of the Earth, but "... salvation does rise or fall on the authority of Scripture. The message of the Gospel comes from these words of Scripture. When that Bible is undermined, he explained, everything it teaches is in doubt."[3]

Britt Beemer's survey above mentions that Sunday school attendees are more likely to defend premarital sex. Surely that can't be true. "Some 80 percent of teenagers who say they have been 'born again' agree that sex outside of marriage is morally wrong,"[4] says Christian sociologist Mark Regnerus. This is hardly a perfect response but at least a high percentage of so-called Christian teenagers say they believe the right thing. So far so somewhat good. "Still, as many as two-thirds of them violate their own beliefs in their actual behavior."[4] Definitely not so good. How did eighty percent saying the right thing turn into something like twenty-seven percent taking the right action? We can blame the culture. "Regnerus gives evidence that correlates the sexual activity in the schools that Christian kids go to with their own behavior."[4] So we can shift the blame to worldly influence?

"But might we also blame the culture of the church?"[4] This reasoning unfortunately makes more sense. "Not only because so many of today's evangelical churches follow the path of cultural conformity as a way to grow bigger and bigger. ..."[4] The problem is two-fold. "Churches used to teach and exemplify self-control, the necessity of keeping one's emotions in check, the discipline of self-denial and mortification of the flesh."[4] Churches have become like the world to be attractive to the world, and they have stopped teaching what the world doesn't want to hear. Unfortunately, there's more blame because of what they are teaching in place of self-denial. "Today the typical evangelical church, in its example and practice, cultivates 'letting go,' emotionalism, self-fulfillment, and an odd religious sensuality."[4] These concepts should sound very familiar by now, because they are straight out of the Secular Humanist playbook. Some contend that the evangelical community has a higher immorality rate than the general populace.

Adult church members are so far in debt that no one has the time to work with teenagers. People don't believe that persecution has already begun in America because they don't see any boxcars with emaciated deportees, piles of bodies in the streets or midnight knocks on the door. But Secular Humanists have learned a thing or two about persecution. Obviously you can destroy one man and perhaps his family by dragging him off to prison and eventually killing him because of what he believes.

But imagine the possibilities if you keep lobbying the government to expand government services, raise the minimum wage, increase business regulations, and demand ever-stricter environmental protections. Each time such measures pass, more private sector businesses go out of business because they can't afford these expanding taxes and government controls. Most liberals/secularists already work for the government and more jobs are being added while the private sector unemployment rises. Analyst Bill Beach discussed the "prognosis" for government expansion after "the recently passed American Recovery and Reinvestment Act ... Beach said he expected 450,000 jobs to be added to the public sector in that time, the largest boost coming with an increase of 130,000 government workers in 2012."[5]

Government employees already earn double what the private sector makes "In 2000, the average compensation (wages and benefits) of federal workers was 66 percent higher than the average compensation in the U.S. private sector. The new data show that average federal compensation is now more than double the average in the private sector."[6] If a Christian man owns his own business, he'll be put out of business. Soon everyone is making too little money to support a family. Wives must work to help the family survive and to pay the taxes. The children must go to public school or public daycare, and the church must fall by the wayside in the weekly schedule because the old days of 8-5 weekday schedules are long gone for many jobs.

But assume this hasn't happened yet and some adults can still come to church and give time to ministering to the youth. They will arrive to find their churches drowning in worldliness. Ships are designed to be in water, but water in the ship will sink it. The Church is designed to be in the world, but it is sinking in sin. Church leaders are so saturated with secularism that they actually drive out those who stand firm for the Word of God and refuse to go along with their secular humanist compromises.

G.B. Trudeau produces a comic strip called *Doonesbury*. In a November 1995 strip. his pastor character makes announcements as follows:

> *"OK, flock, here are this week's activities: This Monday we have a lecture on nutrition by our personal chef ... Tuesday and Thursday will be our 12-step night..."* *"Pastor Scott, is that about drugs or sex addiction?"* *"No, drugs and sex addiction have been cut down to nine steps and meets on Fridays at 6:30 p.m. — right after organic gardening. Also, we have a special treat. Saturday will be aerobic male bonding night! So bring your sneakers! Any questions?"* *"Yes, pastor, is there a church service this week?"* *"No, we had to cancel it. There was a conflict with the self-esteem workshop."*[7]

Trudeau has been known for years for his radical leftist sympathies. This time he has unfortunately hit home. The Scriptures command the church to minister to those in need and help sinners trying to overcome sins. But too many churches have become social clubs and self-help centers, some without realizing it. Maybe they haven't crowded out the sermon yet, but how many people attend the pie socials and never show their faces at the Sunday Morning service? We keep inviting them but they just want free pie, not the Bread of Life. They just keep using us and our nice friendly church, maybe crying on our shoulder once in a while with a "say a prayer for me." We let them get away with it because someday we hope the pastor will get a chance to preach the gospel to them. But we don't tell them about Christ ourselves. They might get "offended" and never come back.

"Designed for those who love praising God with a rock and roll beat,"[8] says the website description for a church's "contemporary worship service" where the music dominates. Why does it? Those microphones, electric guitars, drums and great big amplifiers fill the stage. Those singers sway and "drink" the microphones, voices right in everyone's personal zone. "Bethel's spirited contemporary worship provides a great blend of the familiar and the innovative."[8] That arrhythmic, heart-palpitating beat is louder than the words. There is one preacher and nearly always half a dozen of the "worship leaders."[8]

Worship leaders and their bands are amplified, energized, and just like what every young person sees every day out in the world. Apparently, the Bible was dead before, and it takes the worship band to bring it to life. What spirit makes it spirited? There's nothing "innovative" there. Tribes worshipping any number of demonic spirits got their hearts pounding and their feet thumping to the same beat. But missionaries wept and suffered and died to eradicate that form of worship and take its demonic object off the thrones of people's hearts. Thanks to "contemporary worship" (and Secular Humanism preaching the need to generate emotional excitement to get a message across) we in churches are the heathen now, much in need of conversion.

Everyone was happy when President Bush encouraged "faith-based" services taking the place of government programs. But what are these faith-based groups? "Church Community Services is a faith-based interdenominational non-profit agency that assists people in crisis and empowers them to move out of poverty."[8] Churches help the poor. "Services include a client choice food pantry, emergency financial assistance, plus our Soup of Success Job and Life Skills Training Program."[9] Looking after the needy is scriptural obedience. But some church "ministries" are just social services like this example of a program "which empowers women in poverty to make positive changes toward greater self-sufficiency."[9] They're interdenominational because the theory is that more people can do more good, reach more people. But what are they reaching them with? "We also offer public education on poverty."[9] Good, kind, may-be necessary, but how does that edify souls or build up believers? If Bible-believing churches participate in these programs, are they going to be able to freely preach and teach the Word, or just help stamp out poverty? There's about God, Christ or the Scriptures on the site's homepage. Secularists preach a "do good, feel good" mantra that takes the place of service with eternal rewards.

FDR had a plan to remove care of the needy from the church's ministries and make it exclusively a state function in his State of the Union address of 1934. Later, secularists came up with the new idea of burdening churches with programs that substitute feel good humanism for religious teaching and take up enormous amounts of time and money, such as those promoted by President Bush, no doubt with the best of intentions. Overburdened churches cannot begin to meet the needs of the poor who have no intention of attending church and just want a handout. Such churches are criticized for limiting their outreach to contacts who have at least come to the church or expressed an interest in hearing the Scriptures. They are accused of hating people for having different beliefs, and of neglecting their "duty" to somehow feed, clothe and "show love" to the whole world, when their first duty is to "Preach the Word" (2 Timothy 4:2).

A contemporary-minded church "would proudly proclaim that salvation is by grace alone, through faith alone, in Christ alone. But they have redefined salvation."[10] Redefining words should be a familiar concept to the reader by now. "Salvation is not simply, under the new gospel, the forgiveness of sin and the imputation of righteousness. It is not a deliverance from the wrath of God upon an undeserving and rebellious people."[10] What? Then what is it? Here comes the message, clear and unmistakable. All you have to do is recognize the real source, and realize it's being taught in a staggering number of churches weekly, and be very afraid.

"The new gospel is a liberation from low self-esteem, a freedom from emptiness and loneliness, a means of fulfillment and excitement, a way to receive your heart's desires..."[10] There is no question that this is actually the focus of most of the ministries calling themselves churches today. "The old gospel was about God; the new gospel is about us. ... The old gospel is foolishness to those who are perishing; the new gospel is attractive."[10]

People raised in secular humanistic environments rebel against even the slightest personal discipline. They are dishonest and destructive. When they are welcomed into the church under the banner of evangelism, bad apples turn good apples bad, not the other way around. The Canadian newspaper National Post reported on a homosexual man who "filed a complaint with the Ontario Human Rights Tribunal against a Catholic bishop after he was removed from his volunteer job as an altar server because of his sexual orientation."[11]

A government body called a "human rights tribunal" ought to be looking into war crimes, not hearing complaints against a church for standing up for its beliefs. "The case is the latest involving the human rights tribunal to address whether Church doctrine should be subject to review by a secular body."[11] In a secularist society the government has to control belief somehow. What better way than by claiming to protect human rights?

The paper reports that the Catechism of the Catholic Church says homosexuals "'must be accepted with respect, compassion and sensitivity. [And] every sign of unjust discrimination in their regard should be avoided.' But it adds that "'homosexual persons are called to chastity...'"[11] Members who asked that this man be removed said they understood he was entitled to attend and receive communion, even though the official position of their church states that "... 'homosexual sex is an act of 'grave depravity.'"[11] Church members were forced to either accept this man as a communicant or leave. But they were certain they still had the right to protest his inclusion as an altar attendant.

Joanne McGarry, executive director of the Catholic Civil Rights League circulated an open letter. "...The relationship between the Church and altar servers has none of the attributes that would make it a subject for a complaint to the Ontario Human Rights Tribunal."[11] Seems to be a statement of the obvious. Where is "altar server" on the list of human rights? "No one serves on the altar as a right; it is at the discretion of the pastor, who in turn is at the service of his bishop."[11]

As we said, a "human rights tribunal" ought to be looking into war crimes. Apparently there are lots of war criminals in Canada."...The tribunal ordered *Christian Horizons* -- a religious social agency that cares for 1,400 severely disabled residents -- to pay damages to an employee who was fired for entering into a lesbian relationship."[11] The tribunal has been busy. "Even though the woman signed a morals clause agreeing to the group's beliefs, the tribunal still called it discrimination."[11] These ministries are criminals only in the Secular Humanist war against belief. "The judgment is being appealed. Some observers said at the time that a religious social agency should be able to set its own hiring practices in regards to issues of faith."[11] Unfortunately, at least in the case of the Catholic Church, the Church itself invited this outcome by allowing a person openly embracing an act of "grave depravity" not just in the door but also into the fellowship.

Church leaders are desperate to have an outreach, to make their presence known in the community as doing good, and if they can support a ministry which also purports to train youth, so much the better. Hip-hop recording artist "Minister V" started Youth Ministry Entertainment in 2007. Its website offers "free mentoring support, positive encouragement, and fun ...'Training Up Our Youth' by means of 'Educational Entertainment.'"[12] Minister V wants to own a Hip Hop radio station, to make "cutting edge" youth films, and to have roller rinks and other entertainment facilities for his "ministry." He describes his qualifications for mentoring youth as including his having "received exposure at numerous church events, youth explosions, prisons, and community programs through his membership with Underground Gospel Ministries, Inc."[12]

Minister V's goals are to help youth "... Reach their full potential as leaders. The events, activities, and information ... help ... in making responsible and healthy choices, despite being faced with pressures to conform to risky behaviors prevalent among youth and young adults today."[12] While these are worthy goals, there seems to be something missing. " ... Personal responsibility and community involvement. ... distribution of age appropriate, factual, medically referenced ... Health & Fitness Awareness, Drug & Substance Abuse, and Abuse from Domestic Violence. ..."[12] People can profit by being taught to "Strive for economically and socially productive lives. ... avoid the serious problems of HIV/AIDS infection, teen pregnancy. ... resources necessary to develop them morally, ethically, spiritually, physically and mentally ... accept each person for who they are, ... unconditional atmosphere of love and respect. ... build character, strong bodies and storng [sic] minds ... ignite dreams and build oustanding [sic] leaders!"[12]

This is the actual purpose statement of the organization with just a few omissions for reasons of space. Where is the ministry in this ministry? The Gospel is mentioned once as part of the name of an organization. The founder himself describes no conversion experience, no Scriptures he relies on for his call or founding principles, no biblical principles he intends to teach young people, or anything like a scripture-based program. A Buddhist could teach this stuff, but would probably have more self-denial. It is self-described as empty of any real biblical teaching. It's cool, it's hip, and it's socially responsible. It's a waste of a Christian young person's precious growth-time to participate, and no responsible church should support it in any way.

Young believers who want to serve the Lord lack opportunities. "Ummm ... we need help in the nursery," is one of the answers a teen might get when he asks how he can serve in the church. Church leadership may hesitate to use young people because they are not mature in the faith. Certainly the nursery is a necessary area of service, but young people can do more in a church, and the Scriptures credit them with great potential. "I write to you, young men, because you are strong, and the word of God lives in you," (I John 2:14).

The authors were members of one church which discipled a young man saved out of a rough background and difficult family life. The pastor allowed him to lead opening exercises before Sunday school. He led singing and prepared an object lesson with a scriptural point each week. All the church leadership could be there to observe him and young and old got to watch him mature and take on greater responsibilities. He thrived in a simple position of trust with limitations. Similar assignments can be found throughout a church for young people to develop ministry skills.

There is no excuse, of course, for thrusting an inexperienced Christian or one who still struggles with obvious sin, into a solo teaching position without supervision just because he demands a chance to minister or the church is shorthanded. Young people to whom this has happened often become foolishly proud, embrace heresies, or withdraw in bitterness and frustration. Church leadership must learn to strike a balance between denying a chance to gain experience, helping a young person learn and grow in ministry experience and giving too much responsibility in hopes that the young person will "grow into it."

Missions programs in many churches have been drastically curtailed or discontinued. This happens for various understandable reasons, including a church's dwindling finances or discovering supported ministries cease to meet biblical standards. Sometimes, however, a church decides to spend its money supporting local endeavors. If they are still biblically-based missionary efforts, it may be acceptable to support them, but the Scriptures say "Go into all the world and preach the good news to all creation." (Mark 16:15, NIV). Most Christians interpret this to mean an expanding vision and the need to have some emphasis on distant and foreign missions.

Most of all, churches must beware of allowing a secular emphasis to invade missions programs. The Secular Humanist emphasis on self causes many people to demand that their money support local causes and produce results they can see, with short-term, visible results. Missionaries once went to the field young and labored throughout their lives, teaching and translating, and before any fruit could be seen age forced retirement, or the missionary died there and the next generation labored on. There is also an unhealthy emphasis on physical needs over spiritual ones. Frequently missionaries are also teachers, doctors, builders or pilots who can perform needed humanitarian services. This is excellent and can be invaluable in countries where direct missions are prohibited. But this is beside the point of the call and the going to the field. Secularists would love to have the church's time and resources strangled digging wells, curing diseases and flying supplies back and forth. Criticism ensues if they do not perform endless humanitarian tasks. "Where is your compassion?" Is the cry, when our compassion must be, no matter what the world might say, first and foremost on men's eternal souls?

"Arbeit Macht Frei." "Work sets you free," reads the sign that greeted prisoners sent to *Auschwitz*. Christians are loving and giving people. They will pour their hearts and lives into God's work, for the privilege of serving Him and serving others. Still, one reason the church is losing members is sheer overwork and spiritual starvation. Faithful workers are abused by long hours, low wages and the "reward" of watered-down, shallow messages to "grow the numbers" without feeding the souls of those who are already saved and need meat to continue growing. Their faithfulness is taken for granted while "big names" are exalted from the pulpit. Certain people do work that sticks out or have a "real" ministry. Prominent among these is the class of "Celebrity Sinners." These are people who have been saved after a life in organized crime, former members of street gangs, and one-time drug-addicted rock stars, people with a spectacular testimony who make a ministry of going from church to church telling their stories.

These people may be absolutely sincere, genuinely converted, faithful to God and seeking to do His work. Unfortunately their "ministries" sometimes consist of detailing past sins with a short tribute to God's grace and a "canned" call to accept Christ in the last five minutes. *Catharsis* is a Greek word meaning to purify or purge. Ancient Rome justified the arena games because they said if people witnessed acts of lurid violence they would be purged of the desire to be violent, presumably drained of any desire to rise up against the government. In fact, the games created a lust for more and more excitement, titillation, and violence. Christian people also hunger for stories of "real life" sinful experience. They ignore those with decades or a lifetime of faithfulness to their credit. After all, it's easy to live obedient to God day after day, to stay faithful to a wife or husband for twenty or more years, to get through the rebellious teen years without any rebellion, avoiding the counter-culture altogether, isn't it? The choir director prepares the cantata and gets a few compliments. The nursery director keeps the schedule running smoothly, supplies stocked up, toys clean and organized. That's what they're supposed to do. No real accolades for boring, obedient service.

But let a celebrity sinner show up, and we must praise God for the recital of details of sin after sin, as if hearing about them was essential to appreciating the miraculous work done in this person's life to save him. Burnout and turnover are high where appreciation is low and churches are shallow, seeking the next thrill to fill the pews. Maybe it seems selfish and worldly to want to be noticed for ordinary faithfulness, or to expect the church to feed you in return for your work on its behalf, but it is a biblical principle to mention faithfulness and to reward it. "Remember your Creator in the days of your youth, before the days of trouble come and the years approach when you will say, 'I find no pleasure in them'" (Ecclesiastes 12:1, NIV), sighed world-weary Solomon, a celebrity sinner if there ever was one. He understood how much better it was to just stay faithful than to have to be forgiven for leading the whole nation of Israel into idolatry. In Israel's past the Word was read out to people to make sure they knew it. David had singers and musicians proclaim God's truth through song. God used leadership to feed his people, and their achievements were recognized.

The priests and Levites who served in front of the people are mentioned by name, but so are the men who were skilled to do the work of building the tabernacle and temple. Stephen and his fellow deacons were mostly commissioned to wait tables but every man's name appears in the Scriptures. Church leadership must notice their everyday workers, praise them, encourage them, and if "the strength of the laborers is giving out" (Nehemiah 4:10), be sure it isn't because the church is too deep in worldliness to give them the nourishment from the Word they need to keep going.

---

1 G. Campbell Morgan, *Acts of the Apostles,* 1924.

2 Josephus, Flavius. *Antiquities of the Jews* I: iv: 2) William Whiston, Translator, 1737. William Whiston's footnote #8 in Book One states this tradition. Mathematical calculation from *Like the Master Ministries* (*Never Thirsty.org*) website "Bible Answers." 10,000 people could have been born just Adam and Eve, their children and grandchildren. Assuming that Adam and Eve started having children immediately after God commanded them to be fruitful and multiply (Gen. 1:28). [and] were mature adults who could have children. If we assume that they gave birth to a child every other year, they would have given birth to 65 children by the time they were 130 years of age.
Grandchildren:

If we assume that their children do not start marrying each other until they are about twenty years of age, then the first two children who marry could have given birth to about 56 grandchildren by the time Adam and Eve were 130 years of age. The second two children who marry could have given birth to about 55 grandchildren. The next two children who marry could have given birth to about 55 grandchildren also. If we continue counting we discover that Adam and Eve's children could have given birth to 1,536 grandchildren by the time Adam and Eve were 130 years of age.

Great-Grandchildren:

Next, we must do the same for the grandchildren's children. If we do the math, we discover that the first set of grandchildren could have had 45 great grandchildren. The next two grandchildren from the first set of parents could have 44 great grandchildren. If we continue counting we discover that the first set of 1,536 grandsons or granddaughters or 768 couples could have given birth to over 10,000 children all by themselves. Total: If we continued the process we discover that 10,000 children is a very conservative estimate by the time Adam and Eve are 130 years of age.

3 TESTING THE FAITH "Why are young people leaving the church? Groundbreaking study says Sunday School makes exit more likely." Posted: June 14, 2009 10:11 pm Eastern *WorldNet Daily* Review and interview with Ken Ham of *Answers in Genesis* on book with Britt Beemer, *Already Gone: Why your kids will quit church and what you can do to stop it.* Beemer is a former senior research analyst for the *Heritage Foundation* and founder in 1979 of the *American Research Group*. The

study included 20,000 calls and detailed surveys of 1,000 20 to 29 year olds who used to attend evangelical churches on a regular basis.

4 Mark Regnerus, "Sex and the Evangelical Teen," from *Forbidden Fruit: Sex & Religion in the Lives of American Teenagers,* Oxford University Press, New York, NY, 2007). *World* magazine, THOUGHTS, "Minority report," Aug. 11, 2007, Vol. 22, No. 29.

5 Ryan Byrnes, "Private Sector Jobs Decline, Government Jobs Increase," from Bill Beach, director of center for data analysis at the *Heritage Foundation, CNS News,* Monday, March 09, 2009.

6 Chris Edwards, "Federal Pay Continues Rapid Ascent," *The Cato Institute Website Cato at Liberty.org* featuring The Bureau of Economic Analysis annual data on compensation levels by industry August 24, 2009 @ 11:57 am.

7 G.B. Trudeau, *Doonesbury,* strip published in November, 1995. Universal Press Syndicate. Doonesbury was launched as UPS's first syndicated feature on October 26, 1970.

8 From the *website of Bethel Lutheran Church, Cupertino, CA.*

9 From the *website of Church Community Services, Elkhart, IN.*

10 Gary E. Gilley, *This Little Church Went to Market—Is the Modern Church Reaching Out or Selling Out?* Evangelical Press, July 2005.

11 Charles Lewis, *National Post* (Canada), "Gay altar server Contests firing, Human Rights

Tribunal asked to intervene," Tuesday, July 14, 2009.

12 *y-ment.com*, website of Youth Ministry Entertainment or Y-ME ministries.

4. What Happens to Those Who Practice Secular Humanism?

But he that lacketh these things is blind, and cannot see afar off.
2 Peter 1:9

For such men are slaves, not of our Lord Christ but of their own appetites; and by their smooth and flattering speech they deceive the hearts of the unsuspecting.
Romans 16:18 (NASB)

In former Alaska Governor Sarah Palin's campaign for Vice President of the United States in 2008, she claimed that she took a stand against things that were being handled wrongly by staff members. These included things that were done in her name and on her behalf as a candidate. In some cases they included things she thought ought to have been done that were not done. The operative term here is "thought," because Palin frequently, by her own admission, seems to have thought a great deal about stopping something wrong or doing something right but never got past the "thought" stage.

For example, in her book, *Going Rogue*, Palin commented on a time when a staffer burst into the room and let go an "F-Bomb" while directing that some action be taken or stopped. Sarah commented that she thought, "No more F-Bombs around Piper (her youngest daughter), please."[1] Why did she only *think* that? If she believes it's wrong to use that word around young children why didn't she say so out loud?

Fighting against the tidal wave of profanity, obscenity and vulgarity that assails Christian senses every day may seem hopeless but there was a time when we still fought, and frequently won. We used to fight for ourselves, too, not just our children. Now we just think, "I wish you wouldn't do that," and wonder why people spew garbage at us all day, every day, from bad language to bad philosophy to bad education to bad science. Well, perhaps it's because we let them and only think about objecting. We've been told to be tolerant, so we've become way too tolerant. We think it's being nice. But it's kind of like mental food poisoning. You can tolerate some. Maybe you'll just get a mental "tummy ache." Maybe your organs will fail one by one and you'll die horribly. But at least you were tolerant.

Remember that one vital Secular Humanist tenet is that people should focus on unity rather than being divisive. Nowhere is that philosophy more obvious than in politics. The cry of the liberals is that conservatives are divisive and that nothing can be accomplished because they won't come to the table ready to compromise for the good of the people. If there are politicians who really haven't compromised some principles to get elected they've hidden themselves well from those of us who would love to support them. No one is perfect. Everyone fails. But a candidate who deliberately says, "I have to keep silent on this, this, and this, because getting elected and doing some good is more important than those things" had better be really, really sure where the line should be drawn. He or she can't step backward from serious compromise.

"By their fruit you will recognize them. Do people pick grapes from thornbushes, or figs from thistles?" (Matthew 7:16, NIV). Christians have forgotten that Jesus said error is pretty easy to recognize. They are too busy eating thorns and thistles and trying to get along with the people who produce them. Some Christians are so far gone down that road they have forgotten the taste of grapes and figs. But it is possible to restore discernment to Christians and to teach them to know how to separate good from evil. Unfortunately they're going to discover that evil might be running the food pantry where they volunteer, performing a concert at their local theater, sitting in the pew next to them, teaching their child's Sunday school class, or preaching the morning message. There are as many different kinds of Secular Humanists as there are worshipers of secularism. There are also some characteristics which define all secularists.

The first is a hatred of the truth. The more committed the secularist, the more passionate his hate. You'd think a person who hates the truth would stick out, that Christians would be able to avoid him, and sometimes such a person is easy to spot. Sometimes you can tell a person's philosophy by seeing what he draws inspiration from. Many people enjoy putting up posters with attractive pictures that include an inspirational or motivational statement. Secularists can buy motivational posters, too, with captions like these:

"Just a few more centuries"
(The poster shows ruins of a Christian Church with many modern, advanced buildings and technology examples around/behind it)

The Bible: Because all the works of science cannot equal the wisdom of cattle-sacrificing primitives who thought every animal species in the world lived within walking distance of Noah's house.

Creationism: Because desert goat herders living in tents 3000 years ago knew more about the cosmos and biology than modern-day scientists.

Faith: the leading cause of death and destruction amongst human beings since Horus and Set.

"Is God willing to prevent evil, but not able? Then he is not omnipotent. Is he able, but not willing? Then he is malevolent. Is he both able and willing? Then whence cometh evil? Is he neither able nor willing? Then why call him God?"
Epicurus

Irony: Going to church basements for help with addictions that rose from trauma suffered in church buildings.[2]

They hate the church and they hate God. Obvious. Stay far away.

On the other hand, there are the people who say churches needs to come together, to find strength in numbers, to cooperate to help people. But the reason there are different churches is because while some of them have minor differences, some of them are just plain wrong. Like Charles Briggs, they call it *Bibliolatry* to believe the Scriptures are authoritative. They are still called churches and they still have members eager to do good. But they are lost and mired in Secular Humanism because they hate the truth as represented by the Scriptures just as much as any of those poster-hangers, accepting secularist compromise to "get the work done."

The second is a commitment to self-indulgence. This might be drugs, sex and rock & roll or it might be a stack of books in a locked room. Involvement with drugs and sex would seem obvious, glaring warning signs to stay away. But today it's unloving, divisive, to call sin sin. Christian counseling now deals with "addictions" to sex, drugs, and alcohol just like secular analysts have for years. Some people have legitimate chemical imbalances requiring treatment. But in many cases medications replace searching for scriptural answers to the sins of self-centeredness and a lack of self-control. Sadly, rates for Christian divorce, infidelity in marriage, and fornication among the unmarried are soaring right alongside statistics for the rest of the population.

The same evangelicals who find traditional church services and traditional music boring use CCM (Contemporary Christian Music) for public emotional highs which often end in disastrous private emotional crashes. God designed music to glorify Himself. But in the modern or blended worship service, self-indulgence has replaced self-control. Emotional release has replaced the personal prayers of private worship before and during a service. Seldom is glorifying God even mentioned. Almost every sentence focuses on "I" or "me" or "us." Though the music of Fanny Crosby was condemned by her contemporaries as "bar room" music, no one could question her lyrics.[3] The lyrics of CCM are difficult to hear, and rarely teach doctrine as the hymns of the church have done for two thousand years.

But self-indulgence can also be private as well as public. It is possible to lock yourself away from responsibilities while pursuing studies, "personal enrichment" or "empowerment." Where does it say in the Scriptures that you deserve "me time"? "Me time" is the opposite of personal prayer and Bible study and meditation on the Word of God.

The third defining characteristic is that secularists demand that someone else pay the consequences for their sins. Blame your abusive parents, blame your poverty, blame peer pressure, ADHD, even a bad church. "It's not my fault," worked for the unconverted. Why can't it even work for mothers who neglect their children for a "cause"? Charles Dickens in *Bleak House* depicts a woman who arranged fundraising for missionary endeavors, apparently with the deep spiritual purpose of starting coffee plantations for poor English settlers in *Borrioboola-Gha*, in Africa. Her husband, Mr. Jellyby, spent his home time with his head against the wall, being driven to bankruptcy by his wife's extravagant support of the "mission," helpless to control his filthy household and rebellious children. One day he whispers to his oldest daughter, "Never have a mission, my dear child."[4]

The fourth is a demand that others not only approve of his behavior, but also join him in doing it. "Who knowing the judgment of God, that they which commit such things are worthy of death, not only do the same, but have pleasure in them that do them" (Romans 1:32). The Roman Catholic Church position on homosexuality quoted in the previous chapter demands that to belong to the Church, one must accept homosexuals and allow them communion as long as they are "chaste." The *American Heritage Dictionary* defines chaste as including "morally pure in thought or conduct; decent and modest. Not having experienced sexual intercourse; virginal. Abstaining from unlawful sexual intercourse. Abstaining from all sexual intercourse; celibate." Given that the Roman Catholic Church says, "homosexual sex is an act of 'grave depravity,'" what does "chaste" mean in this context? Why would a person declare himself a homosexual and "marry" his partner if he intended to be celibate? Homosexuals admit that chaste and celibate are not the same, engaging in circular reasoning that seems meant to exhaust anyone trying to understand.

The Church of Rome is giving communion to persons openly embracing what the Bible condemns and demanding that its communicants do the same. According to Rome, the cost for leaving the Roman Catholic Church is made clear."... Because there is no salvation out of the Church."[5] Homosexuals frequently believe that Scriptures condemning homosexuality are misinterpreted. They say that homosexuality as practiced today is not talked about in the Scriptures. These positions cannot be supported unless the truth of Scriptures is rejected. Once again, the problem goes back to rejecting the authority of the Bible. It does clearly speak against homosexuality and anyone who does not accept that has put self ahead of Scriptures and is solidly in the Secular Humanist camp.

Movies, books and television shows provide excellent examples of the fifth common feature of Secular Humanists, the persecution of any kind of opposition. Remember that every writer, whether of books, teleplays or screenplays, has a message in mind. It's never just mindless entertainment. A news story's purpose might be to distract you from bigger and more important news. The attack in that case is against awareness of what's important. In fictional works like those of Charles Dickens the purpose could be to condemn wrong social practices and show a better method of helping the poor and reforming the system. Charles Dickens made a habit of condemning the charitable efforts of members of organized religion for pride and self-centeredness along the way.

Every publisher or producer of these works has his or her own agenda as well. Most are honed in their secularist education to look for ways to promote an agenda of opposing theism. Frequently publishers discriminate against books that openly state scriptural principles as their basis. People who disagree point to bestsellers by committed Christians, especially in the non-fiction category, in which the authors speak openly about God. One thing to remember is that publishers do fundamentally want a bestseller that will make them money and conservative, even religious books, are popular nowadays. Some of the buying market consists of secularists researching to attack the views and some with people who genuinely seek truth.

But how many of these popular conservative authors really support the authority of the Scriptures? Many talk around religion. They mention that they attend church. They agree with basic biblical tenets like purity until marriage and fidelity afterwards. They oppose abortion as the murdering of a human being. Even the books that aren't overtly about politics and social concerns, the ones that purport to teach Christians how to live better lives are missing something.

The bulk of writers who take a Christian viewpoint concern themselves with the here and now, with physical and social life, and have no eternal view. This is a secularist mindset. It's all about the nasty now and now, marriage, children, co-workers and even church relationships. We have to fix this life. Is it because they believe, like secularists, that this life is all? So many people who believe in God do. They forget that the Bible is God-centered, not man-centered. It's designed to get you ready to meet Him, not make the best of your life here.

Secularists have had most Christians as students in public school all their lives, from preschool to public universities. Some people think they made it out unscathed, but secularists have attacked and won on at least one front in the "Christian" books the authors have read. Where is the longing for a future with God?

Some books have it, certainly. But some so-called self-help books just make you discontented and obsessed with making this life perfect. Happiness is not the same as "godliness with contentment," (I Timothy 6:6) but it's clearly synonymous in many Christians' minds.

Many Christians still don't go to movies or watch television. They may be the wisest among us. Others think they deserve to be entertained after a hard day's work and say they want to "relax" in front of the TV. One family the authors knew had a plaque on top of their TV that read, "I will set no wicked thing before mine eyes" (Psalm 101:3), as a reminder to be discerning in the program choices. For those of us who do watch TV and movies, there is much secularism to guard against in the messages of plots and programs.

The first message of most of TV is that men are stupid, or scum, or only capable of "solving" crimes by prematurely shooting or beating suspects to death. If the men do not fall into any of these categories, they fall into the "tender" category and are just women with different equipment, sometimes homosexuals, talented, sympathetic, full of great advice, perfect shopping buddies. A very few others may be permitted to be rude but coldly efficient, with a warm and giving side seldom displayed. One popular "real male" type is one who is deeply wounded, or with a very wicked past which has made him savvy enough to be good at his job and get on with his tormented life.

The second message is that women are tough, rational, sometimes hiding a tender secret about saving a man from disgrace or death, but usually just plain more competent to handle life than men. They are unrealistically attractive or else outwardly unattractive but wiser and more beautiful inside than the rest of the cast. Mothers don't leave their kids. Dads do, unless it's a plot in which the man needs a strong woman to overcome his inability to cope with the kids. Sometimes women are portrayed as ruthless, evil, grasping power and making subordinates' lives miserable. But the triumph of the assistant comes through "peasant cunning," an ancient fairytale technique where the poorer, weaker character overcomes by deceit. Women will have sex outside of marriage just as often as men, maybe more.

Many movies follow the same pattern, but have more scope and so can take on bigger issues than male-female conflicts. The destruction of the world is a popular topic for movies. Since the advent of the nuclear age moviemakers have been obsessed with the idea that we will somehow be to blame for destroying the Earth. Either someone will deliberately try to wipe out the Earth or some natural disaster will occur, such as an asteroid or conquering aliens from space. Environmentalism teaches that we are by neglect destroying the ozone layer, using up all the natural resources, etc., and the clock is ticking for mankind if he doesn't change. Of course, man can save himself or, if necessary, recover from such misuse of resources. This is a sort of Armageddon without God plotline. No spiritual forces will intervene in judgment, just man possibly messing things up but man also fixing them or rising from the ashes to start anew. Man will go on and the Earth or someplace like it that he has fixed will continue eternally.

The other major plotline in movies today is some form of spirituality involving good versus evil. Vampire movies might seem as earthly as you can get but there are spiritual forces clearly at work in vampire stories. Vampires are usually evil, and the people who combat them or fall in love with them represent the power of good. Thus in modern vampire stories the vampire can change, give up bloodsucking, become good. Nothing is clearly right or wrong and nothing is black and white. Sometimes the vampires are better morally than the living characters. There is also the aspect of immortality because a vampire can live forever.

This principle works in "space opera"/scifi or fantasy movies as well. Sometimes characters switch back and forth, good to evil and evil to good. Good characters lie, cheat, steal, kill to do good. Breaking the rules is good and necessary because the rule makers are too dogmatic and isolated from what is happening around them. Evil characters behave according to a stricter code of conduct, exhibit more discipline, are bound by their promises, but these things are bad, don't you see? Emotion, dead spirits, and mystical powers guide heroes. Immortality is a factor here, too because the dead can come back to advise the hero. Their decisions are made without regard to any living or known good counselors, who are usually in turmoil, paralyzed by blindness or somehow confined and limited in power. "Trust your feelings" is the mantra repeated over and over again. The young are wiser than the old, at least in part because they allow their passions to goad them into action.

A few movies actually mention what seems to be the true God. In some cases they show superficial respect for religion, though the hero is rarely a believer. In any case that respect has a twist to it. Usually the hero is in error about the facts of the Scriptures, wrong about what its plain teaching says in relationship to the movie storyline. The "fun" is in twisting those facts, turning them inside out, and making man come out on top. Frequently his hard work is rewarded. Sometimes he is unconditionally loved no matter what outrageous wrong he does. Standards are fluid. He might be celibate. It's unlikely that he'll be happily married.

The secular humanist convert enters his new religion confused and upset, perhaps even angry. Perhaps he once believed in God but like the stony ground part of the sower parable (Matthew 13:18ff) he had his "belief" shattered by some tragedy or instance of God's "unfairness." He sees life as something like Max Heller's *Catch 22*, hopelessly entangled in circular reasoning. This is, surprisingly enough, a mindset dangerous to the Secular Humanist priesthood, because there is a very high suicide rate among these people. If the person is not reeducated he may enter the next stage, apathy, complete indifference even to simple personal hygiene. This can manifest to the world as a drug addict who lives only for the next fix or overdoses because he just doesn't care about anything else. Christians might define this stage as despair. Secularists avoid that term, understanding that it belongs to believers who couple it with the hope that a person might get so low he "looks up" to find God.

The goal of Secular Humanism is to "progress" the convert out of this state to a blind utopian faith in man's ability to evolve into something better. Older Science Fiction preached this dogma. Man could achieve anything if he just left theism behind. He could even become a god, creating livable landscapes on alien worlds or making new worlds entirely. He could create intelligent life just as easily, but not with a God who was the True Creator and to whom man remained inferior. Reality will intrude and the sin nature will destroy honest belief in Secular Humanism. That is where the Secular Humanist priests come in. They will attempt to deny the validity of honest debate, censor disagreement, and will not hesitate to lie to protect their religion.

Lies rarely end up being consistent and uniform, which is why there is so much disagreement among secularists and so many contradictions in belief on so many subjects. Opposition to true belief is their only point of unity since they are mostly out to gratify and exalt themselves. The final result is that many people in positions of privilege and power are fighting to maintain their positions. Those believers in Secular Humanism who are not in positions of privilege and power oscillate between irrational optimism and deadly despair. Without any real hope because of the belief that this brief material life is all there is to existence, Secular Humanist priests must do their best to control these mood swings and rely on one of two cultural methods to address the situation. One uses the artificial stimulation of drugs, entertainment, music and self-indulgence and allows these to become a way of life. The other disdains these artificial stimulants. It recreates the

Spartan culture, using the continual distraction of terrorism and outright war with obsessive state-centered propaganda masquerading as patriotism to divert its believers.

Some secularists will overcome this turmoil and will seem to have achieved serenity. Their outward calm masks a form or stoicism. Their consciences are thoroughly seared against the working of truth and they have achieved the state that Marcus Aurelius described in this way: "If thou art pained by any external thing, it is not this that disturbs thee, but thy own judgment about it. And it is in thy power to wipe out this judgment now."[6]

---

1 Sarah Palin, *Going Rogue: An American Life*, Harper Collins, New York: NY, 2009.

2 From *scottklarr.com*, the website of Scott Klarr Jr.

3 Regi Fowler, Church/ Community Vice President, "Tolerating Thoughts on Tolerance," *Texas Sings, Volume 13*, number 2, Fall 1997. [Fowler quotes a "high church" sentiment from the time when hymnwriters began to write original songs instead of relying on the Psalms for worship:] "Contemporary music is not worshipful; there is no reverence involved. It is a worldly influence on sacred ground." When Isaac Watts (1674-1748) wrote, "When I Survey the Wondrous Cross" in the 1700's, he was severely criticized for his new, contemporary style. Fanny Crosby (1820-1915), who wrote the text to some of our most beautiful hymns such as "Blessed Assurance," "Near the Cross," and "Have Thine Own Way, Lord," was criticized for having her words set to

what was perceived as barroom music. ... These God-inspired hymns have withstood the test of time, and are considered reverent and standard repertoire in our worship services today."

4 Charles Dickens, *Bleak House,* Chapter 30, originally published serially from March 1852 to September 1853.

5 The original saying by Saint Cyprian of Carthage (3rd century AD) is found his *Letter LXXII, Ad Jubajanum de haereticis baptizandis,* and in Latin reads: *"Salus extra ecclesiam non est."* (Literally, "salvation outside the church is not.") Translated by Robert Ernest Wallis. From *Ante-Nicene Fathers,* Vol. 5. Edited by Alexander Roberts, James Donaldson, and A. Cleveland Coxe. (Buffalo, NY: Christian Literature Publishing Co., 1886.)

6 Marcus Aurelius, Translated by George Long, *Meditations,* (VIII. 47).1862.

5. What Can We Do About Secular Humanism?

"History is more or less bunk."[1]
Henry Ford

*For our struggle is not against flesh and blood,
but against the rulers, against the authorities,
against the powers of this dark world and against
the spiritual forces of evil in the heavenly realms.*
Ephesians 6:12

This is the part where we ask, "What can we do?"
We begin with trust. Over and over we have
defined belief, faith, and trust and by now it
should be clear that trust in God means relying on
the tested evidence of Who and what God is. God
is omnipotent and sufficient to overcome whatever
the world throws at us. The battle is the Lord's.
Victory is not possible through our schemes. The
warfare is spiritual, as Ephesians 6:12 says.

Secularists have tried to hide the spiritual aspect of
life, to bury it by denying its existence. While it is
wrong to become wrapped up in emotional,
mystical "experiences," life has a true spiritual
component. There is a God. Not only do the
experiences of every human ever born tell us that
there is a God; the Bible tells us so. It says that He
is a Spirit. It also says that there is a devil, Satan,

and that he has spirits who go through the world influencing men. Hiding the enemy does not make him go away. Secularism is a form of camouflage behind which "the spiritual forces of evil" can hide while working man's destruction.

Throughout history secularism has masked its true purpose, creating camouflage to distort historical truth. Frequently Secular Humanists are successful at completely burying the true motives behind an event. Wars are a favorite topic for rewrites of history, twisting a just purpose into a nasty one that will make people despise and distrust those who believed a "just" war was right and necessary. Motives fall prey to revisionist history and the truth gets buried so deeply hardly anyone knows what it was.

Are you a secular bigot? It is easy to "go along with the crowd." When "everyone" is telling you what to believe, do you go along? The winners write history, but they don't always write the truth.

"I was raised by one of the greatest men in the world," testified Rev William Mack Lee, former slave and cook to Robert E. Lee and the other Confederate Generals until after the Civil War. "There was never one born of a woman greater than Gen. Robert E. Lee, according to my judgment. All of his servants were set free ten years before the war, but all remained on the plantation until after the surrender."[3] Though Robert E. Lee was forced by law to manage his father-in-law's slave-holding estate until the will allowed him to free them,[4] Robert E. Lee opposed slavery.[5] "There are few, I believe, in this enlightened age, who will not acknowledge that slavery as an institution is a moral and political evil." (Robert E. Lee, letter dated December 27, 1856, five years before the beginning of the Civil War.)

Did you know this? Have you heard it before? This book is not about the War Between the States. It is about us today. If you cannot accept this truth about Lee and many others of the Southern leadership, then you are a secular bigot. The authors of this work grew up in Arizona and New York. We lived in Pennsylvania for twenty years. We do not support the Confederacy. We only use The War Between the States because it is a good example of secular bigotry. Secularists have turned many in the twenty first century into bigots over the issue of slavery.

Before the first shots were fired, Robert E. Lee was asked by Abraham Lincoln to lead the Northern armies. He refused because of his principled opposition to the policies of the Federal government of the United States.[2]

The winners of the War Between the States have written millions of volumes claiming that it was fought over slavery. Chatter on the Internet wonders if Lee fathered slave children. The US Marine Corps recently refused a recruit for no other reason than a tattoo of a Confederate flag on his shoulder.

Ulysses S. Grant thought slavery an issue not worth fighting over.[6] Abraham Lincoln said, "My paramount object in this struggle is to save the Union, and is not either to save or to destroy slavery."[6] The issues of preservation of the Union, states' rights and Federal encroachment upon them are hardly ever mentioned. Yes, the North also fought for principle. Near the end of the war ending the great evil of slavery became one of the important issues. The North, however, might have been more racist than the South. In the South, slaves were armed and fought alongside whites. In the South there were black officers. There were no records of their numbers because those blacks were simply considered Southern soldiers. In the North, blacks were segregated and fought in divisions separate from whites, commanded only by white officers.

The Confederates were not fools. These men actually believed they had the superior financial position. They believed that they could hold out against invaders from the North. The effective censorship by the winners has conditioned us to think of the Confederate leadership as fools. The truth is that Secular Humanism is the established state religion of the Federal Government and it will fight with as much determination as Abraham Lincoln's troops to maintain that position.

Does anyone even know the circumstances today? We now know that the South was wrong but few know upon what they based their original confidence.

Throughout the world in the Middle Ages people wore silk, leather, felt or homespun wool or linen. Most of these materials were quite expensive and could not be washed readily. These clothes attracted insects and gave breeding grounds to disease-causing organisms. Though many things brought about the end of the Middle Ages, one of the most important was a magic cloth which made clothes less expensive and washable. Cleaner clothes actually extended life spans as much as a decade or more.

This magic material was machine-made cotton cloth. We call the production and distribution of this fabric the industrial revolution. English, American and European ships used this cotton cloth in sails and flags. English, American and European ships carried cotton in their holds and traded it for every kind of luxury imaginable all over the world. State churches preached that women needed to cover themselves with layers of clothing, usually cotton cloth. Houses and public buildings had curtains, tapestries, tablecloths, sheets, pillowcases and furniture coverings, all using cotton cloth. The trade of the world was based on cotton cloth.

Production of this cloth demanded a dependable supply of raw cotton. By 1860 the Confederate States of America supplied more than fifty percent of the world's raw cotton. More trade was carried on the steamboats of the Mississippi River system than all the ocean-going ships of the world. Jefferson Davis and the Confederate leadership believed that they had assurances that foreign customers of Confederate cotton would not allow the North to interrupt the supply of cotton.[7]

We should not put our trust in foreign governments, as when Hezekiah trusted the Babylonians. Do not put your trust in princes, in mortal men, who cannot save. (Psalm 146:3 NIV) We should not put our trust in alliances, as when Solomon married the daughters of kings. Nor should we trust our own government or our own abilities. We should trust in the Lord our God. The Southern leadership boldly proclaimed that they trusted in the Lord, but in 20/20 hindsight their actions seem to be blinded by pride.

The pride of being in the right on some issues has crippled more than one cause throughout history. It isn't enough to be right about the truth of the authority of the Scriptures. It isn't enough to be right about the dangers of Secular Humanism. We can make all the right arguments, express them perfectly, and still be defeated by our own human pride. Moses killed the Egyptian because he thought he was good enough to free the Israelites on his own. He had all the learning of Egypt. He had the Israelite heritage. He alone had freedom when all his people were slaves. Instead he had to flee for his life and spend forty more years, leaving the slaves in misery for that long as well, while he became a meek (humble) man God could use (Numbers 12:3, KJV).

The second point is faith. We are certain of the eventual outcome because God's Word is clear that His will is going to triumph. Because of that knowledge, not because of what the secularists call blind superstition, we work as if everything depends on us. Marriage is the biblical picture of our relationship to the Lord, which is why the Accuser is so desperate to destroy marriage. Marriage is not a 50/50 relationship. It is 100%/100%. "Your labor is not in vain in the Lord" (I Corinthians 15:58). We pray and trust the Lord God completely, give Him all the glory for the victory, but work as if everything depended on us. "Whatsoever thy hand findeth to do, do it with all thy might; for there is no work, nor device, nor knowledge, nor wisdom, in the grave, whither thou goest" (Ecclesiastes 9:10).

Our greatest enemy is Satan and his most effective tool in the Twenty-first century is the Establishment of Religion in America. The most pressing need of the hour is to disestablish America's established church. The only way to do this is to cut off her federal funds and court-appointed power. The question is how. If we blow up IRS buildings we will be branded terrorists, hunted down as criminals and executed without trials. We will be treated worse than real terrorists. Even worse, the rubble of the destroyed buildings will be honored as shrines and the government criminals will be honored as martyrs. So our final condition will be worse than our current condition.

If we do nothing, our children and our property will be taken from us as the Nazis, Soviets and Communists all over the world have done, as secularist governments who claim they are "just here to help" are already doing in Europe and on a smaller scale here in America. Some of these attempts to regulate churches and homelife are overturned by public outcry. Secularists may jump the gun once in a while. They may misjudge the level of power and support they have in particular localities. They will step back and wait until they have put in place a few more activist judges. They will insert a few more officeholders who will urge everyone to put aside their differences for the common good. Governments at all levels are already in a chokehold with social service mandates passed down from the federal welfare state. They must generate more revenue, and they will do it by closing the "loopholes" that protect our freedoms from being replaced by taxation. Eventually those who refuse to worship the Established Religion of Secular Humanism will be unable first to work. The next step will be making it impossible to buy or sell. People might still protest, but eventually anyone who opposes the Established Religion will be sent to re-education camps to be worked to death.

The real solution is found in the New Testament, in the Church of Jesus Christ. The mission of the Church is evangelism. The mission in the Church is education. While thousands have seen the need for evangelism, telling the unbeliever about Jesus Christ, for over a hundred years any further education has been handed over to liberals to undermine the faith of new believers. This is the reason the most important event in US history is the Briggs heresy trial. Briggs was a heretic. He denied the inspiration and authority of the Bible. He denied the doctrines of the Bible. Yet he took the position of a Bible college professor. He needed the position of a Bible teacher to attack the Bible. He dedicated his life to destroying the faith by indoctrinating students in the liberal foundations of Secular Humanism.

Though there is no single solution for everyone, there exists a set of principles which must be followed if we are to exercise our faith. The first principle is a close personal relationship with Jesus Christ. Since Christianity is both a religion and a relationship, a close relationship with Jesus Christ is impossible without a close relationship to his bride, the Church. With great sorrow, we see churches, mission boards, universities, publishers and every conceivable type of ministry abandoning the faith and becoming Secular Humanist social clubs where the greatest possible sin is hurting someone else's feelings.

For most believers, growth in Christ must either occur with small groups within the Church or outside the Church. While this seems impossible, Churches throughout America have become mission fields.

The second principle of our faith which we must exercise is a proper relationship with people around us. The standard in the Word of God is "telling the truth in love." The human tendency is to either care about someone so much that we do not love them enough to tell them the truth or to be so honest that we fail to be kind. We need to let our speech be always with grace, seasoned with salt. It is also our responsibility to know how to answer every man.

Though it is God's responsibility to provide opportunities for us, it is our responsibility to seek opportunities. There will be far fewer opportunities when we are in debt. One of the most important ways to live at peace with all men is to stay out of debt. Nothing will turn an otherwise honest man into a dishonest man faster than debt. If we control our appetites then we will have far fewer problems with money. It is God's will that we have the material resources to support the ministries of others. It is not God's will that we should be slaves to either our appetites or the government.

Esther did not choose, did not want, to risk her life to save her people. We are approaching similar times in America, when we will be thrust into a life or death situation, perhaps not of our choosing, but where our influence may make a difference. In preparation for such a situation, we must make certain that we have a right relationship with Jesus

Christ, that we are well grounded in God's Word, that as much as possible we have a right relationship with others, that we have no debt. At that point we will be ready and should be willing to work in our political system to restrain evil.

The political goal, within the constraints of the United States Constitution, is the elimination of income taxes, capital gains taxes and estate taxes while eliminating the federal debt. The only way this can be done is by a massive reduction in federal spending. Without federal money, the establishment of religion in America will collapse. The political principles of disestablishmentarianism can be oversimplified into a bumper sticker phrase: no income tax, no capital gains tax, no estate tax and no deficit spending.

The other politically necessary goal is the appointment of men to federal courts who respect the Constitution. Though there are tens of thousands of examples, probably the two best-known examples of this lack of respect for the United States Constitution are the infamous Supreme Court decisions *Brown v Board of Education* and *Roe v Wade*. Courts only have jurisdiction over issues specifically spelled out in the Constitution. This was promised in the *Federalist Papers* before the Constitution was even voted on. Everything else is expressly forbidden and left to the states. Local school district control and "a woman's right to choose" are in no way among those spelled-out issues. Both of these decisions are necessary to Secular Humanism. Secular Humanists support the results, while ignoring the fact that these two decisions have absolutely no Constitutional basis. Short of war, the only way to overturn these decisions is to replace the Secular Humanists who currently sit in the US Senate with honest Senators. Only good men running for local party offices can make this change. As Stalin is reputed to have said and politicians through the years have reiterated, "It's not who votes that counts, but who counts the votes."

Though many Christians believe that the major problems of America would be solved if a committed believer was elected President, that is simply not true. A believer obedient to the Word of God in the office of President could do much good. He could appoint judges who uphold the constitution, remove unconstitutional regulation and taxes and veto new socialist legislation. These changes, however, will be shallow and temporary without the changed lives of individuals throughout the country. America as a nation has, like the Church at Ephesus of Revelation 2:4, left her first love, and needs to return to the Lord.

Just as God told Elijah that there were left to Him 7,000 in Israel who had not bowed to Baal or kissed him, so there is a faithful remnant in America. If this remnant is unwilling to obey the Word of God in every aspect of life, then America will go down the same path as Nazi Germany, Soviet Russia and Communist China. This is only possible result of allowing Secular Humanism to continue as America's Establishment of Religion. Do not fall for the lie that "I am just one person so it really does not matter what I do."

An establishment of religion is the educational and charitable work of religion supported by the government and the religion and government mutually influencing and supporting each other's actions. With most Established Religions in most governments throughout time and throughout the world, both the religion and the government have been corrupt and dangerous. Secular Humanism became America's Establishment of Religion when it followed the pattern of taking over education and social services, attacking and stifling opposition, and attaching itself to the government through judicial legislation. True Science is an essential basis for all knowledge. Secular Humanism has tried to tear it loose from its scriptural moorings and turn it into a false religious dogma supporting its own power structure. Secularism promotes itself as the only path to peace, prosperity and true advancement. Finally, the outcome of that policy is oppressive government, churches teaching self-worship and individuals unwilling or unable to understand and apply God's teachings in the Scriptures.

The political fight, as distasteful as it is, is necessary. And today, as it has always been, the real decisions are made out of sight in backrooms. The level of involvement in the political process is a decision each believer needs to make. There are no two believers who will be led by God's Spirit in the same way. Jesus called twelve men to follow men as disciples. Others he sent home after healing them.

Our suggestions to fight secularism are incomplete. There are many other possibilities. Please, do not read this and do nothing.

"A good man leaves an inheritance to his children's children, And the wealth of the sinner is

stored up for the righteous."
Proverbs 13:22

What are you leaving your grandchildren?

---

1 Henry Ford, interview with Charles N. Wheeler, *Chicago Tribune*, May 25, 1916.

2 Robert E. Lee, (General Lee's son), *Recollections and Letters of General Robert E. Lee,* letter to Reverdy Johnson (United States Senate), Washington, D. C., Lexington, Virginia, February 25, 1868. "Mr. Francis Preston Blair ... at the instance of President Lincoln [made the request to Lee]. After listening to his remarks, I declined the offer that he made me, to take command of the army that was to be brought into the field; stating, as candidly and courteously as I could, that, though opposed to secession and deprecating war, I could take no part in an invasion of the Southern States." From the website *quillspirit.org*

3 William Mack Lee, from his History of the Life of William Mack Lee, a pamphlet he wrote and published in 1910. Lee was a servant to Robert E. Lee until he became a Baptist Missionary Preacher. The pamphlet bears the inscription "Still living under the protection of the Southern States."

4 From an undated excerpt of Lee's letters to his family, probably in 1862, "...As regards the liberation of the people, I wish to progress in it as far as I can. Those hired in Richmond can still find employment there if they choose. Those in the country can do the same or remain on the farms. I hope they will all do well and behave themselves. I should like, if I could, to attend to their wants and see them placed to the best advantage. But that is

impossible. All that choose can leave the State before the war closes..." From the *website quillspirit.org*

5 In a letter dated December 27, 1856, five years before the war began, Lee said, "There are few, I believe, in this enlightened age, who will not acknowledge that slavery as an institution is a moral and political evil."

6 Paul Taylor, Series Editor, Elizabeth Deane, Program Executive Producer, American Experience, Ulysses S. Grant, *PBS, WGBH Educational Foundation,* 2002. This presentation quoted Grant as saying, "I deplored the agitation of abolitionists, but talk of dissolution of the Union made my blood run cold."

7 Response to Horace Greeley's abolitionist editorial in the *New York Tribune*, August 22, 1862.

8 In 1858 Senator James Henry Hammond of South Carolina replied to Senator William H. Seward of New York:
"Without the firing of a gun, without drawing a sword, should they [Northerners] make war upon us [Southerners], we could bring the whole world to our feet. What would happen if no cotton was furnished for three years ... England would topple headlong and carry the whole civilized world with her. No, you dare not make war on cotton! No power on earth dares make war upon it. Cotton is King."

Appendixes

Appendix One: Court Cases

Church of the Holy Trinity v. United States 1892 U.S. Supreme Court Church of the Holy Trinity v. United States, 143 U.S. 457 (1892) No. 143

Argued and submitted January 7, 1892 Decided February 29, 1892 143 U.S. 457

ERROR TO THE CIRCUIT COURT OF THE UNITED

STATES FOR THE SOUTHERN DISTRICT OF NEW YORK

Syllabus

The Act of February 26, 1880, "to prohibit the importation and migration of foreigners and aliens under contract or agreement to perform labor in the United States, its Territories, and the District of Columbia," 23 Stat. 332, c. 164, does not apply to a contract between an alien, residing out of the United States, and a religious society incorporated under the laws of a state, whereby he engages to remove to the United States and to enter into the service of the society as its rector or minister.

THE case is stated in the opinion.

MR. JUSTICE BREWER delivered the opinion of the Court.

Plaintiff in error is a corporation duly organized and incorporated as a religious society under the laws of the State of New York. E. Walpole Warren was, prior to September, 1887, an alien residing in England. In that month the plaintiff in error made a contract with him by which he was to remove to the City of New York and enter into its service as rector and pastor, and in pursuance of such contract, Warren did so remove and enter upon such service. It is claimed by the United States that this contract on the part of the plaintiff in error was forbidden by 23 Stat. 332, c. 164, and an action was commenced to recover the penalty prescribed by that act. The circuit court held that the contract was within the prohibition of the statute, and rendered judgment accordingly, 36 F.3d 3, and the single question presented for our determination is whether it erred in that conclusion.

The first section describes the act forbidden, and is in these words:

"Be it enacted by the Senate and House of Representatives of the United States of America in Congress assembled, that from and after the passage of this act it shall be unlawful for any person, company, partnership, or corporation, in any manner whatsoever, to prepay the transportation, or in any way assist or encourage the importation or migration, of any alien or aliens, any foreigner or foreigners, into the United States, its territories, or the District of Columbia under contract or agreement, parol or special, express or implied, made previous to the importation or migration of such alien or aliens, foreigner or foreigners, to perform labor or service of any kind in the United States, its territories, or the District of Columbia."

We find, therefore, that the title of the act, the evil which was intended to be remedied, the circumstances surrounding the appeal to Congress, the reports of the committee of each house, all concur in affirming that the intent of Congress was simply to stay the influx of this cheap unskilled labor.

But, beyond all these matters, no purpose of action against religion can be imputed to any legislation, state or national, because this is a religious people. This is historically true. From the discovery of this continent to the present hour, there is a single voice making this affirmation.

The commission to Christopher Columbus, prior to his sail westward, is from "Ferdinand and Isabella, by the grace of God, King and Queen of Castile," etc., and recites that "it is hoped that by God's assistance some of the continents and islands in the ocean will be discovered," etc. The first colonial grant, that made to Sir Walter Raleigh in 1584, was from "Elizabeth, by the grace of God, of England, Fraunce and Ireland, Queene, defender of the faith," etc., and the grant authorizing him to enact statutes of the government of the proposed colony provided that "they be not against the true Christian faith nowe professed in the Church of England." The first charter of Virginia, granted by King James I in 1606, after reciting the application of certain parties for a charter, commenced the grant in these words:

"We, greatly commending, and graciously accepting of, their Desires for the Furtherance of so noble a Work, which may, by the Providence of Almighty God, hereafter tend to the Glory of his Divine Majesty, in propagating of Christian Religion to such People, as yet live in Darkness and miserable Ignorance of the true Knowledge and Worship of God, and may in time bring the Infidels and Savages, living in those parts, to human Civility, and to a settled and quiet government; DO, by these our Letters-Patents, graciously accept of, and agree to, their humble and well intended Desires."

Language of similar import may be found in the subsequent charters of that colony, from the same king, in 1609 and 1611, and the same is true of the various charters granted to the other colonies. In language more or less emphatic is the establishment of the Christian religion declared to be one of the purposes of the grant. The celebrated compact made by the pilgrims in the *Mayflower*, 1620, recites:

"Having undertaken for the Glory of God, and Advancement of the Christian Faith, and the Honour of our King and Country, a Voyage to plant the first Colony in the northern Parts of Virginia; Do by these Presents, solemnly and mutually, in the Presence of God and one another, covenant and combine ourselves together into a civil Body Politick, for our better Ordering and Preservation, and Furtherance of the Ends aforesaid."

The fundamental orders of Connecticut, under which a provisional government was instituted in 1638-39, commence with this declaration:

"Forasmuch as it hath pleased the Allmighty God by the wise disposition of his diuyne pruidence so to Order and dispose of things that we the Inhabitants and Residents of Windsor, Hartford, and Wethersfield are now cohabiting and dwelling in and vppon the River of Conectecotte and the Lands thereunto adioyneing; And well knowing where a people are gathered togather the word of God requires that to mayntayne the peace and vnion of such a people there should be an orderly and decent Gouerment established according to God, to order and dispose of the affayres of the people at all seasons as occation shall require; doe therefore assotiate and conioyne our selues to be as one Publike state or Comonwelth, and doe, for our selues and our Successors and such as shall be adioyned to vs att any tyme hereafter, enter into Combination and Confederation togather, to mayntayne and presearue the liberty and purity of the gospell of our Lord Jesus weh we now prfesse, as also the disciplyne of the Churches, weh according to the truth of the said gospell is now practiced amongst vs."

In the charter of privileges granted by William Penn to the province of Pennsylvania, in 1701, it is recited:

"Because no People can be truly happy, though under the greatest Enjoyment of Civil Liberties, if abridged of the Freedom of their Consciences, as to their Religious Profession and Worship; And Almighty God being the only Lord of Conscience, Father of Lights and Spirits, and the Author as well as Object of all divine Knowledge, Faith, and Worship, who only doth enlighten the Minds, and persuade and convince the Understandings of People, I do hereby grant and declare," etc.

Coming nearer to the present time, the declaration of independence recognizes the presence of the Divine in human affairs in these words:

"We hold these truths to be self-evident, that all men are created equal, that they are endowed by their Creator with certain unalienable Rights, that among these are Life, Liberty, and the pursuit of Happiness. . . . We therefore the Representatives of the United States of America, in General Congress, Assembled, appealing to the Supreme Judge of the world for the rectitude of our intentions, do, in the Name and by Authority of the good these Colonies, solemnly publish and declare," etc.; "And for the support of this Declaration, with a firm reliance on the Protection of Divine Providence, we mutually pledge to each other our Lives, our Fortunes, and our sacred Honor."

If we examine the constitutions of the various states, we find in them a constant recognition of religious obligations. Every Constitution of every one of the forty-four states contains language which, either directly or by clear implication, recognizes a profound reverence for religion, and an assumption that its influence in all human affairs is essential to the wellbeing of the community. This recognition may be in the preamble, such as is found in the Constitution of Illinois, 1870: "We, the people of the State of Illinois, grateful to Almighty God for the civil, political, and religious liberty which He hath so long permitted us to enjoy, and looking to Him for a blessing upon our endeavors to secure and transmit the same unimpaired to succeeding generations," etc.

It may be only in the familiar requisition that all officers shall take an oath closing with the declaration, "so help me God." It may be in clauses like that of the Constitution of Indiana, 1816, Art. XI, section 4: "The manner of administering an oath or affirmation shall be such as is most consistent with the conscience of the deponent, and shall be esteemed the most solemn appeal to God." Or in provisions such as are found in Articles 36 and 37 of the declaration of rights of the Constitution of Maryland, 1867: "That, as it is the duty of every man to worship God in such manner as he thinks most acceptable to Him, all persons are equally entitled to protection in their religious liberty, wherefore no person ought, by any law, to be molested in his person or estate on account of his religious persuasion or profession, or for his religious practice, unless, under the color of religion, he shall disturb the good order, peace, or safety of the state, or shall infringe the laws of morality, or injure others in their natural, civil, or religious rights; nor ought any person to be compelled to frequent or maintain or contribute, unless on contract, to maintain any place of worship or any ministry; nor shall any person, otherwise competent, be deemed incompetent as a witness or juror on account of his religious belief, provided he believes in the existence of God, and that, under his dispensation, such person will be held morally accountable for his acts, and be rewarded or punished therefore, either in this world or the world to come. That no religious test ought ever to be required as a qualification for any office of profit or trust in this state, other than a declaration of belief in the existence of God; nor shall the legislature prescribe any other oath of office than the oath prescribed by this constitution."

Or like that in Articles 2 and 3 of part 1st of the Constitution of Massachusetts, 1780: "It is the right as well as the duty of all men in society publicly, and at stated seasons, to worship the Supreme Being, the great Creator and Preserver of the universe. . . . As the happiness of a people and the good order and preservation of civil government essentially depend upon piety, religion, and morality, and as these cannot be generally diffused through a community but by the institution of the public worship of God and of public instructions in piety, religion, and morality, therefore, to promote their happiness, and to secure the good order and preservation of their government, the people of this commonwealth have a right to invest their legislature with power to authorize and require, and the legislature shall, from time to time, authorize and require, the several towns, parishes, precincts, and other bodies politic or religious societies to make suitable provision at their own expense, for the institution of the public worship of God and for the support and maintenance of public Protestant teachers of piety, religion, and morality, in all cases where such provision shall not be made voluntarily."

Or, as in sections 5 and 14 of Article 7 of the Constitution of Mississippi, 1832: "No person who denies the being of a God, or a future state of rewards and punishments, shall hold any office in the civil department of this state. . . . Religion morality, and knowledge being necessary to good government, the preservation of liberty, and the happiness of mankind, schools, and the means of education, shall forever be encouraged in this state."

Or by Article 22 of the Constitution of Delaware, (1776), which required all officers, besides an oath of allegiance, to make and subscribe the following declaration: "I, A. B., do profess faith in God the Father, and in Jesus Christ His only Son, and in the Holy Ghost, one God, blessed for evermore, and I do acknowledge the Holy Scriptures of the Old and New Testament to be given by divine inspiration."

Even the Constitution of the United States, which is supposed to have little touch upon the private life of the individual, contains in the First Amendment a declaration common to the constitutions of all the states, as follows: "Congress shall make no law respecting an establishment of religion, or prohibiting the free exercise thereof," etc., and also provides in Article I, Section 7, a provision common to many constitutions, that the executive shall have ten days (Sundays excepted) within which to determine whether he will approve or veto a bill.

There is no dissonance in these declarations. There is a universal language pervading them all, having one meaning. They affirm and reaffirm that this is a religious nation. These are not individual sayings, declarations of private persons. They are organic utterances. They speak the voice of the entire people. While, because of a general recognition of this truth, the question has seldom been presented to the courts, yet we find that in

Updegraph v. Commonwealth, 11 S. & R. 394, 400, it was decided that "Christianity, general Christianity, is, and always has been, a part of the common law of Pennsylvania; . . . not Christianity with an established church and tithes and spiritual courts, but Christianity with liberty of conscience to all men."

And in People v. Ruggles, 8 Johns. 290, 294-295, Chancellor Kent, the great commentator on American law, speaking as Chief Justice of the Supreme Court of New York, said: "The people of this state, in common with the people of this country, profess the general doctrines of Christianity as the rule of their faith and practice, and to scandalize the author of these doctrines is not only, in a religious point of view, extremely impious, but, even in respect to the obligations due to society, is a gross violation of decency and good order. . . . The free, equal, and undisturbed enjoyment of religious opinion, whatever it may be, and free and decent discussions on any religious subject, is granted and secured; but to revile, with malicious and blasphemous contempt, the religion professed by almost the whole community is an abuse of that right. Nor are we bound by any expressions in the Constitution, as some have strangely supposed, either not to punish at all, or to punish indiscriminately the like attacks upon the religion of Mahomet or of the Grand Lama, and for this plain reason, that the case assumes that we are a Christian people, and the morality of the country is deeply engrafted upon Christianity, and not upon the doctrines or worship of those impostors."

And in the famous case of Vidal v. Girard's Ex'rs, 2 How. 127, 198, this Court, while sustaining the will of Mr. Girard, with its provision for the creation of a college into which no minister should be permitted to enter, observed: "It is also said, and truly, that the Christian religion is a part of the common law of Pennsylvania."

If we pass beyond these matters to a view of American life, as expressed by its laws, its business, its customs, and its society, we find everywhere a clear recognition of the same truth. Among other matters, note the following: the form of oath universally prevailing, concluding with an appeal to the Almighty; the custom of opening sessions of all deliberative bodies and most conventions with prayer; the prefatory words of all wills,"In the name of God, amen;" the laws respecting the observance of the Sabbath, with the general cessation of all secular business, and the closing of courts, legislatures, and other similar public assemblies on that day; the churches and church organizations which abound in every city, town, and hamlet; the multitude of charitable organizations existing every where under Christian auspices; the gigantic missionary associations, with general support, and aiming to establish Christian missions in every quarter of the globe. These, and many other matters which might be noticed, add a volume of unofficial declarations to the mass of organic utterances that this is a Christian nation. In the face of all these, shall it be believed that a Congress of the United States intended to make it a misdemeanor for a church of this country to contract for the services of a Christian minister residing in another nation?

Suppose, in the Congress that passed this act, some member had offered a bill which in terms declared that if any Roman Catholic church in this country should contract with Cardinal Manning to come to this country and enter into its service as pastor and priest, or any Episcopal church should enter into a like contract with Canon Farrar, or any Baptist church should make similar arrangements with Rev. Mr. Spurgeon, or any Jewish synagogue with some eminent rabbi, such contract should be adjudged unlawful and void, and the church making it be subject to prosecution and punishment. Can it be believed that it would have received a minute of approving thought or a single vote? Yet it is contended that such was, in effect, the meaning of this statute. The construction invoked cannot be accepted as correct. It is a case where there was presented a definite evil, in view of which the legislature used general terms with the purpose of reaching all phases of that evil, and thereafter, unexpectedly, it is developed that the general language thus employed is broad enough to reach cases and acts which the whole history and life of the country affirm could not have been intentionally legislated against. It is the duty of the courts under those circumstances to say that, however broad the language of the statute may be, the act, although within the letter, is not within the intention of the legislature, and therefore cannot be within the statute.

The judgment will be reversed, and the case remanded for further proceedings in accordance with this opinion.

Epperson vs. Arkansas, 1968, United States Supreme Court

(Author's Note: Italicized material represents direct quotations. Material in regular type represents the author's comments.)

(The following paragraph is not part of a trial transcript, but is quoted from the website *Voices For Evolution*.)

In 1968, in Epperson v. Arkansas, the United States Supreme Court invalidated an Arkansas statute that prohibited the teaching of evolution. The Court held the statute unconstitutional on grounds that the First Amendment to the U.S. Constitution does not permit a state to require that teaching and learning must be tailored to the principles or prohibitions of any particular religious sect or doctrine.

(Epperson v. Arkansas (1968) 393 U.S. 97, 37 U.S. Law Week 4017, 89S. Ct. 266, 21 L. Ed 228)

Following are excerpts from the Supreme Court transcript of this trial, taken from the website www.bc.edu/ bc_org/avp/cas/comm/ free_speech/epperson. Background material in the transcript explains that a teacher hired in 1964 to teach High School Biology completed her first year without incident. Her second year, however, a new textbook was obtained for her class which included a chapter on Darwin's theory. The teacher was apparently aware of the state's constitutional issue and decided to protect herself from disciplinary action before any was taken by suing the state to have the statue voided. The excerpt begins by stating the position of the attorney representing the State of Arkansas explaining how the state would interpret the statute.

On the other hand, counsel for the State, in oral argument in this Court, candidly stated that, despite the State Supreme Court's equivocation, Arkansas would interpret the statute "to mean that to make a student aware of the theory . . . just to teach that there was [103] such a theory" would be grounds for dismissal and for prosecution under the statute; and he said "that the Supreme Court of Arkansas' opinion should be interpreted in that manner." He said: "If Mrs. Epperson would tell her students that 'Here is Darwin's theory, that man ascended or descended from a lower form of being,' then I think she would be under this statute liable for prosecution."

In any event, we do not rest our decision upon the asserted vagueness of the statute. On either interpretation of its language, Arkansas' statute cannot stand. It is of no moment whether the law is deemed to prohibit mention of Darwin's theory, or to forbid any or all of the infinite varieties of communication embraced within the term "teaching." Under either interpretation, the law must be stricken because of its conflict with the constitutional prohibition of state laws respecting an establishment of religion or prohibiting the free exercise thereof. The overriding fact is that Arkansas' law selects from the body of knowledge a particular segment which it proscribes for the sole reason that it is deemed to conflict with a particular religious doctrine; that is, with a particular interpretation of the Book of Genesis by a particular religious group.

The following excerpt includes the specific opinion of Justice Black on this matter.

MR. JUSTICE BLACK, concurring.

120

I am by no means sure that this case presents a genuinely justiciable case or controversy. Although Arkansas Initiated Act No. 1, the statute alleged to be unconstitutional, was passed by the voters of Arkansas in 1928, we are informed that there has never been even a single attempt by the State to enforce it. And the pallid, unenthusiastic, even apologetic defense of the Act presented by the State in this Court indicates that the State would make no attempt to enforce the law should it remain on the books for the next century. Now, nearly 40 years after the law has slumbered on the books as though dead, a teacher alleging fear that the State might arouse from its lethargy and try to punish her has asked for a declaratory judgment holding the law unconstitutional. She was subsequently joined by a parent who alleged his interest in seeing that his two then school-age sons "be informed of all scientific theories and hypotheses ..."

Notwithstanding my own doubts as to whether the case presents a justiciable controversy, the Court brushes aside these doubts and leaps headlong into the middle of the very broad problems involved in federal intrusion into state powers to decide what subjects and schoolbooks it may wish to use in teaching state pupils. ... But, agreeing to consider this as a genuine case or controversy, I cannot agree to thrust the Federal Government's long arm the least bit further into state school curriculums than decision of this particular case requires. And the Court, in order to invalidate the Arkansas law as a violation of the First Amendment, has been compelled to give the State's law a broader meaning than the State Supreme Court was willing to give it. The Arkansas

Supreme Court's opinion, in its entirety, stated that:

"Upon the principal issue, that of constitutionality, the court holds that Initiated Measure No. 1 of 1928, Ark. Stat. Ann. § 80-1627 and § 80-1628 (Repl. 1960), is a valid exercise of the state's power to specify the curriculum in its public schools. The court expresses no opinion on the question whether the Act prohibits any explanation of the theory of evolution or merely prohibits teaching that the theory is true; the answer not being necessary to a decision in the case, and the issue not having been raised."

It is plain that a state law prohibiting all teaching of human development or biology is constitutionally quite different from a law that compels a teacher to teach as true only one theory of a given doctrine. It would be difficult to make a First Amendment case out of a state law eliminating the subject of higher mathematics, or astronomy, or biology from its curriculum. And, for all the Supreme Court of Arkansas has said, this particular Act may prohibit that and nothing else. This Court, however, treats the Arkansas Act as though it made it a misdemeanor to teach or to use a book that teaches that evolution is true. But it is not for this Court to arrogate to itself the power to determine the scope of Arkansas statutes. Since the highest court of Arkansas has deliberately refused to give its statute that meaning, we should not presume to do so.

The Supreme Court struck down this Arkansas statue partly because it believed the state was violating the first and fourteenth amendments and partly because it believed the law to be too vaguely worded. The significant fact is in Black's statement that Arkansas had a chance to deal with the issue without federal interference and failed to do so. Black did not like even the idea that a Federal hand might be reaching into a state issue. Education specifics were supposed to be up to the states in those days. Arkansas gave away its state's right, and the rights of states in the future, by allowing the Supreme Court to establish this precedent.

The important issue of this case is just what Black said. The federal government made a ruling in a state issue and that shouldn't have happened. Time after time cases like this one have whittled away autonomy and replaced it with precedent. The power of the federal courts took away, little by little, the control of states over education and transferred it to the federal government. The Supreme Court has been a powerful tool in taking away our protection, our freedom, our rights and our property.

Segraves vs. State of California, 1981

(Author's Note: Italicized material represents direct quotations. Material in regular type represents the author's comments.)

(The following paragraph is not part of a trial transcript, but is quoted from the website Voices For Evolution)

In 1981, in Segraves v. State of California the Court found that the California State Board of Education's Science Framework, as written and as qualified by its anti-dogmatism policy, gave sufficient accommodation to the views of Segraves, contrary to his contention that class discussion of evolution prohibited his and his children's free exercise of religion. The anti-dogmatism policy provided that class discussions of origins should emphasize that scientific explanations focus on "how", not "ultimate cause," and that any speculative statements concerning origins, both in texts and in classes, should be presented conditionally, not dogmatically. The court's ruling also directed the Board of Education to widely disseminate the policy, which in 1989 was expanded to cover all areas of science, not just those concerning issues of origins. (Segraves v. California (1981) Sacramento Superior Court #278978)

Following are excerpts from the oral presentation of the case. Superior Court Judge Irving Perluss adopted a very friendly and informal tone, insisting on the oral format, making light of the need for huge amounts of documentation, and so it's a bit difficult to find a clean copy of this transcript to draw from. Most of the sections are the opinion of the judge, but there is an instance where a witness, Dr. Meyer, is called upon to speak.

These excerpts come from a personal website built by Frank Fire, who says he is "a firefighter/paramedic. (with a name like that, what else would I be?) I also built it to promote critical thinking and to promote the defense of the First Amendment." The text contained a number of typos and formatting errors which have been corrected for ease of reading, but the basic format is that of the original transcript.

The judge's tone seemed to imply that the case was not important enough to be recorded and everyone should just get together as friends and settle things. It established an important precedent, however, and Frank Fire performed an important service by posting a copy of the transcript.

And isn't it truly wonderful that in our country we can seek to invoke the awesome authority of the courts to assuage the feelings of a single child, a child. And in the final analysis, I believe that is what this case is all about. The play between establishment on the one hand, in terms of accommodation, and free exercise on the other. Now, fortunately -- I say "fortunately" because I'm the fellow that has to make the decision -- the issues have been narrowed here to the point where we are not faced with such a dilemma, and thus there is on contention here that evolution should not be taught in the public schools. I think you've heard me say on several occasions that if there were, it would be rejected as an impermissible accommodation, for that battle was fought and resolved by the Supreme Court of the United States, in Epperson versus Arkansas. Now, moreover, the Plaintiffs have disclaimed any interest in an accommodation which would require the teaching of special creation in the public schools. And I might say, in -- and of course, this is what they call, "dicta," this is not part of the decision in this case, but this is my -- my view -- that is was appropriate that they do so, for I have no doubt, whatever, that such an accommodation would be held to be violated with the establishment clause, and forbidden. I think this is so, as a matter of law. It was basically held to be such in the -- in the opinion of the California Attorney General in 58 Attorney General Opinions, 262. And of course, it was held in the decision of

Daniels versus Waters in the Sixth Circuit, which was referred to during the course of our trial.

Now, the issue, simply stated, accordingly, is whether or not the free exercise of religion by Mr. Segraves and his children was thwarted by the instruction in science that children had received in school, and if so, has there been sufficient accommodation for their views?

The Court, in addition, is prepared to find and does find that the science framework, as written, and if qualified by the policy of the Board exemplified by Exhibit N, does provide sufficient accommodation for the views of the Plaintiff. This is so, in my judgment, even if, as was alluded to by Mr. Turner, there is some problem about whether that was ever officially adopted as a policy by the Board because the fact is now that by virtue of the statement of the representative of the Board, more than one, not only the Attorney General but the representatives of the Board, that is current Board policy and shall remain as current Board policy until a Board changes it. I think all teachers -- I hope all teachers endeavor to follow the Code of Ethics and the administrative regulation that we have read 80130 of Title Five. But nevertheless, all of us conclude, and I conclude myself, sometimes are needed -- we need to be reminded of our responsibilities. It seems to me that what has happened here has developed from a lack of communication from the Board to the school to the classroom teacher. I think it is the emphasis on tolerance and understanding that should be communicated as a fundamental policy of the State Board of Education. This is true not only in science, but it's true throughout the entire public school system. I must add that it seems to the Court, also, that persons seeking tolerance and understanding must practice it, also. Only in this way can all of us enjoy the religious liberty which is our fundamental right.

Mr. Turner has already quoted from the concurring opinion of Justice Stewart, and Sherbert versus Vernor. I think it's worth repeating because those are resounding and beautiful words where he said, "I am convinced that no liberty is more essential to the continued vitality of the free society which our constitution guarantees than is the religious liberty protected by the free exercise clause explicit in the First Amendment and embedded in the Fourteenth." I think Justice Stewart has spoken well.

In the final analysis, ladies and gentlemen, counsel, all that Plaintiffs seek, in the Court's view, presently is contained in Board policy. It appears, however, that this Board policy may not have been communicated to all who should know of it, and who should be guided by that policy. As this is a Court of equity, it seems to the Court that an appropriate remedy may be fashioned.

It will be the order of the Court that there shall be disseminated to all the publishers, institutions, school districts, schools, and persons regularly receiving the science framework a copy of the Board policy set forth in Exhibit N. By this, the Court means, insofar as possible, the policies shall -- the policy shall be sent to those who have received the framework in the past. It shall be included in the framework disseminated in the future. It follows that if there are violations of this policy when disseminated it becomes a matter of concern for students and parents to adjust with their local teachers, their local schools, and their local school boards.

"Now, when you begin to think of textbooks that talk about belief, now to me belief is not a scientific word. One knows, one accumulates data, one has a comprehension of, one understands, one does a lot of things, but to me belief always, in my situation, has been something I associate with my theology. I would not like to see my theology and my science get mixed. I have never dealt with a scientific process where somebody says, 'I believe.' I have dealt with theological processes where one believes. In short, I think at that point you begin to mix epistemologies, and that's confusing."

And then I said to him,

"But I see, as I comprehend this case, we are talking about the very kind of disclaimer that you have just told us about, that you have just told us about, that at the beginning of a science textbook should there not be a statement --because not everyone is a scientist and knows all the background of scientists -- but shouldn't there be a statement saying, 'this does not deal with theology?'"

Dr. Mayer,

"Absolutely. I would -- I would say there should be a clear explanation that perhaps should run through the entire textbook within the student's mind what it is he's dealing with. He's dealing with science. We are not making a pretense to teach him music, art, poetry, theology, or any other discipline. Science does these things, and outside of that realm, science is not only moot, but might even be harmful."

Court,

"And, moreover, science is not dogmatic in that it is open ended and there is an absence of preset conclusions?"

The witness,

"Yes sir."

Now, there is one additional statement from Justice Stewart -- forgive me if I quote from him often, but our son clerked for him as a clerk, and so I -- I think he's a great man.

Justice Stewart also said in the concurring opinion, and in the Sherbert case, and these are the words that I felt were most pertinent to our case where he said, "And I think that the guarantee of religious liberty embodied in the free exercise clause affirmatively requires government to create an atmosphere of hospitality and accommodation to individual belief or disbelief. In short, I think our constitution commands the positive protection by government of religious freedom, not only for a minority, however small, not only for the majority, however large, but for each of us." I don't think any of us could really quarrel with that.

As I view this case, accordingly, counsel, I really don't believe that either side has lost. I truly believe that both sides have won. I think that we have all won because hopefully what we have achieved in this case is understanding.

California had a policy to make sure teachers didn't make evolution a dogma. The judge made a very kind and inclusive statement that everybody won but the man and his children lost the case.

The anti-dogmatism policy provided that class discussions of origins should emphasize that scientific explanations focus on "how," not "ultimate cause," and that any speculative statements concerning origins, both in texts and in classes, should be presented conditionally, not dogmatically.

This California statute may or may not have been sufficient to protect the religious beliefs of students. The intended result seems to have been that each side is free to believe what it will about origins. A consequence that may have been unintended is that by accepting and operating under this standard, by attempting to place both sides on an equal footing, Evolutionists reveal that they really do regard Evolution as a set of beliefs, in spite of the judge's contention that Science doesn't deal with beliefs.

McLean v. Arkansas Board of Education, 1982

(Author's Note: Italicized material represents direct quotations. Material in regular type represents the author's comments.)

(The following paragraph is not part of a trial transcript, but is quoted from the website Voices For Evolution.)

In 1982, in McLean v. Arkansas Board of Education, a federal court held that a "balanced treatment" statute violated the Establishment Clause of the U.S. Constitution. The Arkansas statute required public schools to give balanced treatment to "creation-science" and "evolution-science". In a decision that gave a detailed definition of the term "science," the court declared that "creation science" is not in fact a science. The court also found that the statute did not have a secular purpose, noting that the statute used language peculiar to creationist literature in emphasizing origins of life as an aspect of the theory of evolution. While the subject of life's origins is within the province of biology, the scientific community does not consider the subject as part of evolutionary theory, which assumes the existence of life and is directed to an explanation of how life evolved after it originated. The theory of evolution does not presuppose either the absence or the presence of a creator. (McLean v. Arkansas Board of Education (1982) 529 F. Supp. 1255, 50 U.S. Law Week 2412)

Following are excerpts from the trial transcript. The source is *www.talkorigins.org/faqs/mclean-v-arkansas*.

Special attention should be paid to the notation in the preceding paragraph, however, the one that says While the subject of life's origins is within the province of biology, the scientific community does not consider the subject as part of evolutionary theory, which assumes the existence of life and is directed to an explanation of how life evolved after it originated. The theory of evolution does not presuppose either the absence or the presence of a creator. Keep this idea in mind for later consideration.

On March 19, 1981, the Governor of Arkansas signed into law Act 590 of 1981, entitled "Balanced Treatment for Creation-Science and Evolution-Science Act." The Act is codified as Ark. Stat. Ann. &80-1663, et seq., (1981 Supp.). Its essential mandate is stated in its first sentence: "Public schools within this State shall give balanced treatment to creation-science and to evolution-science." On May 27, 1981, this suit was filed challenging the constitutional validity of Act 590 on three distinct grounds.

First, it is contended that Act 590 constitutes an establishment of religion prohibited by the First Amendment to the Constitution, which is made applicable to the states by the Fourteenth Amendment. Second, the plaintiffs argue the Act violates a right to academic freedom which they say is guaranteed to students and teachers by the Free Speech Clause of the First Amendment. Third, plaintiffs allege the Act is impermissibly vague and thereby violates the Due Process Clause of the Fourteenth Amendment.

The following excerpt is significant because it tells you that the courts have taken upon themselves the right to sole and indisputable power to tell us what the Constitution says and what it means. The courts can tell you how to think about this because people let them tell you how to think about it before. Now you're stuck.

There is no controversy over the legal standards under which the Establishment Clause portion of this case must be judged. The Supreme Court has on a number of occasions expounded on the meaning of the clause, and the pronouncements are clear. Often the issue has arisen in the context of public education, as it has here. In Everson v. Board of Education, 330 U.S. 1, 15-16 (1947), Justice Black stated:

The "establishment of religion" clause of the First Amendment means at least this: Neither a state nor the Federal Government can set up a church. Neither can pass laws which aid one religion, aid all religions, or prefer one religion over another. Neither can force nor influence a person to go to or to remain away from church against his will or force him to profess a belief or disbelief in any religion. No person can be punished for entertaining or professing religious beliefs or disbeliefs, for church-attendance or non-attendance. No tax, large or small, can be levied to support any religious activities or institutions, whatever they may be called, or what ever form they may adopt to teach or practice religion. Neither a state nor the Federal Government can, openly or secretly, participate in the affairs of any religious organizations or groups and vice versa. In the words of Jefferson, the clause ... was intended to erect "a wall of separation between church and State."

The Establishment Clause thus enshrines two central values: voluntarism and pluralism. And it is in the area of the public schools that these values must be guarded most vigilantly.

Designed to serve as perhaps the most powerful agency for promoting cohesion among a heterogeneous democratic people, the public school must keep scrupulously free from entanglement in the strife of sects. The preservation of the community from divisive conflicts, of Government from irreconcilable pressures by religious groups, or religion from censorship and coercion however subtly exercised, requires strict confinement of the State to instruction other than religious, leaving to the individual's church and home, indoctrination in the faith of his choice. [McCollum v. Board of Education, 333 U.S. 203, 216-217 (1948), (Opinion of Frankfurter, J., joined by Jackson, Burton, and Rutledge, J.J.)]

What Black said was proper and correct, up to the point where he inserted Jefferson's explanation about the "wall of separation." People have gotten to think that that's actually in the Constitution because of mentions like this, but it isn't. And it's been used to promote the idea that all mention of any religion must be excised from education because education must be a state function. What Thomas Jefferson actually meant is just the opposite of what Justice Black says. Thomas Jefferson, the extreme leftist of his day, meant that the state must not interfere in the affairs of the Church; the wall was to protect the Church from the state. Thomas Jefferson meant what all of the founding fathers meant. No aspect of the federal government, including the courts, had any power, any authority to do anything at all with any aspect an establishment of religion. An Establishment of Religion is welfare, education and worship. Yet Justice Black in this case doesn't even stop there. He goes on to quote Frankfurter, and Frankfurter goes too far. He presupposes that the government must be the teacher or the people can't be cohesive.

Education wasn't originally a state function. It was usurped by the state from religious leaders and parents. In every society from ancient times to the present, where the government took over teaching the children, the seeds of that government's destruction were sown. The teaching of religion doesn't automatically mean that there will be strife or coercion or even indoctrination. Who puts up a fuss about religious instruction? People who don't want to be reminded that they are responsible to God. Look for them, and you'll see where the strife and coercion is coming from.

In the second place, no one even pretends that all religion has been excised from the public school. Yoga classes are taught in Physical Education. Teaching the Crusades in History class can't be done without bringing up religious issues, wrong ones and right ones. Teachers interweave culture and religion with Foreign Language study, and even studying Science brings up medical treatments at the Temple of Aesclipius and Egyptian pharmaceutical papyri ceremonially buried with priests.

The term "scientific creationism" first gained currency around 1965 following publication of *The Genesis Flood* in 1961 by Whitcomb and Morris. There is undoubtedly some connection between the appearance of the BSCS texts emphasizing evolutionary thought and efforts of Fundamentalist to attach the theory. (Mayer)

In the 1960's and early 1970's, several Fundamentalist organizations were formed to promote the idea that the Book of Genesis was supported by scientific data. The terms "creation science" and "scientific creationism" have been adopted by these Fundamentalists as descriptive of their study of creation and the origins of man. Perhaps the leading creationist organization is the Institute for Creation Research (ICR), which is affiliated with the Christian heritage College and supported by the Scott Memorial Baptist Church in San Diego, California. The ICR, through the Creation-Life Publishing Company, is the leading publisher of creation science material. other creation science organizations include the Creation Science Research Center (CSRC) of San Diego and the Bible Science Association of Minneapolis, Minnesota. In 1963, the Creation Research Society (CRS) was formed from a schism in the American Scientific Affiliation (ASA). It is an organization of literal Fundamentalists who have the equivalent of a master's degree in some recognized area of science. A purpose of the organization is "to reach all people with the vital message of the scientific and historical truth about creation." Nelkin, The Science Textbook Controversies and the Politics of Equal Time, 66.

The preceding quote sets up the case being presented, the argument, not about whether teachers should have the freedom to teach what they believe is important and right, but whether a particular teaching must be attacked, discredited and beaten out of the schools. The court has already made itself the authority on what the state is and what religion is and how they can't be in the same room together. That includes the concept that the school is the state. A lengthy summary of the history of Fundamentalism is included in the transcript, because it's necessary for an inextricable bond to be formed between Creation Science and religious extremists. The transcript contends that proponents of this bill were on a religious crusade and that they attempted to conceal the fact to allow their bill to pass.

Senator James L. Holsted [was chosen to] introduce the act. Holsted, a self-described "born again" Christian Fundamentalist, introduced the act in the Arkansas Senate. He did not consult the State Department of Education, scientists, science educators or the Arkansas Attorney General. The Act was not referred to any Senate committee for hearing and was passed after only a few minutes' discussion on the Senate floor. In the House of Representatives, the bill was referred to the Education Committee which conducted a perfunctory fifteen minute hearing. No scientist testified at the hearing, nor was any representative from the State Department of Education called to testify.

The State failed to produce any evidence which would warrant an inference or conclusion that at any point in the process anyone considered the legitimate educational value of the Act. It was simply and purely an effort to introduce the Biblical version of creation into the public school curricula. The only inference which can be drawn from these circumstances is that the Act was passed with the specific purpose by the General Assembly of advancing religion. The Act therefore fails the first prong of the three-pronged test, that of secular legislative purpose, as articulated in Lemon v. Kurtzman, supra, and Stone v. Graham, supra.

An immediate attack is made on the bill's credentials. There were no scientists, no Department of Education input, no senate committee ruled on it, so it can't be valid. More about the issue of scientists later, but at least the last two entities can be identified as instruments of government control. The state must retain sole power here. A bill merely created and submitted by earnest, intelligent citizens is no good on its face.

A presentation of the basic tenets of Creation Science and Evolutionary Science follows in the transcript, setting the two in opposition to each other. An attack is made on this method of presentation as follows and the "true" definition of science is arrived at so that Creation Science can quickly be excluded entirely from serious consideration. The statement that "in a free society, knowledge does not require the imprimatur of legislation in order to become science" is almost laughable if it weren't such a lie. This whole case is about legislating what is and isn't Science.

In addition to the fallacious pedagogy of the two model approach, Section 4(a) lacks legitimate educational value because "creation-science" as defined in that section is simply not science. Several witnesses suggested definitions of science. A descriptive definition was said to be that science is what is "accepted by the scientific community" and is "what scientists do." The obvious implication of this description is that, in a free society, knowledge does not require the imprimatur of legislation in order to become science.

More precisely, the essential characteristics of science are:(1) It is guided by natural law;

(2) It has to be explanatory by reference to nature law;(3) It is testable against the empirical world;(4) Its conclusions are tentative, i.e. are not

necessarily the final word; and (5) It is falsifiable. (Ruse and other science witnesses).

The term "Natural Law" comes from Plato and Aristotle. Aristotle acknowledged the possibility of an "unmoved mover," but Plato is famous for having thrown "the gods" (and the true God) out of his perfect society thousands of years ago. This court has taken an adversarial position carefully devised to exclude the possibility of Creation and set its own position up as the only possible fact. It's not fact, it's philosophy. The entire "definition" of Science presented here is Naturalism, a philosophy designed to exclude God, not true Science at all but a way to set up the worship of man's intellect as an extension of nature.

As many times as the transcript argues that Creation Science proofs don't prove anything, you would think that it would become clear that this premise as a definition of Science doesn't prove anything. About the only thing true about "Science" as defined here is that its conclusions certainly are tentative. Yet the position taken is that they are the final word. This is the dogma of a belief, a religion, not Science.

Note the folksy statements that Science is "what scientists do." Naturally that excludes Creationists, even though most of these proponents of Creation Science hold advanced degrees from accredited institutions in recognized scientific fields. Unless you presuppose that a Creationist can't be a scientist you would have to grant that these people really are scientists and therefore they also do what scientists do.

Creation science as described in Section 4(a) fails to meet these essential characteristics. First, the section revolves around 4(a)(1) which asserts a sudden creation "from nothing." Such a concept is not science because it depends upon a supernatural intervention which is not guided by natural law. It is not explanatory by reference to natural law, is not testable and is not falsifiable.

The same arguments are applicable to Evolution, or would be if Evolution were forced to justify its tenets by actually coming up with a viable theory to cover origins. Instead it is allowed to slide by with the explanation that it doesn't deal with origins. Actually, it does, but more along the lines of Eastern religions which allow for an endless cycle of time, progressively more billions of years. How can the statement that it presupposes the existence of life be satisfactory? It allows for all of Evolutionary theory to be based on presuppositions, and indeed that's all it is, suppositions based on the founding premise that we suppose there isn't any God who started everything.

Creation science as defined in Section 4(a), not only fails to follow the canons of dealing with scientific theory, it also fails to fit the more general descriptions of "what scientists think" and "what scientists do." The scientific community consists of individuals and groups, nationally and internationally, who work independently in such varied fields as biology, paleontology, geology, and astronomy. Their work is published and subject to review and testing by their peers. The journals for publication are both numerous and varied. There is, however, not one recognized scientific journal which has published an article espousing the creation science theory described in Section 4(a). Some of the State's witnesses suggested that the scientific community was "close-minded" on the subject of creationism and that explained the lack of acceptance of the creation science arguments. Yet no witness produced a scientific article for which publication has been refused. Perhaps some members of the scientific community are resistant to new ideas. It is, however, inconceivable that such a loose knit group of independent thinkers in all the varied fields of science could, or would, so effectively censor new scientific thought.

The reader is directed to Dr. Richard Sternberg's discussion of what happened to him when he published an article by Dr. Stephen Meyer which contained material related to Intelligent Design, not even espousing Creationism. (See the Section Three Appendix for specific examples of attacks on recognized members of the scientific community because of a connection with Intelligent Design.)

The trial transcript simply dismisses the possibility that the scientific community could be narrow minded. No doubt thousands of articles and books which have been refused publication could have been produced as evidence of this narrow-mindedness. The transcript later brings up the fact that a woman who was charged with developing curriculum materials was unable to find any that met her criteria for inclusion. In other words, her fruitless search proves one of two points, either that reputable scientists cannot get creationist material published or that her criteria is narrow-minded and exclusive of this material.

141

The defendants' argument would be more persuasive if, in fact, there were only two theories or idea about the origins of life and the world. That there are a number of theories was acknowledge by the State's witnesses, Dr. Wickramasinghe and Dr. Geisler. Dr. Wickramasinghe testified at length in support of a theory that life on earth was "seeded" by comets which delivered genetic material and perhaps organisms to the earth's surface from interstellar dust far outside the solar system. The "seeding" theory further hypothesizes that the earth remains under the continuing influence of genetic material from space which continues to affect life. While Wickramasinghe's theory about the origins of life on earth has not received general acceptance within the scientific community, he has, at least, used scientific methodology to produce a theory of origins which meets the essential characteristics of science.

It is a logical fallacy to create a definition and then make it the only definition anybody can use to prove anything. The preceding exposition of the theory of "genetic seeding" by Dr. Wickramasinghe is presented to prove that creation science isn't allowed to set itself off against Evolution because Evolution isn't the only theory of how things are the way they are. There's this one, which the Scientific community doesn't recognize and won't even fund further study about. Excellent choice. A theory with a completely unprovable, unexaminable and already generally discarded premise is at least good Science.

Robert Gentry's discovery of radioactive polonium haloes in granite and coalified woods is, perhaps, the most recent scientific work which the creationists use as argument for a "relatively recent inception" of the earth and a "worldwide flood." The existence of polonium haloes in granite and coalified wood is thought to be inconsistent with radiometric dating methods based upon constant radioactive decay rates. Mr. Gentry's findings were published almost ten years ago and have been the subject of some discussion in the scientific community. The discoveries have not, however, led to the formulation of any scientific hypothesis or theory which would explain a relatively recent inception of the earth or a worldwide flood. Gentry's discovery has been treated as a minor mystery which will eventually be explained. It may deserve further investigation, but the National Science Foundation has not deemed it to be of sufficient import to support further funding.

The National Science Foundation has decided not to fund this promising area of research for only one reason: It might disprove a few presuppositions Evolutionists cling to. If ever there was an example of narrow-mindedness in the scientific community, here it is. Demanding that Creationists must produce something "new" before they will get a hearing is a humorous thought coming from someone who resurrects Plato to craft a definition of Science. This is a common dismissal of Creationist evidence, that it's old so it isn't valid. How is age a worthy criteria for judging evidentiary value? If you can prove you were born in the United States thirty years ago is that evidence too old to be admitted as proof of citizenship?

In any event, if Act 590 is implemented, many teachers will be required to teach materials in support of creation science which they do not consider academically sound. Many teachers will simply forego teaching subjects which might trigger the "balanced treatment" aspects of Act 590 even though they think the subjects are important to a proper presentation of a course.

Implementation of Act 580 will have serious and untoward consequences for students, particularly those planning to attend college. Evolution is the cornerstone of modern biology, and many courses in public schools contain subject matter relating to such varied topics as the age of the earth, geology and relationships among living things. Any student who is deprived of instruction as to the prevailing scientific thought on these topics will be denied a significant part of science education. Such a deprivation through the high school level would undoubtedly have an impact upon the quality of education in the State's colleges and universities, especially including the pre-professional and professional programs in the health sciences.

"Evolution is the cornerstone of modern biology," certainly gives enormous weight to a theoretical teaching that is not supposed to be presented as dogma. While it's true that eliminating evolution from the curriculum would severely limit what can be taught, this bill did not ask for that to be done. It asked for balance, for equal time, to present the opposing viewpoint. This transcript direly predicts that instead teachers will live n fear of reprisals from wild-eyed religionists and children's education will suffer. They will be denied a full preparation and have stunted opportunities and a blighted future. Who would not fear the possibility that their children might fail to learn important things, things they need to go on in their education?

The defendants argue in their brief that evolution is, in effect, a religion, and that by teaching a religion which is contrary to some students' religious views, the State is infringing upon the student's free exercise rights under the First Amendment. Mr. Ellwanger's legislative findings, which were adopted as a finding of fact by the Arkansas Legislature in Act 590, provides:

Evolution-science is contrary to the religious convictions or moral values or philosophical beliefs of many students and parents, including individuals of many different religious faiths and with diverse moral and philosophical beliefs. Act 590, &7(d).

The defendants argue that the teaching of evolution alone presents both a free exercise problem and an establishment problem which can only be redressed by giving balanced treatment to creation science, which is admittedly consistent with some religious beliefs. This argument appears to have its genesis in a student note written by Mr. Wendell Bird, "Freedom of Religion and Science Instruction in Public Schools," 87 Yale L.J. 515 (1978). The argument has no legal merit.

If creation science is, in fact, science and not religion, as the defendants claim, it is difficult to see how the teaching of such a science could "neutralize" the religious nature of evolution.

Assuming for the purposes of argument, however, that evolution is a religion or religious tenet, the remedy is to stop the teaching of evolution, not establish another religion in opposition to it. Yet it is clearly established in the case law, and perhaps also in common sense, that evolution is not a religion and that teaching evolution does not violate the Establishment Clause, Epperson v. Arkansas, supra, Willoughby v. Stever, No. 15574-75 (D.D.C. May 18, 1973); aff'd. 504 F.2d 271 (D.C. Cir. 1974), cert. denied , 420 U.S. 924 (1975); Wright v. Houston Indep. School Dist., 366 F. Supp. 1208 (S.D. Tex 1978), aff.d. 486 F.2d 137 (5th Cir. 1973), cert. denied 417 U.S. 969 (1974).

As proof that Evolution is not a religion, the transcript cites precedent, case law. This is circular reasoning if there ever was such a thing. The court rules that Evolution is not a religion because another court has already ruled that Evolution is not a religion. Case closed.

The Court closes this opinion with a thought expressed eloquently by the great Justice Frankfurter:

We renew our conviction that "we have at stake the very existence of our country on the faith that complete separation between the state and religion is best for the state and best for religion." Everson v. Board of Education, 330 U.S. at 59. If nowhere else, in the relation between Church and State, "good fences make good neighbors." [McCollum v. Board of Education, 333 U.S. 203, 232 (1948)]

Once again Justice Frankfurter claims for the state the sole right to educate, and to dictate what shall and shall not be allowed in the scope of that education.

The quote from Robert Frost's 1914 poem "Mending Wall" is extremely significant in this context. The narrator of the poem objects to the metaphorical walls dividing people from one another. If the state is that neighbor on the other side, I feel the same as the narrator of Frost's poem:

> *Before I built a wall I'd ask to know*
> *What I was walling in or walling out,*
> *And to whom I was like to give offense.*
> *Something there is that doesn't love a*
> *wall,*
> *That wants it down.'*
> *I could say 'Elves' to him,*
> *But it's not elves exactly, and I'd rather*
> *He said it for himself. I see him there*
> *Bringing a stone grasped firmly by the*
> *top*
> *In each hand, like an old-stone savage*
> *armed.*
> *He moves in darkness as it seems to me,*
> *Not of woods only and the shade of trees.*
> *He will not go behind his father's saying,*
> *And he likes having thought of it so well*
> *He says again,*
> *'Good fences make good neighbors.'*

Edwards v. Aguillard, U.S. Supreme Court, 1987

(Author's Note: Italicized material represents direct quotations.

Material in regular type represents the author's comments.)

(The following paragraph is not part of a trial transcript, but is quoted from the website Voices For Evolution)

In 1987, in Edwards v. Aguillard, the U.S. Supreme Court held unconstitutional Louisiana's "Creationism Act." This statute prohibited the teaching of evolution in public schools, except when it was accompanied by instruction in "creation science." The Court found that, by advancing the religious belief that a supernatural being created humankind, which is embraced by the term creation science, the act impermissibly endorses religion. In addition, the Court found that the provision of a comprehensive science education is undermined when it is forbidden to teach evolution except when creation science is also taught. (Segraves v. State of California (1981) Sacramento Superior Court #278978)

Instead of excerpts from the full trial transcript, which is essentially the same issue as that treated in the case of McLean v. Arkansas Board of Education, 1982, what follows is Justice Antonin Scalia's dissenting opinion, which was shared by the Chief Justice William Rehnquist. This material is taken from www.talkorigins.org/faqs/ edwards-v-aguillard. It is lengthy and includes many notes and references but his statement is in vocabulary easy to understand and well worth reading. It is possible to get through the notes and references with patient effort. There is no inserted commentary because the justice's statements are those of a straightforward, honest man honestly frustrated by his inability to stop an injustice. They need no real explanation and would be difficult to improve upon.

Even if I agreed with the questionable premise that legislation can be invalidated under the Establishment Clause on the basis of its motivation alone, without regard to its effects, I would still find no justification for today's decision. The Louisiana legislators who passed the "Balanced Treatment for Creation-Science and Evolution-Science Act" (Balanced Treatment Act), La. Rev. Stat. Ann. 17:286.1-17:286.7 (West 1982), each of whom had sworn to support the Constitution were well aware of the potential Establishment Clause problems and considered that aspect of the legislation with great care. After seven hearings and several months of study, resulting in substantial revision of the original proposal, they approved the Act overwhelmingly and specifically articulated the secular purpose they meant it to serve.

Although the record contains abundant evidence of the sincerity of that purpose (the only issue pertinent to this case), the Court today holds, essentially on the basis of "its visceral knowledge regarding what must have motivated the legislators," 778 F.2d 225, 227 (CA5 1985) (Gee, J., dissenting) (emphasis added), that the members of the Louisiana Legislature knowingly violated their oaths and then lied about it. I dissent. Had requirements of the Balanced Treatment Act that are not apparent on its face been clarified by an interpretation of the Louisiana Supreme Court, or by the manner of its implementation, the Act might well be found unconstitutional; but the question of its constitutionality cannot rightly be disposed of on the gallop, by impugning the motives of its supporters.

I

This case arrives here in the following posture: The Louisiana Supreme Court has never been given an opportunity to interpret the Balanced Treatment Act, State officials have never attempted to implement it, and it has never been the subject of a full evidentiary hearing. We can only guess at its meaning. We know that it forbids instruction in either "creation-science" or "evolution-science" without instruction in the other, @ 17:286.4A, but the parties are sharply divided over what creation science consists of. Appellants insist that it is a collection of educationally valuable scientific data that has been censored from classrooms by an embarrassed scientific establishment. Appellees insist it is not science at all but thinly veiled religious doctrine. Both interpretations of the intended meaning of that phrase find considerable support in the legislative history.

At least at this stage in the litigation, it is plain to me that we must accept appellants' view of what the statute means. To begin with, the statute itself defines "creation-science" as "the scientific evidences for creation and inferences from those scientific evidences." @ 17:286.3(2) (emphasis added). If, however, that definition is not thought sufficiently helpful, the means by which the Louisiana Supreme Court will give the term more precise content is quite clear -- and again, at this stage in the litigation, favors the appellants' view. "Creation science" is unquestionably a "term of art," see Brief for 72 Nobel Laureates et al. as Amici Curiae 20, and thus, under Louisiana law, is "to be interpreted according to [its] received meaning and acceptation with the learned in the art, trade or profession to which [it] refer[s]." La. Civ. Code Ann., Art. 15 (West 1952). The only evidence in the record of the "received meaning and acceptation" of "creation science" is found in five affidavits filed by appellants. In those affidavits, two scientists, a philosopher, a theologian, and an educator, all of whom claim extensive knowledge of creation science, swear that it is essentially a collection of scientific data supporting the theory that the physical universe and life within it appeared suddenly and have not changed substantially since appearing. See App. to Juris. Statement A-19 (Kenyon); id., at A-36 (Morrow); id., at A-41 (Miethe). These experts insist that creation science is a strictly scientific concept that can be presented without religious reference. See id., at A-19 -- A-20, A-35 (Kenyon); id., at A-36 -- A-38 (Morrow); id., at A-40, A-41, A-43 (Miethe); id., at A-47, A-48 (Most); id., at A-49 (Clinkert). At this point, then, we must assume that the Balanced Treatment Act does not require the presentation of religious doctrine.

Nothing in today's opinion is plainly to the contrary, but what the statute means and what it requires are of rather little concern to the Court. Like the Court of Appeals, 765 F.2d 1251, 1253, 1254 (CA5 1985), the Court finds it necessary to consider only the motives of the legislators who supported the Balanced Treatment Act, ante, at 586, 593-594, 596. After examining the statute, its legislative history, and its historical and social context, the Court holds that the Louisiana Legislature acted without "a secular legislative purpose" and that the Act therefore fails the "purpose" prong of the three-part test set forth in Lemon v. Kurtzman, 403 U.S. 602, 612 (1971). As I explain below, infra, at 636-640, I doubt whether that "purpose" requirement of Lemon is a proper interpretation of the Constitution; but even if it were, I could not agree with the Court's assessment that the requirement was not satisfied here.

This Court has said little about the first component of the Lemon test. Almost invariably, we have effortlessly discovered a secular purpose for measures challenged under the Establishment Clause, typically devoting no more than a sentence or two to the matter. See, e. g., Witters v. Washington Dept. of Services for Blind, 474 U.S. 481, 485-486 (1986); Grand Rapids School District v. Ball, 473 U.S. 373, 383 (1985); Mueller v. Allen, 463 U.S. 388, 394-395 (1983); Larkin v. Grendel's Den, Inc., 459 U.S. 116, 123-124 (1982); Widmar v. Vincent, 454 U.S. 263, 271 (1981); Committee for Public Education & Religious Liberty v. Regan, 444 U.S. 646, 654, 657 (1980); Wolman v. Walter, 433 U.S. 229, 236 (1977) (plurality opinion); Meek v. Pittenger, 421 U.S. 349, 363 (1975); Committee for Public Education & Religious Liberty v. Nyquist, 413 U.S. 756, 773 (1973); Levitt v. Committee for Public Education & Religious Liberty, 413 U.S. 472, 479-480, n. 7 (1973); Tilton v. Richardson, 403 U.S. 672, 678-679 (1971) (plurality opinion); Lemon v. Kurtzman, supra, at 613. In fact, only once before deciding Lemon, and twice since, have we invalidated a law for lack of a secular purpose. See Wallace v. Jaffree, 472 U.S. 38 (1985); Stone v. Graham, 449 U.S. 39 (1980) (per curiam); Epperson v. Arkansas, 393 U.S. 97 (1968).

Nevertheless, a few principles have emerged from our cases, principles which should, but to an unfortunately large extent do not, guide the Court's application of Lemon today. It is clear, first of all, that regardless of what "legislative purpose" may mean in other contexts, for the purpose of the Lemon test it means the "actual" motives of those responsible for the challenged action. The Court recognizes this, see ante, at 585, as it has in the past, see, e. g., Witters v. Washington Dept. of Services for Blind, supra, at 486; Wallace v. Jaffree, supra, at 56. Thus, if those legislators who supported the Balanced Treatment Act in fact acted with a "sincere" secular purpose, ante, at 587, the Act survives the first component of the Lemon test, regardless of whether that purpose is likely to be achieved by the provisions they enacted.

Our cases have also confirmed that when the Lemon Court referred to "a secular . . . purpose," 403 U.S., at 612, it meant "a secular purpose." The author of Lemon, writing for the Court, has said that invalidation under the purpose prong is appropriate when "there [is] no question that the statute or activity was motivated wholly by religious considerations." Lynch v. Donnelly, 465 U.S. 668, 680 (1984) (Burger, C. J.) (emphasis added); see also id., at 681, n. 6; Wallace v. Jaffree, supra, at 56 ("The First Amendment requires that a statute must be invalidated if it is entirely motivated by a purpose to advance religion") (emphasis added; footnote omitted). In all three cases in which we struck down laws under the Establishment Clause for lack of a secular purpose, we found that the legislature's sole motive was to promote religion. See Wallace v. Jaffree, supra, at 56, 57, 60; Stone v. Graham, supra, at 41, 43, n. 5; Epperson v. Arkansas, supra, at 103, 107-108; see also Lynch v. Donnelly, supra, at 680 (describing Stone and Epperson as cases in which we invalidated laws "motivated wholly by religious

153

considerations"). Thus, the majority's invalidation of the Balanced Treatment Act is defensible only if the record indicates that the Louisiana Legislature had no secular purpose.

It is important to stress that the purpose forbidden by Lemon is the purpose to "advance religion." 403 U.S., at 613; accord, ante, at 585 ("promote" religion); Witters v. Washington Dept. of Services for Blind, supra, at 486 ("endorse religion"); Wallace v. Jaffree, 472 U.S., at 56 ("advance religion"); ibid. ("endorse . . . religion"); Committee for Public Education & Religious Liberty v. Nyquist, supra, at 788 ("'advancing' . . . religion"); Levitt v. Committee for Public Education & Religious Liberty, supra, at 481 ("advancing religion"); Walz v. Tax Comm'n of New York City, 397 U.S. 664, 674 (1970) ("establishing, sponsoring, or supporting religion"); Board of Education v. Allen, 392 U.S. 236, 243 (1968) ("'advancement or inhibition of religion'") (quoting Abington School Dist. v. Schempp, 374 U.S. 203, 222 (1963)). Our cases in no way imply that the Establishment Clause forbids legislators merely to act upon their religious convictions. We surely would not strike down a law providing money to feed the hungry or shelter the homeless if it could be demonstrated that, but for the religious beliefs of the legislators, the funds would not have been approved. Also, political activism by the religiously motivated is part of our heritage. Notwithstanding the majority's implication to the contrary, ante, at 589-591, we do not presume that the sole purpose of a law is to advance religion merely because it was supported strongly by organized religions or by adherents of particular faiths. See Walz v. Tax Comm'n of New York City, supra, at 670; cf. Harris

v. McRae, 448 U.S. 297, 319-320 (1980). To do so would deprive religious men and women of their right to participate in the political process. Today's religious activism may give us the Balanced Treatment Act, but yesterday's resulted in the abolition of slavery, and tomorrow's may bring relief for famine victims. Similarly, we will not presume that a law's purpose is to advance religion merely because it "'happens to coincide or harmonize with the tenets of some or all religions,'" Harris v. McRae, supra, at 319 (quoting McGowan v. Maryland, 366 U.S. 420, 442 (1961)), or because it benefits religion, even substantially. We have, for example, turned back Establishment Clause challenges to restrictions on abortion funding, Harris v. McRae, supra, and to Sunday closing laws, McGowan v. Maryland, supra, despite the fact that both "agre[e] with the dictates of [some] Judaeo-Christian religions," id., at 442. "In many instances, the Congress or state legislatures conclude that the general welfare of society, wholly apart from any religious considerations, demands such regulation." Ibid. On many past occasions we have had no difficulty finding a secular purpose for governmental action far more likely to advance religion than the Balanced Treatment Act. See, e. g., Mueller v. Allen, 463 U.S., at 394-395 (tax deduction for expenses of religious education); Wolman v. Walter, 433 U.S., at 236 (plurality opinion) (aid to religious schools); Meek v. Pittenger, 421 U.S., at 363 (same); Committee for Public Education & Religious Liberty v. Nyquist, 413 U.S., at 773 (same); Lemon v. Kurtzman, 403 U.S., at 613 (same); Walz v. Tax Comm'n of New York City, supra, at 672 (tax exemption for church property);

155

Board of Education v. Allen, supra, at 243 (textbook loans to students in religious schools). Thus, the fact that creation science coincides with the beliefs of certain religions, a fact upon which the majority relies heavily, does not itself justify invalidation of the Act.

Finally, our cases indicate that even certain kinds of governmental actions undertaken with the specific intention of improving the position of religion do not "advance religion" as that term is used in Lemon. 403 U.S., at 613. Rather, we have said that in at least two circumstances government must act to advance religion, and that in a third it may do so.

First, since we have consistently described the Establishment Clause as forbidding not only state action motivated by the desire to advance religion, but also that intended to "disapprove," "inhibit," or evince "hostility" toward religion, see, e. g., ante, at 585 ("'disapprove'") (quoting Lynch v. Donnelly, supra, at 690 (O'CONNOR, J., concurring)); Lynch v. Donnelly, supra, at 673 ("hostility"); Committee for Public Education & Religious Liberty v. Nyquist, supra, at 788 ("'inhibi[t]'"); and since we have said that governmental "neutrality" toward religion is the preeminent goal of the First Amendment, see, e. g., Grand Rapids School District v. Ball, 473 U.S., at 382; Roemer v. Maryland Public Works Bd., 426 U.S. 736, 747 (1976) (plurality opinion); Committee for Public Education & Religious Liberty v. Nyquist, supra, at 792-793; a State which discovers that its employees are inhibiting religion must take steps to prevent them from doing so, even though its purpose would clearly be to advance religion. Cf.

156

Walz v. Tax Comm'n of New York City, supra, at 673. Thus, if the Louisiana Legislature sincerely believed that the State's science teachers were being hostile to religion, our cases indicate that it could act to eliminate that hostility without running afoul of Lemon's purpose test.

Second, we have held that intentional governmental advancement of religion is sometimes required by the Free Exercise Clause. For example, in Hobbie v. Unemployment Appeals Comm'n of Fla., 480 U.S. 136 (1987); Thomas v. Review Bd., Indiana Employment Security Div., 450 U.S. 707 (1981); Wisconsin v. Yoder, 406 U.S. 205 (1972); and Sherbert v. Verner, 374 U.S. 398 (1963), we held that in some circumstances States must accommodate the beliefs of religious citizens by exempting them from generally applicable regulations. We have not yet come close to reconciling Lemon and our Free Exercise cases, and typically we do not really try. See, e. g., Hobbie v. Unemployment Appeals Comm'n of Fla., supra, at 144-145; Thomas v. Review Bd., Indiana Employment Security Div., supra, at 719-720. It is clear, however, that members of the Louisiana Legislature were not impermissibly motivated for purposes of the Lemon test if they believed that approval of the Balanced Treatment Act was required by the Free Exercise Clause.

We have also held that in some circumstances government may act to accommodate religion, even if that action is not required by the First Amendment. See Hobbie v. Unemployment Appeals Comm'n of Fla., supra, at 144-145. It is well established that "the limits of permissible state accommodation to religion are by no means co-extensive with the noninterference mandated by the Free Exercise Clause." Walz v. Tax Comm'n of New York City, supra, at 673; see also Gillette v. United States, 401 U.S. 437, 453 (1971). We have implied that voluntary governmental accommodation of religion is not only permissible, but desirable. See, e. g., ibid. Thus, few would contend that Title VII of the Civil Rights Act of 1964, which both forbids religious discrimination by private-sector employers, 78 Stat. 255, 42 U. S. C. @ 2000e-2(a)(1), and requires them reasonably to accommodate the religious practices of their employees, @ 2000e(j), violates the Establishment Clause, even though its "purpose" is, of course, to advance religion, and even though it is almost certainly not required by the Free Exercise Clause. While we have warned that at some point, accommodation may devolve into "an unlawful fostering of religion," Hobbie v. Unemployment Appeals Comm'n of Fla., supra, at 145, we have not suggested precisely (or even roughly) where that point might be. It is possible, then, that even if the sole motive of those voting for the Balanced Treatment Act was to advance religion, and its passage was not actually required, or even believed to be required, by either the Free Exercise or Establishment Clauses, the Act would nonetheless survive scrutiny under Lemon's purpose test.

One final observation about the application of that test: Although the Court's opinion gives no hint of it, in the past we have repeatedly affirmed "our reluctance to attribute unconstitutional motives to the States." Mueller v. Allen, supra, at 394; see also Lynch v. Donnelly, 465 U.S., at 699 (BRENNAN, J., dissenting). We "presume that legislatures act in a constitutional manner."

Illinois v. Krull, 480 U.S. 340, 351 (1987); see also Clements v. Fashing, 457 U.S. 957, 963 (1982) (plurality opinion); Rostker v. Goldberg, 453 U.S. 57, 64

(1981); McDonald v. Board of Election Comm'rs of Chicago, 394 U.S. 802, 809 (1969). Whenever we are called upon to judge the constitutionality of an act of a state legislature, "we must have 'due regard to the fact that this Court is not exercising a primary judgment but is sitting in judgment upon those who also have taken the oath to observe the Constitution and who have the responsibility for carrying on government.'" Rostker v. Goldberg, supra, at 64 (quoting Joint Anti-Fascist Refugee Committee v. McGrath, 341 U.S. 123, 164 (1951) (Frankfurter, J., concurring)). This is particularly true, we have said, where the legislature has specifically considered the question of a law's constitutionality. Ibid.

With the foregoing in mind, I now turn to the purposes underlying adoption of the Balanced Treatment Act.

II

II A

We have relatively little information upon which to judge the motives of those who supported the Act. About the only direct evidence is the statute itself and transcripts of the seven committee hearings at which it was considered. Unfortunately, several of those hearings were sparsely attended, and the legislators who were present revealed little about their motives. We have no committee reports, no floor debates, no remarks inserted into the legislative history, no statement from the

Governor, and no postenactment statements or testimony from the bill's sponsor or any other legislators. Cf. Wallace v. Jaffree, 472 U.S., at 43, 56-57. Nevertheless, there is ample evidence that the majority is wrong in holding that the Balanced Treatment Act is without secular purpose.

At the outset, it is important to note that the Balanced Treatment Act did not fly through the Louisiana Legislature on wings of fundamentalist religious fervor -- which would be unlikely, in any event, since only a small minority of the State's citizens belong to fundamentalist religious denominations. See B. Quinn, H. Anderson, M. Bradley, P. Goetting, & P. Shriver, Churches and Church Membership in the United States 16 (1982). The Act had its genesis (so to speak) in legislation introduced by Senator Bill Keith in June 1980. After two hearings before the Senate Committee on Education, Senator Keith asked that his bill be referred to a study commission composed of members of both Houses of the Louisiana Legislature. He expressed hope that the joint committee would give the bill careful consideration and determine whether his arguments were "legitimate." 1 App. E-29

-- E-30. The committee met twice during the interim, heard testimony (both for and against the bill) from several witnesses, and received staff reports. Senator Keith introduced his bill again when the legislature reconvened. The Senate Committee on Education held two more hearings and approved the bill after substantially amending it (in part over Senator Keith's objection). After approval by the full Senate, the bill was referred to the House Committee on Education. That committee conducted a lengthy hearing, adopted further amendments, and sent the bill on to the full House, where it received favorable consideration. The Senate concurred in the House amendments and on July 20, 1981, the Governor signed the bill into law.

Senator Keith's statements before the various committees that considered the bill hardly reflect the confidence of a man preaching to the converted. He asked his colleagues to "keep an open mind" and not to be "biased" by misleading characterizations of creation science. Id., at E-33. He also urged them to "look at this subject on its merits and not on some preconceived idea." Id., at E-34; see also 2 id., at E-491. Senator Keith's reception was not especially warm. Over his strenuous objection, the Senate Committee on Education voted 5-1 to amend his bill to deprive it of any force; as amended, the bill merely gave teachers permission to balance the teaching of creation science or evolution with the other. 1 id., at E-442 -- E-461. The House Committee restored the "mandatory" language to the bill by a vote of only 6-5, 2 id., at E-626 -- E-627, and both the full House (by vote of 52-35), id., at E-700 -- E-706, and full Senate (23-15), id., at E-735 -- E-738, had to repel further efforts to gut the bill.

The legislators understood that Senator Keith's bill involved a "unique" subject, 1 id., at E-106 (Rep. M. Thompson), and they were repeatedly made aware of its potential constitutional problems, see, e. g., id., at E-26 -- E-28 (McGehee); id., at E-38 -- E-39 (Sen. Keith); id., at E-241 -- E-242 (Rossman); id., at E-257 (Probst); id., at E-261 (Beck); id., at E-282 (Sen. Keith). Although the

161

Establishment Clause, including its secular purpose requirement, was of substantial concern to the legislators, they eventually voted overwhelmingly in favor of the Balanced Treatment Act: The House approved it 71-19 (with 15 members absent), 2 id., at E-716 -- E-722; the Senate 26-12 (with all members present), id., at E-741 -- E-744. The legislators specifically designated the protection of "academic freedom" as the purpose of the Act. La. Rev. Stat. Ann. @ 17:286.2 (West 1982). We cannot accurately assess whether this purpose is a "sham," ante, at 587, until we first examine the evidence presented to the legislature far more carefully than the Court has done.

Before summarizing the testimony of Senator Keith and his supporters, I wish to make clear that I by no means intend to endorse its accuracy. But my views (and the views of this Court) about creation science and evolution are (or should be) beside the point. Our task is not to judge the debate about teaching the origins of life, but to ascertain what the members of the Louisiana Legislature believed. The vast majority of them voted to approve a bill which explicitly stated a secular purpose; what is crucial is not their wisdom in believing that purpose would be achieved by the bill, but their sincerity in believing it would be.

Most of the testimony in support of Senator Keith's bill came from the Senator himself and from scientists and educators he presented, many of whom enjoyed academic credentials that may have been regarded as quite impressive by members of the Louisiana Legislature. To a substantial extent, their testimony was devoted to

162

lengthy, and, to the layman, seemingly expert scientific expositions on the origin of life. See, e. g., 1 App. E-11 -- E-18 (Sunderland); id., at E-50 -- E-60 (Boudreaux); id., at E-86 -- E-89 (Ward); id., at E-130 -- E-153 (Boudreaux paper); id., at E-321 -- E-326 (Boudreaux); id., at E-423 -- E-428 (Sen. Keith). These scientific lectures touched upon, inter alia, biology, paleontology, genetics, astronomy, astrophysics, probability analysis, and biochemistry. The witnesses repeatedly assured committee members that "hundreds and hundreds" of highly respected, internationally renowned scientists believed in creation science and would support their testimony. See, e. g., id., at E-5 (Sunderland); id., at E-76 (Sen. Keith); id., at E-100 -- E-101 (Reiboldt); id., at E-327 -- E-328 (Boudreaux); 2 id., at E-503 -- E-504 (Boudreaux).

Senator Keith and his witnesses testified essentially as set forth in the following numbered paragraphs:

(1) There are two and only two scientific explanations for the beginning of life -- evolution and creation science. 1 id., at E-6 (Sunderland); id., at E-34 (Sen. Keith); id., at E-280 (Sen. Keith); id., at E-417 -- E-418 (Sen. Keith). Both are bona fide "sciences." Id., at E-6 -- E-7 (Sunderland); id., at E-12 (Sunderland); id., at E-416 (Sen. Keith); id., at E-427 (Sen. Keith); 2 id., at E-491 -- E-492 (Sen. Keith); id., at E-497 -- E-498 (Sen. Keith). Both posit a theory of the origin of life and subject that theory to empirical testing. Evolution posits that life arose out of inanimate chemical compounds and has gradually evolved over millions of years. Creation science posits that all life forms now on earth appeared suddenly and

relatively recently and have changed little. Since there are only two possible explanations of the origin of life, any evidence that tends to disprove the theory of evolution necessarily tends to prove the theory of creation science, and vice versa. For example, the abrupt appearance in the fossil record of complex life, and the extreme rarity of transitional life forms in that record, are evidence for creation science. 1 id., at E-7 (Sunderland); id., at E-12 -- E-18 (Sunderland); id., at E-45 -- E-60 (Boudreaux); id., at E-67 (Harlow); id., at E-130 -- E-153 (Boudreaux paper); id., at E-423 -- E-428 (Sen. Keith).

(2) The body of scientific evidence supporting creation science is as strong as that supporting evolution. In fact, it may be stronger. Id., at E-214 (Young statement); id., at E-310 (Sen. Keith); id., at E-416 (Sen. Keith); 2 id., at E-492 (Sen. Keith). The evidence for evolution is far less compelling than we have been led to believe. Evolution is not a scientific "fact," since it cannot actually be observed in a laboratory. Rather, evolution is merely a scientific theory or "guess." 1 id., at E-20 -- E-21 (Morris); id., at E-85 (Ward); id., at E-100 (Reiboldt); id., at E-328 -- E-329 (Boudreaux); 2 id., at E-506 (Boudreaux). It is a very bad guess at that. The scientific problems with evolution are so serious that it could accurately be termed a "myth." 1 id., at E-85 (Ward); id., at E-92 -- E-93 (Kalivoda); id., at E-95 -- E-97 (Sen. Keith); id., at E-154 (Boudreaux paper); id., at E-329 (Boudreaux); id., at E-453 (Sen. Keith); 2 id., at E-505 -- E-506 (Boudreaux); id., at E-516 (Young).

(3) Creation science is educationally valuable. Students exposed to it better understand the

current state of scientific evidence about the origin of life. 1 id., at E-19 (Sunderland); id., at E-39 (Sen. Keith); id., at E-79 (Kalivoda); id., at E-308 (Sen. Keith); 2 id., at E-513 -- E-514 (Morris). Those students even have a better understanding of evolution. 1 id., at E-19 (Sunderland). Creation science can and should be presented to children without any religious content. Id., at E-12 (Sunderland); id., at E-22 (Sanderford); id., at E-35 -- E-36 (Sen. Keith); id., at E-101 (Reiboldt); id., at E-279 -- E-280 (Sen. Keith); id., at E-282 (Sen. Keith).

(4) Although creation science is educationally valuable and strictly scientific, it is now being censored from or misrepresented in the public schools. Id., at E-19 (Sunderland); id., at E-21 (Morris); id., at E-34 (Sen. Keith); id., at E-37 (Sen. Keith); id., at E-42 (Sen. Keith); id., at E-92 (Kalivoda); id., at E-97 -- E-98 (Reiboldt); id., at E-214 (Young statement); id., at E-218 (Young statement); id., at E-280 (Sen. Keith); id., at E-309 (Sen. Keith); 2 id., at E-513 (Morris). Evolution, in turn, is misrepresented as an absolute truth. 1 id., at E-63 (Harlow); id., at E-74 (Sen. Keith); id., at E-81 (Kalivoda); id., at E-214 (Young statement); 2 id., at E-507 (Harlow); id., at E-513 (Morris); id., at E-516 (Young). Teachers have been brainwashed by an entrenched scientific establishment composed almost exclusively of scientists to whom evolution is like a "religion." These scientists discriminate against creation scientists so as to prevent evolution's weaknesses from being exposed. 1 id., at E-61 (Boudreaux); id., at E-63 -- E-64 (Harlow); id., at E-78 -- E-79 (Kalivoda); id., at E-80 (Kalivoda); id., at E-95 -- E-97 (Sen. Keith); id., at E-129 (Boudreaux paper);

id., at E-218 (Young statement); id., at E-357 (Sen. Keith); id., at E-430 (Boudreaux).

(5) The censorship of creation science has at least two harmful effects. First, it deprives students of knowledge of one of the two scientific explanations for the origin of life and leads them to believe that evolution is proven fact; thus, their education suffers and they are wrongly taught that science has proved their religious beliefs false. Second, it violates the Establishment Clause. The United States Supreme Court has held that secular humanism is a religion. Id., at E-36 (Sen. Keith) (referring to Torcaso v. Watkins, 367 U.S. 488, 495, n. 11 (1961)); 1 App. E-418 (Sen. Keith); 2 id., at E-499 (Sen. Keith). Belief in evolution is a central tenet of that religion. 1 id., at E-282 (Sen. Keith); id., at E-312 -- E-313 (Sen. Keith); id., at E-317 (Sen. Keith); id., at E-418 (Sen. Keith); 2 id., at E-499 (Sen. Keith). Thus, by censoring creation science and instructing students that evolution is fact, public school teachers are now advancing religion in violation of the Establishment Clause. 1 id., at E-2 -- E-4 (Sen. Keith); id., at E-36 -- E-37, E-39 (Sen. Keith); id., at E-154 -- E-155 (Boudreaux paper); id., at E-281 -- E-282 (Sen. Keith); id., at E-313 (Sen. Keith); id., at E-315 -- E-316 (Sen. Keith); id., at E-317 (Sen. Keith); 2 id., at E-499 -- E-500 (Sen. Keith).

Senator Keith repeatedly and vehemently denied that his purpose was to advance a particular religious doctrine. At the outset of the first hearing on the legislation, he testified: "We are not going to say today that you should have some kind of religious instructions in our schools. . . . We are not talking about religion today. . . . I am not proposing that we take the Bible in each science class and read the first chapter of Genesis." 1 id., at E-35. At a later hearing, Senator Keith stressed: "To . . . teach religion and disguise it as creationism . . . is not my intent. My intent is to see to it that our textbooks are not censored." Id., at E-280. He made many similar statements throughout the hearings. See, e. g., id., at E-41; id., at E-282; id., at E-310; id., at E-417; see also id., at E-44 (Boudreaux); id., at E-80 (Kalivoda).

We have no way of knowing, of course, how many legislators believed the testimony of Senator Keith and his witnesses. But in the absence of evidence to the contrary (4), we have to assume that many of them did. Given that assumption, the Court today plainly errs in holding that the Louisiana Legislature passed the Balanced Treatment Act for exclusively religious purposes.

II B

Even with nothing more than this legislative history to go on, I think it would be extraordinary to invalidate the Balanced Treatment Act for lack of a valid secular purpose. Striking down a law approved by the democratically elected representatives of the people is no minor matter. "The cardinal principle of statutory construction is to save and not to destroy. We have repeatedly held that as between two possible interpretations of a statute, by one of which it would be unconstitutional and by the other valid, our plain duty is to adopt that which will save the act." NLRB v. Jones & Laughlin Steel Corp., 301 U.S. 1, 30 (1937). So, too, it seems to me, with discerning statutory purpose. Even if the legislative history were silent or ambiguous about the existence of a secular purpose -- and here it is not -- the statute should survive Lemon's purpose test. But even more validation than mere legislative history is present here. The Louisiana Legislature explicitly set forth its secular purpose ("protecting academic freedom") in the very text of the Act. La. Rev. Stat. @ 17:286.2 (West 1982). We have in the past repeatedly relied upon or deferred to such expressions, see, e. g., Committee for Public Education & Religious Liberty v. Regan, 444 U.S., at 654; Meek v. Pittenger, 421 U.S., at 363, 367-368; Committee for Public Education & Religious Liberty v. Nyquist, 413 U.S., at 773; Levitt v. Committee for Public Education & Religious Liberty, 413 U.S., at 479-480, n. 7; Tilton v. Richardson, 403 U.S., at 678-679 (plurality opinion); Lemon v. Kurtzman, 403 U.S., at 613; Board of Education v. Allen, 392 U.S., at 243.

The Court seeks to evade the force of this expression of purpose by stubbornly misinterpreting it, and then finding that the provisions of the Act do not advance that misinterpreted purpose, thereby showing it to be a sham. The Court first surmises that "academic freedom" means "enhancing the freedom of teachers to teach what they will," ante, at 586 -- even though "academic freedom" in that sense has little scope in the structured elementary and secondary curriculums with which the Act is concerned. Alternatively, the Court suggests that it might mean "maximiz[ing] the comprehensiveness and effectiveness of science instruction," ante, at 588 -- though that is an exceedingly strange interpretation of the words, and one that is refuted on the very face of the statute. See @ 17:286.5. Had the Court devoted to this central question of the meaning of the legislatively expressed purpose a small fraction of the research into legislative history that produced its quotations of religiously motivated statements by individual legislators, it would have discerned quite readily what "academic freedom" meant: students' freedom from indoctrination. The legislature wanted to ensure that students would be free to decide for themselves how life began, based upon a fair and balanced presentation of the scientific evidence -- that is, to protect "the right of each [student] voluntarily to determine what to believe (and what not to believe) free of any coercive pressures from the State." Grand Rapids School District v. Ball, 473 U.S., at 385. The legislature did not care whether the topic of origins was taught; it simply wished to ensure that when the topic was taught, students would receive "'all of the evidence.'" Ante, at 586 (quoting Tr. of Oral Arg. 60).

As originally introduced, the "purpose" section of the Balanced Treatment Act read: "This Chapter is enacted for the purposes of protecting academic freedom . . . of students . . . and assisting students in their search for truth." 1 App. E-292 (emphasis added). Among the proposed findings of fact contained in the original version of the bill was the following: "Public school instruction in only evolution-science . . . violates the principle of academic freedom because it denies students a choice between scientific models and instead indoctrinates them in evolution science alone." Id., at E-295 (emphasis added). Senator Keith unquestionably understood "academic freedom" to mean "freedom from indoctrination." See id., at E-36 (purpose of bill is "to protect academic freedom by providing student choice"); id., at E-283

(purpose of bill is to protect "academic freedom" by giving students a "choice" rather than subjecting them to "indoctrination on origins")

If one adopts the obviously intended meaning of the statutory term "academic freedom," there is no basis whatever for concluding that the purpose they express is a "sham." Ante, at 587. To the contrary, the Act pursues that purpose plainly and consistently. It requires that, whenever the subject of origins is covered, evolution be "taught as a theory, rather than as proven scientific fact" and that scientific evidence inconsistent with the theory of evolution (viz., "creation science") be taught as well. La. Rev. Stat. Ann. @ 17:286.4A (West 1982). Living up to its title of "Balanced Treatment for Creation-Science and Evolution-Science Act," @ 17.286.1, it treats the teaching of creation the same way. It does not mandate instruction in creation science, @ 17:286.5; forbids teachers to present creation science "as proven scientific fact," @ 17:286.4A; and bans the teaching of creation science unless the theory is (to use the Court's terminology) "discredit[ed] '. . . at every turn'" with the teaching of evolution. Ante, at 589 (quoting 765 F.2d, at 1257). It surpasses understanding how the Court can see in this a purpose "to restructure the science curriculum to conform with a particular religious viewpoint," ante, at 593,"to provide a persuasive advantage to a particular religious doctrine," ante, at 592,"to promote the theory of creation science which embodies a particular religious tenet," ante, at 593, and "to endorse a particular religious doctrine," ante, at 594.

The Act's reference to "creation" is not convincing evidence of religious purpose. The Act defines creation science as "scientific evidenc[e]," @ 17:286.3(2) (emphasis added), and Senator Keith and his witnesses repeatedly stressed that the subject can and should be presented without religious content. See supra, at 623. We have no basis on the record to conclude that creation science need be anything other than a collection of scientific data supporting the theory that life abruptly appeared on earth. See n. 4, supra. Creation science, its proponents insist, no more must explain whence life came than evolution must explain whence came the inanimate materials from which it says life evolved. But even if that were not so, to posit a past creator is not to posit the eternal and personal God who is the object of religious veneration. Indeed, it is not even to posit the "unmoved mover" hypothesized by Aristotle and other notably nonfundamentalist philosophers. Senator Keith suggested this when he referred to "a creator however you define a creator." 1 App. E-280 (emphasis added).

The Court cites three provisions of the Act which, it argues, demonstrate a "discriminatory preference for the teaching of creation science" and no interest in "academic freedom." Ante, at 588. First, the Act prohibits discrimination only against creation scientists and those who teach creation science. @ 17:286.4C. Second, the Act requires local school boards to develop and provide to science teachers "a curriculum guide on presentation of creation-science." @ 17:286.7A. Finally, the Act requires the Governor to designate seven creation scientists who shall, upon request, assist local school boards in developing the curriculum guides. @ 17:286.7B. But none of these provisions casts doubt upon the sincerity of the legislators' articulated purpose of "academic freedom" -- unless, of course, one gives that term the obviously erroneous meanings preferred by the Court. The Louisiana legislators had been told repeatedly that creation scientists were scorned by most educators and scientists, who themselves had an almost religious faith in evolution. It is hardly surprising, then, that in seeking to achieve a balanced,"nonindoctrinating" curriculum, the legislators protected from discrimination only those teachers whom they thought were suffering from discrimination. (Also, the legislators were undoubtedly aware of Epperson v. Arkansas, 393 U.S. 97 (1968), and thus could quite reasonably have concluded that discrimination against evolutionists was already prohibited.) The two provisions respecting the development of curriculum guides are also consistent with "academic freedom" as the Louisiana Legislature understood the term. Witnesses had informed the legislators that, because of the hostility of most scientists and educators to creation science, the topic had been censored from or badly misrepresented in elementary and secondary school texts. In light of the unavailability of works on creation science suitable for classroom use (a fact appellees concede, see Brief for Appellees 27, 40) and the existence of ample materials on evolution, it was entirely reasonable for the legislature to conclude that science teachers attempting to implement the Act would need a curriculum guide on creation science, but not on evolution, and that those charged with developing the guide would need an easily accessible group of creation scientists. Thus, the provisions of the Act of so much concern to the Court support the conclusion that the legislature acted to advance "academic freedom."

The legislative history gives ample evidence of the sincerity of the Balanced Treatment Act's articulated purpose. Witness after witness urged the legislators to support the Act so that students would not be "indoctrinated" but would instead be free to decide for themselves, based upon a fair presentation of the scientific evidence, about the origin of life. See, e. g., 1 App. E-18 (Sunderland) ("all that we are advocating" is presenting "scientific data" to students and "letting [them] make up their own mind[s]"); id., at E-19 -- E-20 (Sunderland) (Students are now being "indoctrinated" in evolution through the use of "censored school books. . . . All that we are asking for is [the] open unbiased education in the classroom . . . your students deserve"); id., at E-21 (Morris) ("A student cannot [make an intelligent decision about the origin of life] unless he is well informed about both [evolution and creation science]"); id., at E-22 (Sanderford) ("We are asking very simply [that] . . . creationism [be presented] alongside . . . evolution and let people make their own mind[s] up"); id., at E-23 (Young) (the bill would require teachers to live up to their "obligation to present all theories" and thereby enable "students to make judgments themselves"); id., at E-44 (Boudreaux) ("Our intention is truth and as a scientist, I am interested in truth"); id., at E-60 -- E-61 (Boudreaux) ("We [teachers] are guilty of a lot of brainwashing. . . . We have a duty to . . . [present the] truth" to students "at all levels from gradeschool on through the college level");

173

id., at E-79 (Kalivoda) ("This [hearing] is being held I think to determine whether children will benefit from freedom of information or if they will be handicapped educationally by having little or no information about creation"); id., at E-80 (Kalivoda) ("I am not interested in teaching religion in schools. . . . I am interested in the truth and [students] having the opportunity to hear more than one side"); id., at E-98 (Reiboldt) ("The students have a right to know there is an alternate creationist point of view. They have a right to know the scientific evidences which suppor[t] that alternative"); id., at E-218 (Young statement) (passage of the bill will ensure that "communication of scientific ideas and discoveries may be unhindered"); 2 id., at E-514 (Morris) ("Are we going to allow [students] to look at evolution, to look at creationism, and to let one or the other stand or fall on its own merits, or will we by failing to pass this bill . . . deny students an opportunity to hear another viewpoint?"); id., at E-516 -- E-517 (Young) ("We want to give the children here in this state an equal opportunity to see both sides of the theories"). Senator Keith expressed similar views. See, e. g., 1 id., at E-36; id., at E-41; id., at E-280; id., at E-283.

Legislators other than Senator Keith made only a few statements providing insight into their motives, but those statements cast no doubt upon the sincerity of the Act's articulated purpose. The legislators were concerned primarily about the manner in which the subject of origins was presented in Louisiana schools -- specifically, about whether scientifically valuable information was being censored and students misled about evolution. Representatives Cain, Jenkins, and F.

174

Thompson seemed impressed by the scientific evidence presented in support of creation science. See 2 id., at E-530 (Rep. F. Thompson); id., at E-533 (Rep. Cain); id., at E-613 (Rep. Jenkins). At the first study commission hearing, Senator Picard and Representative M. Thompson questioned Senator Keith about Louisiana teachers' treatment of evolution and creation science. See 1 id., at E-71 -- E-74. At the close of the hearing, Representative M. Thompson told the audience:

"We as members of the committee will also receive from the staff information of what is currently being taught in the Louisiana public schools. We really want to see [it]. I . . . have no idea in what manner [biology] is presented and in what manner the creationist theories [are] excluded in the public school[s]. We want to look at what the status of the situation is." Id., at E-104.

Legislators made other comments suggesting a concern about censorship and misrepresentation of scientific information. See, e. g., id., at E-386 (Sen. McLeod); 2 id., at E-527 (Rep. Jenkins); id., at E-528 (Rep. M. Thompson); id., at E-534 (Rep. Fair).

It is undoubtedly true that what prompted the legislature to direct its attention to the misrepresentation of evolution in the schools (rather than the inaccurate presentation of other topics) was its awareness of the tension between evolution and the religious beliefs of many children. But even appellees concede that a valid secular purpose is not rendered impermissible simply because its pursuit is prompted by concern for religious sensitivities. Tr. of Oral Arg. 43, 56. If a history teacher falsely told her students that the bones of Jesus Christ had been discovered, or a physics teacher that the Shroud of Turin had been conclusively established to be inexplicable on the basis of natural causes, I cannot believe (despite the majority's implication to the contrary, see ante, at 592-593) that legislators or school board members would be constitutionally prohibited from taking corrective action, simply because that action was prompted by concern for the religious beliefs of the misinstructed students.

In sum, even if one concedes, for the sake of argument, that a majority of the Louisiana Legislature voted for the Balanced Treatment Act partly in order to foster (rather than merely eliminate discrimination against) Christian fundamentalist beliefs, our cases establish that that alone would not suffice to invalidate the Act, so long as there was a genuine secular purpose as well. We have, moreover, no adequate basis for disbelieving the secular purpose set forth in the Act itself, or for concluding that it is a sham enacted to conceal the legislators' violation of their oaths of office. I am astonished by the Court's unprecedented readiness to reach such a conclusion, which I can only attribute to an intellectual predisposition created by the facts and the legend of Scopes v. State, 154 Tenn. 105, 289 S. W. 363 (1927) -- an instinctive reaction that any governmentally imposed requirements bearing upon the teaching of evolution must be a manifestation of Christian fundamentalist repression. In this case, however, it seems to me the Court's position is the repressive one. The people of Louisiana, including those who are Christian fundamentalists, are quite entitled, as a secular matter, to have whatever scientific evidence there may be against evolution presented in their schools, just as Mr. Scopes was entitled to present whatever scientific evidence there was for it. Perhaps what the Louisiana Legislature has done is unconstitutional because there is no such evidence, and the scheme they have established will amount to no more than a presentation of the Book of Genesis. But we cannot say that on the evidence before us in this summary judgment context, which includes ample uncontradicted testimony that "creation science" is a body of scientific knowledge rather than revealed belief. Infinitely less can we say (or should we say) that the scientific evidence for evolution is so conclusive that no one could be gullible enough to believe that there is any real scientific evidence to the contrary, so that the legislation's stated purpose must be a lie. Yet that illiberal judgment, that Scopes-in-reverse, is ultimately the basis on which the Court's facile rejection of the Louisiana Legislature's purpose must rest.

Since the existence of secular purpose is so entirely clear, and thus dispositive, I will not go on to discuss the fact that, even if the Louisiana Legislature's purpose were exclusively to advance religion, some of the well-established exceptions to the impermissibility of that purpose might be applicable -- the validating intent to eliminate a perceived discrimination against a particular religion, to facilitate its free exercise, or to accommodate it. See supra, at 617-618. I am not in any case enamored of those amorphous exceptions, since I think them no more than unpredictable correctives to what is (as the next Part of this opinion will discuss) a fundamentally unsound rule. It is surprising, however, that the

Court does not address these exceptions, since the context of the legislature's action gives some reason to believe they may be applicable. (6)

Because I believe that the Balanced Treatment Act had a secular purpose, which is all the first component of the Lemon test requires, I would reverse the judgment of the Court of Appeals and remand for further consideration.

III

I have to this point assumed the validity of the Lemon "purpose" test. In fact, however, I think the pessimistic evaluation that THE CHIEF JUSTICE made of the totality of Lemon is particularly applicable to the "purpose" prong: it is "a constitutional theory [that] has no basis in the history of the amendment it seeks to interpret, is difficult to apply and yields unprincipled results ..." Wallace v. Jaffree, 472 U.S., at 112 (REHNQUIST, J., dissenting).

Our cases interpreting and applying the purpose test have made such a maze of the Establishment Clause that even the most conscientious governmental officials can only guess what motives will be held unconstitutional. We have said essentially the following: Government may not act with the purpose of advancing religion, except when forced to do so by the Free Exercise Clause (which is now and then); or when eliminating existing governmental hostility to religion (which exists sometimes); or even when merely accommodating governmentally uninhibited religious practices, except that at some point (it is unclear where) intentional accommodation results in the fostering of religion, which is of course unconstitutional. See supra, at 614-618.

But the difficulty of knowing what vitiating purpose one is looking for is as nothing compared with the difficulty of knowing how or where to find it. For while it is possible to discern the objective "purpose" of a statute (i. e., the public good at which its provisions appear to be directed), or even the formal motivation for a statute where that is explicitly set forth (as it was, to no avail, here), discerning the subjective motivation of those enacting the statute is, to be honest, almost always an impossible task. The number of possible motivations, to begin with, is not binary, or indeed even finite. In the present case, for example, a particular legislator need not have voted for the Act either because he wanted to foster religion or because he wanted to improve education. He may have thought the bill would provide jobs for his district, or may have wanted to make amends with a faction of his party he had alienated on another vote, or he may have been a close friend of the bill's sponsor, or he may have been repaying a favor he owed the Majority Leader, or he may have hoped the Governor would appreciate his vote and make a fundraising appearance for him, or he may have been pressured to vote for a bill he disliked by a wealthy contributor or by a flood of constituent mail, or he may have been seeking favorable publicity, or he may have been reluctant to hurt the feelings of a loyal staff member who worked on the bill, or he may have been settling an old score with a legislator who opposed the bill, or he may have been mad at his wife who opposed the bill, or he may have been intoxicated and utterly unmotivated when the vote was called, or he may have accidentally voted "yes" instead of "no," or, of course, he may have had (and very likely did have) a combination of some of the above and many other motivations. To look for the sole purpose of even a single legislator is probably to look for something that does not exist.

Putting that problem aside, however, where ought we to look for the individual legislator's purpose? We cannot of course assume that every member present (if, as is unlikely, we know who or even how many they were) agreed with the motivation expressed in a particular legislator's preenactment floor or committee statement. Quite obviously, "what motivates one legislator to make a speech about a statute is not necessarily what motivates scores of others to enact it." United States v. O'Brien, 391 U.S. 367, 384 (1968). Can we assume, then, that they all agree with the motivation expressed in the staff-prepared committee reports they might have read -- even though we are unwilling to assume that they agreed with the motivation expressed in the very statute that they voted for? Should we consider postenactment floor statements? Or postenactment testimony from legislators, obtained expressly for the lawsuit? Should we consider media reports on the realities of the legislative bargaining? All of these sources, of course, are eminently manipulable. Legislative histories can be contrived and sanitized, favorable media coverage orchestrated, and postenactment recollections conveniently distorted. Perhaps most valuable of all would be more objective indications -- for example, evidence regarding the individual legislators' religious affiliations. And if that, why not evidence regarding the fervor or tepidity of their beliefs?

Having achieved, through these simple means, an assessment of what individual legislators intended, we must still confront the question (yet to be addressed in any of our cases) how many of them must have the invalidating intent. If a state senate approves a bill by vote of 26 to 25, and only one of the 26 intended solely to advance religion, is the law unconstitutional? What if 13 of the 26 had that intent? What if 3 of the 26 had the impermissible intent, but 3 of the 25 voting against the bill were motivated by religious hostility or were simply attempting to "balance" the votes of their impermissibly motivated colleagues? Or is it possible that the intent of the bill's sponsor is alone enough to invalidate it -- on a theory, perhaps, that even though everyone else's intent was pure, what they produced was the fruit of a forbidden tree?

Because there are no good answers to these questions, this Court has recognized from Chief Justice Marshall, see Fletcher v. Peck, 6 Cranch 87, 130 (1810), to Chief Justice Warren, United States v. O'Brien, supra, at 383-384, that determining the subjective intent of legislators is a perilous enterprise. See also Palmer v. Thompson, 403 U.S. 217, 224-225 (1971); Epperson v. Arkansas, 393 U.S., at 113 (Black, J., concurring). It is perilous, I might note, not just for the judges who will very likely reach the wrong result, but also for the legislators who find that they must assess the validity of proposed legislation -- and risk the condemnation of having voted for an unconstitutional measure -- not on the basis of what the legislation contains, nor even on the basis of what they themselves intend, but on the basis of what others have in mind.

Given the many hazards involved in assessing the subjective intent of governmental decision makers, the first prong of Lemon is defensible, I think, only if the text of the Establishment Clause demands it. That is surely not the case. The Clause states that "Congress shall make no law respecting an establishment of religion." One could argue, I suppose, that any time Congress acts with the intent of advancing religion, it has enacted a "law respecting an establishment of religion"; but far from being an unavoidable reading, it is quite an unnatural one. I doubt, for example, that the Clayton Act, 38 Stat. 730, as amended, 15 U. S. C. @ 12 et seq., could reasonably be described as a "law respecting an establishment of religion" if bizarre new historical evidence revealed that it lacked a secular purpose, even though it has no discernible nonsecular effect. It is, in short, far from an inevitable reading of the Establishment Clause that it forbids all governmental action intended to advance religion; and if not inevitable, any reading with such untoward consequences must be wrong.

In the past we have attempted to justify our embarrassing Establishment Clause jurisprudence (7) on the ground that it "sacrifices clarity and predictability for flexibility. " Committee for Public Education & Religious Liberty v. Regan, 444 U.S., at 662. One commentator has aptly characterized this as "a euphemism . . . for . . . the absence of any principled rationale." Choper, supra n. 7, at 681. I think it time that we sacrifice some "flexibility" for "clarity and predictability." Abandoning Lemon's purpose test -- a test which exacerbates the tension between the Free Exercise and Establishment Clauses, has no basis in the language or history of the Amendment, and, as today's decision shows, has wonderfully flexible consequences -- would be a good place to start.

Notes:

1. Article VI, cl. 3, of the Constitution provides that "the Members of the several State Legislatures . . . shall be bound by Oath or Affirmation, to support this Constitution."

2. Thus the popular dictionary definitions cited by JUSTICE POWELL, ante, at 598-599 (concurring opinion), and appellees, see Brief for Appellees 25, 26; Tr. of Oral Arg. 32, 34, are utterly irrelevant, as are the views of the school superintendents cited by the majority, ante, at 595, n. 18. Three-quarters of those surveyed had "no" or "limited" knowledge of "creation-science theory," and not a single superintendent claimed "extensive" knowledge of the subject. 2 App. E-798.

3. Although creation scientists and evolutionists also disagree about the origin of the physical universe, both proponents and opponents of Senator Keith's bill focused on the question of the beginning of life.

4. Although appellees and amici dismiss the testimony of Senator Keith and his witnesses as pure fantasy, they did not bother to submit evidence of that to the District Court, making it difficult for us to agree with them. The State, by contrast, submitted the affidavits of two scientists, a philosopher, a theologian, and an educator, whose academic credentials are rather impressive. See App. to Juris. Statement A-17 -- A-18 (Kenyon); id., at A-36 (Morrow); id., at A-39 -- A-40 (Miethe); id., at A-46 -- A-47 (Most); id., at A-

49 (Clinkert). Like Senator Keith and his witnesses, the affiants swear that evolution and creation science are the only two scientific explanations for the origin of life, see id., at A-19 -- A-20 (Kenyon); id., at A-38 (Morrow); id., at A-41 (Miethe); that creation science is strictly scientific, see id., at A-18 (Kenyon); id., at A-36 (Morrow); id., at A-40 -- A-41 (Miethe); id., at A-49 (Clinkert); that creation science is simply a collection of scientific data that supports the hypothesis that life appeared on earth suddenly and has changed little, see id., at A-19 (Kenyon); id., at A-36 (Morrow); id., at A-41 (Miethe); that hundreds of respected scientists believe in creation science, see id., at A-20 (Kenyon); that evidence for creation science is as strong as evidence for evolution, see id., at A-21 (Kenyon); id., at A-34 -- A-35 (Kenyon); id., at A-37 -- A-38 (Morrow); that creation science is educationally valuable, see id., at A-19 (Kenyon); id., at A-36 (Morrow); id., at A-38 -- A-39 (Morrow); id., at A-49 (Clinkert); that creation science can be presented without religious content, see id., at A-19 (Kenyon); id., at A-35 (Kenyon); id., at A-36 (Morrow); id., at A-40 (Miethe); id., at A-43 -- A-44 (Miethe); id., at A-47 (Most); id., at A-49 (Clinkert); and that creation science is now censored from classrooms while evolution is misrepresented as proven fact, see id., at A-20 (Kenyon); id., at A-35 (Kenyon); id., at A-39 (Morrow); id., at A-50 (Clinkert). It is difficult to conclude on the basis of these affidavits -- the only substantive evidence in the record -- that the laymen serving in the Louisiana Legislature must have disbelieved Senator Keith or his witnesses.

5. The majority finds it "astonishing" that I would cite a portion of Senator Keith's original bill that

was later deleted as evidence of the legislature's understanding of the phrase "academic freedom." Ante, at 589, n. 8. What is astonishing is the majority's implication that the deletion of that section deprives it of value as a clear indication of what the phrase meant -- there and in the other, retained, sections of the bill. The Senate Committee on Education deleted most of the lengthy "purpose" section of the bill (with Senator Keith's consent) because it resembled legislative "findings of fact," which, committee members felt, should generally not be incorporated in legislation. The deletion had absolutely nothing to do with the manner in which the section described "academic freedom." See 1 App. E-314 -- E-320; id., at E-440 -- E-442.

6. As the majority recognizes, ante, at 592, Senator Keith sincerely believed that "secular humanism is a bona fide religion," 1 App. E-36; see also id., at E-418; 2 id., at E-499, and that "evolution is the cornerstone of that religion," 1 id., at E-418; see also id., at E-282; id., at E-312 -- E-313; id., at E-317; 2 id., at E-499. The Senator even told his colleagues that this Court had "held" that secular humanism was a religion. See 1 id., at E-36, id., at E-418; 2 id., at E-499. (In Torcaso v. Watkins, 367 U.S. 488, 495, n. 11 (1961), we did indeed refer to "Secular Humanism" as a "religio[n].") Senator Keith and his supporters raised the "religion" of secular humanism not, as the majority suggests, to explain the source of their "disdain for the theory of evolution," ante, at 592, but to convince the legislature that the State of Louisiana was violating the Establishment Clause because its teachers were misrepresenting evolution as fact and depriving students of the information necessary to

185

question that theory. 1 App. E-2 -- E-4 (Sen. Keith); id., at E-36 -- E-37, E-39 (Sen. Keith); id., at E-154 -- E-155 (Boudreaux paper); id., at E-281 -- E-282 (Sen. Keith); id., at E-317 (Sen. Keith); 2 id., at E-499 -- E-500 (Sen. Keith). The Senator repeatedly urged his colleagues to pass his bill to remedy this Establishment Clause violation by ensuring state neutrality in religious matters, see, e. g., 1 id., at E-36; id., at E-39; id., at E-313, surely a permissible purpose under Lemon. Senator Keith's argument may be questionable, but nothing in the statute or its legislative history gives us reason to doubt his sincerity or that of his supporters.

7. Professor Choper summarized our school aid cases thusly:

"[A] provision for therapeutic and diagnostic health services to parochial school pupils by public employees is invalid if provided in the parochial school, but not if offered at a neutral site, even if in a mobile unit adjacent to the parochial school. Reimbursement to parochial schools for the expense of administering teacher-prepared tests required by state law is invalid, but the state may reimburse parochial schools for the expense of administering state-prepared tests. The state may lend school textbooks to parochial school pupils because, the Court has explained, the books can be checked in advance for religious content and are 'self-policing'; but the state may not lend other seemingly self-policing instructional items such as tape recorders and maps. The state may pay the cost of bus transportation to parochial schools, which the Court has ruled are 'permeated' with religion; but the state is forbidden to pay for field trip transportation visits 'to governmental, industrial, cultural, and scientific centers designed to enrich the secular studies of students.'" Choper, The Religion Clauses of the First Amendment: Reconciling the Conflict, 41 U. Pitt. L. Rev. 673, 680-681 (1980) (footnotes omitted).

Since that was written, more decisions on the subject have been rendered, but they leave the theme of chaos securely unimpaired. See, e. g., Aguilar v.Felton, 473 U.S. 402 (1985); Grand Rapids School District v. Ball, 473 U.S. 373 (1985).

Webster v. New Lenox School District, 1990, the Seventh Circuit Court of Appeals

(Author's Note: Italicized material represents direct quotations. Material in regular type represents the author's comments.)

(The following paragraph is not part of a trial transcript, but is quoted from the website Voices For Evolution)

In 1990, in Webster v. New Lenox School District, the Seventh Circuit Court of Appeals found that a school district may prohibit a teacher from teaching creation science, in fulfilling its responsibility to ensure that the First Amendment's establishment clause is not violated, and religious beliefs are not injected into the public school curriculum. The court upheld a district court finding that the school district had not violated Webster's free speech rights when it prohibited him from teaching "creation science," since it is a form of religious advocacy. (Webster v. New Lenox School District #122, 917 F. 2d 1004)

This case stands out among the others because it does not deal directly with Science teaching. The

187

plaintiff in this case was a junior-high Social Studies teacher. As shown in the background section of the transcript, Webster's classroom textbook contained a statement that the world was more than four billion years old. It didn't propose it as a theory. It didn't say there was a possibility it might not be four billion years old. It just made a statement without qualification.

The one thing that ought to be noticed here is, in the case of Segrave vs State of California, 1981, that state had an anti-dogmatism law. This should mean, in simplest terms, that theories can't be taught as facts. Yet if you look at the thousands of textbooks and millions of even quasi-educational materials on every possible subject available to children, from post-graduate doctoral material to preschool "world explorer" cartoons, this is the way they always state their dogma. Not "studies suggest an age of four billion years for the earth," or "Scientists have said the earth may be more than four billion years old." It's stated as a fact. Our eyes run right past it now because it's so common. History books begin with Cro-Magnon and Neanderthal man, or maybe even Australopithecus Afarensis, the so-called "Lucy" fossil. Literature survey books cover "prehistory" such as cave paintings and attribute them to an earlier link to modern man. And the information is presented as factual, not theoretical.

Author's Note: The format of this transcript is somewhat unusual so the following should help to clarify its presentation here. The transcript is presented in its original format. Structure and headings (such as the Roman numeral I and the heading entitled Background) are part of the original document. All quoted material appears in italic type. Commentary by the author appears in regular type, in various places throughout. Occasionally the author picks up a quote to repeat, and this material also appears in italic type. The heading information from the very beginning of the original document, with the title of the case and various legal listings has been omitted. The transcript reproduced here begins with the name of the presiding judge and a statement of the case.

Ripple, Circuit Judge. Ray Webster sought injunctive and declaratory relief based on his claim that the New Lenox School District violated his first and fourteenth amendment rights by prohibiting him from teaching a nonevolutionary theory of creation in the classroom. He appeals the dismissal of his complaint for failure to state a claim. For the following reasons, we affirm the judgment of the district court.

I

Background

The district court dismissed Mr. Webster's suit for failure to state a claim upon which relief can be granted. See Fed. R. Civ. P. 12(b)(6). The grant of a motion to dismiss is, of course, reviewed de novo. Villegas v. Princeton Farms, Inc., 893 F.2d 919, 924 (7th Cir. 1990); Corcoran v. Chicago Park Dist., 875 F2d 609, 611 (7th Cir. 1989). It is well settled that, when reviewing the grant of a motion to dismiss, we must assume the truth of all well-pleaded factual allegations and make all possible inferences in favor of the plaintiff. Janowsky v. United States, No. 89-2219, slip op. at 4 (7th Cir.

Sept. 17, 1990); Rogers v. United States, 902, F.2d 1268, 1269 (7th Cir. 1990).

A complaint should not be dismissed "unless it appears beyond doubt that the plaintiff can prove no set of facts in support of his claim which would entitle him to relief." Conley v. Gibson, 355 U. S. 41, 45-46 (1957). This obligation is especially serious when, as here, we deal with allegations involving the freedom of expression protected by the first amendment. See Stewart v. District of Columbia Armory Bd., 863 F.2d 1013, 1017-18 (D.C. Cir. 1988) ("where government action is challenged on first amendment grounds, a court should be especially 'unwilling to decide the legal questions posed by the parties without a more thoroughly developed record of proceedings in which the parties have an opportunity to prove those disputed factual assertions upon which they rely'") (quoting City of Los Angeles v. Preferred Communications, 476 U.S. 488, 494 (1986)). Courts may, however, consider exhibits attached to the complaint as part of the pleadings. Beam v. IPCO Corp., 838 F.2d 242, 244 (1988). With these constraints in mind, we set forth the pertinent facts.

A. Facts

Ray Webster teaches social studies at the Oster-Oakview Junior High School in New Lenox, Illinois. In the spring of 1987, a student in Mr. Webster's social studies class complained that Mr. Webster's teaching methods violated principles of separation between church and state. In addition to the student, both the American Civil Liberties Union and the Americans United for the Separation of Church and State objected to Mr.

Webster's teaching practices. Mr. Webster denied the allegations. On July 31, 1987, the New Lenox school board (school board), through its superintendent, advised Mr. Webster by letter that he should restrict his classroom instruction to the curriculum and refrain from advocating a particular religious viewpoint.

Believing the superintendent's letter vague, Mr. Webster asked for further clarification in a letter dated September 4, 1987. In this letter, Mr. Webster also set forth his teaching methods and philosophy. Mr. Webster stated that the discussion of religious issues in his class was only for the purpose of developing an open mind in his students. For example, Mr. Webster explained that he taught nonevolutionary theories of creation to rebut a statement in the social studies textbook indicating that the world is over four billion years old. Therefore, his teaching methods in no way violated the doctrine of separation between church and state. Mr. Webster contended that, at most, he encouraged students to explore alternative viewpoints.

The superintendent responded to Mr. Webster's letter on October 13, 1987. The superintendent reiterated that advocacy of a Christian viewpoint was prohibited, although Mr. Webster could discuss objectively the historical relationship between church and state when such discussions were an appropriate part of the curriculum. Mr. Webster was specifically instructed not to teach creation science, because the teaching of this theory had been held by the federal courts to be religious advocacy.

Mr. Webster brought suit, principally arguing that the school board's prohibitions constituted censorship in violation of the first and fourteenth amendments. In particular, Mr. Webster argued that the school board should permit him to teach a nonevolutionary theory of creation in his social studies class.

Unfortunately the actual correspondence that preceded this case is not available, only summaries which in themselves seem biased in favor the school district. It would also be interesting to know exactly what the student's original complaint was and how all of this got started. It would seem necessary to know how Webster worded his letters or even how he presented his material in the classroom. But these facts are not deemed important enough to be included, apparently. We only know that Webster said he only wished to present a "nonevolutionary" theory (not a fact, not a religious belief, only a theory) to balance the statement in the textbook, which was not presented as a theory, but as a fact. The students would logically assume their textbook taught them facts, unless it told them it was presenting a theory.

B. The District Court

The district court concluded that Mr. Webster did not have a first amendment right to teach creation science in a public school. The district court began by noting that, in deciding whether to grant the school district's motion to dismiss, the court was entitled to consider the letters between the superintendent and Mr. Webster because Mr. Webster had attached these letters to his complaint as exhibits. In particular, the district court determined that the October 13, 1987 letter was critical; this letter clearly indicated exactly what conduct the school district sought to proscribe. Specifically, the October 13 letter directed that Mr. Webster was prohibited from teaching creation science and was admonished not to engage in religious advocacy. Furthermore, the superintendent's letter explicitly stated that Mr. Webster could discuss objectively the historical relationship between church and state.

The case here rests on whether Webster was denied the freedom to teach what he as an educator thought was right for his students to know. He thought it was right for his students to know that determining the age of the earth is theoretical. He taught them that there was more than one theory used to determine this information and that more than one conclusion could be reached. That is his statement of what he did and why he did it. Unless he committed perjury and lied about what he taught, it is necessary to accept his statement as fact.

In order to explain how it is possible that the factual statement in the textbook might not in fact be a fact, it was necessary to bring up an alternate theory for determining the age of the earth. It should be significant to note that it was apparently not sufficient for Webster to say, "this statement about the age of the earth is part of a theory, the theory of evolution. There are other theories about how to determine how old the earth is, but you already know all about them, so we'll just leave it at that."

He was unable to do that, because it's extremely likely that the students in his classroom had no idea that statement wasn't a fact or what any other theories that challenge it might be. We are not privy to the discussion in the classroom. It wasn't drawn out in interviews and made part of the case writings. It is possible, however, to speculate based on the modern teaching texts and quasi-educational materials available that students are not being given more than one theory to consider. They are being presented with statements of fact about things that are in reality still theories. It was therefore necessary for Webster to spell out another theory that encompasses how to determine the age of the earth. It was necessary to point out that the textbook had a fact that wasn't a fact. It was then necessary to explain why it wasn't a fact. He was a teacher. It was his job to tell students things they didn't know, even if those things weren't part of the curriculum.

The letter Webster got from the school district, the one considered critical to the disposition of the case, tells him he was prohibited from teaching creation science and was admonished not to engage in religious advocacy. Furthermore, the superintendent's letter explicitly stated that Mr. Webster could discuss objectively the historical relationship between church and state. Propping itself up on the crutch of previous court decisions, the school district considered teaching creation science teaching religion. Apparently it was not just teaching religion, but advocating it. It must not be possible to teach a concept without advocating it. Webster presented creation science as a concept in his classroom. Therefore he advocated it. Therefore he must be proscribed from it. Of course he was permitted to deal with historic church and state relationships. He was permitted to teach something, even though it really had nothing to do with correcting the error in his textbook. Because he was allowed to teach something about religion, his free speech wasn't infringed upon. Case dismissed.

The district court noted that a school board generally has wide latitude in setting the curriculum, provided the school board remains within the boundaries established by the constitution. Because the establishment clause prohibits the enactment of any law "respecting an establishment of religion," the school board could not enact a curriculum that would inject religion into the public schools. U.S. Const. amend. I. Moreover, the district court determined that the school board had the responsibility to ensure that the establishment clause was not violated.

The district court then framed the issue as whether Mr. Webster had the right to teach creation science. Relying on Edwards v. Aguillard, 482 U.S. 578 (1987), the district court determined that teaching creation science would constitute religious advocacy in violation of the first amendment and that the school board correctly prohibited Mr. Webster from teaching such material. The court further noted:

Webster has not been prohibited from teaching any nonevolutionary theories or from teaching anything regarding the historical relationship between church and state. Martino's [the superintendent] letter of October 13, 1987 makes it clear that the religious advocacy of Webster's teaching is prohibited and nothing else. Since no other constraints were placed on Webster's teaching, he had no basis for his complaint and it must fail.

Webster v. New Lenox School Dist., Mem. op, at 4-5 (N.D. Ill. May 25 1989). Accordingly, the district court dismissed the complaint.

II

Analysis

At the outset, we note that a narrow issue confronts us: Mr. Webster asserts that he has a first amendment right to determine the curriculum content of his junior high school class. He does not, however, contest the general authority of the school board, acting through its executive agent, the superintendent, to set the curriculum.

This case does not present a novel issue. We have already confirmed the right of those authorities charged by state law with curriculum development to require the obedience of subordinate employees, including the classroom teacher. Judge Wood expressed the controlling principle succinctly in Palmer v. Board of Educ., 603 F.2d 1271, 1274 (7th Cir. 1979), cert. denied, 444 U.S. 1026 (1980), when he wrote:

Parents have a vital interest in what their children are taught. Their representatives have in general prescribed a curriculum. There is a compelling state interest in the choice and adherence to a suitable curriculum for the benefit of our young citizens and society. It cannot be left to individual teachers to teach what they please.

Yet Mr. Webster, in effect, argues that the school board must permit him to teach what he pleases. The first amendment is "not a teacher license for uncontrolled expression at variance with established curricular content." Id. at 1273. See also Clard v. Holmes, 474 F.2d 928 (7th Cir.) (holding that individual teacher has no constitutional prerogative to override the judgment of his superiors as to proper course content), cert. denied, 411 U.S. 972 (1973). Clearly, the school board had the authority and the responsibility to ensure that Mr. Webster did not stray from the established curriculum by injecting religious advocacy into the classroom. "Families entrust public schools with the education of their children, but condition their trust on the understanding that the classroom will not purposely be used to advance religious views that may conflict with the private beliefs of the student and his or her family." Edwards v. Aguillard, 482 U.S. 578, 584 (1987).

There is no indication that Webster said he had a right to determine the curriculum content of his junior high school class, nor that Mr. Webster, in effect, argues that the school board must permit him to teach what he pleases. (already cited) The court acknowledges that he accepted the authority of the board. He had the required textbook and was teaching from it, or he wouldn't have run across the passage in question. He would have saved himself from a great deal of trouble if he had simply not assigned his class to read that part of the book. Yet Webster was not interested in stifling even what he considered to be a lie, or at least not a fact. He presented the statement, and then he offered an alternative. It seems extreme to state that he was guilty of "uncontrolled expression at variance with established curricular content." He also was not guilty of betraying the trust of the

School District families by abusing his position to advance conflicting religious views. The key word is "advancing." It implies putting something forward as superior, similar to the idea of "advocacy." A teacher presents a concept in his class, and the board and the court assumes he is in favor of it, that he wants his students to believe it, not just listen to it. But it seems that is only the case if the teacher presents Creation Science. He can objectively present anything else. Not that.

A teacher may say, "the 'Final Solution' for dealing with the Jews was to put them in concentration camps and kill them." Is the teacher advocating death camps for Jews? Of course not. He is presenting to his class a historical position. Unless the teacher is insane, his position is quite opposite from advocating what he states. Surely other "solutions" were possible for Hitler (granting that there was a problem of the nature under discussion, which, again, no sane person would agree with) and may even have been presented to Hitler at the time of this historical event. But Hitler wanted this one. Only this one. He may even have proscribed his advisors from bringing any other theories up. He certainly would not have been interested in possible solutions that appeared to advocate or advance a religious position.

If we ever would have wanted a government to permit the presentation of an alternate theory to deal with an issue, even a religious-based theory, that would have been the time. Alternate theories were apparently stifled, because, ironically enough, survival of the fittest, one of Evolution's foundational tenets, one upon which Hitler based many of his actions, couldn't survive on its own. It had to be protected then, and it has to be protected by the American justice system now.

A junior high school student's immature stage of intellectual development imposes a heightened responsibility upon the school board to control the curriculum. See Zykan v. Warsaw Community School Corp., 631 F.2d 1300, 1304 (7th Cir. 1980). We have noted that secondary school teachers occupy a unique position for influencing secondary school students, thus creating a concomitant power in school authorities to choose the teachers and regulate their pedagogical methods. Id. "The state exerts great authority and coercive power through mandatory attendance requirements, and because of the students' emulation of teachers as role models and the children's susceptibility to peer pressure." Edwards, 482 U.S. at 584 (footnote omitted).

It is true that the discretion lodged in school boards is not completely unfettered. For example, school boards may not fire teachers for random classroom comments. Zykan, 631 F.2d at 1305. Moreover, school boards may not require instruction in a religiously inspired dogma to the exclusion of other points of view. Epperson v. Arkansas, 393 U.S. 97, 106 (1968).

Interesting that Epperson v. Arkansas is brought up to support exactly the opposite of what it accomplished. Creation Science, another point of view, was squashed and the religious dogma of Evolution was exclusively preferred.

This complaint contains no allegation that school authorities have imposed "a pall of orthodoxy" on the offerings of the entire public school curriculum, Keyishian v. Board of Regents, 385 U.S. 589, 603 (1967)," which might either implicate the state in the propagation of an identifiable religious creed or otherwise impair permanently the student's ability to investigate matters that arise in the natural course of intellectual inquiry." Zykan, 631 F2d at 1306. Therefore, this case does not present the issue of whether, or under what circumstances, a school board may completely eliminate material from the curriculum. Cf. Zykan, 631 F.2d at 1305-06 (school may not flatly prohibit teachers from mentioning relevant material). Rather, the principle that an individual teacher has no right to ignore the directives of duly appointed education authorities is dispositive of this case. Today, we decide only that, given the allegations of the complaint, the school board has successfully navigated the narrow channel between impairing intellectual inquire and propagating a religious creed.

The wording of the previous opinion implies that the school board must be guilty of promoting a religion throughout the entire curriculum before it can be said to be in violation of the separation principle or infringing upon an individual teacher's free expression right. A teacher, however, can be denied the right to express one idea, apparently. Never mind that the entire curriculum required by the state and the school board is riddled with evolutionary language. This case is a perfect example of that. Who would have thought evolution would be an issue in a social studies class?

This is a concept appearing absolutely everywhere in curriculum. It can't be repeated often enough that it exists in every subject, often in incidental but purposeful references, as a fact, not as a theory. The state and the school boards absolutely are guilty of promoting this dogma exclusive of any other, in every subject. Try to find a state-approved textbook in any academic subject that does not bring up the subject of billions of years of earth age, or discuss man as being at first entirely primitive and gradually becoming civilized, or note that the extinction of certain types of animals or plants also indicates that more adaptable types replaced them. These are evolutionary concepts.

Here, the superintendent concluded that the subject matter taught by Mr. Webster created serious establishment clause concerns. Cf. Edwards, 482 U.S. at 583-84 ("The Court has been particularly vigilant in monitoring compliance with the Establishment Clause in elementary and secondary schools."); Epperson, 393 U.S at 106 (school may not adopt programs that aid or oppose any religion). As the district court noted, the superintendent's letter is directed to this concern. "[E]ducators do not offend the First Amendment so long as their actions are reasonably related to legitimate pedagogical concerns." Hazelwood School Dist. v. Kuhlmier, 484 U.S 260, 278 (1988). Given the school board's important pedagogical interest in establishing the curriculum and legitimate concern with possible establishment clause violations, the school board's prohibition on the teaching of creation science to junior high students was appropriate. See Palmer v. Board of Educ., 603 F.2d 1274 (7th Cir. 1979) (school board has "compelling" interest in setting the curriculum). Accordingly, the district court properly dismissed Mr. Webster's complaint.

The school in this case adopted a program that both aided one religion and opposed another. The dogma of evolution was once again aided, and the truth was opposed.

Peloza v. Capistrano School District, 1994

(Author's Note: Italicized material represents direct quotations. Material in regular type represents the author's comments. This section also has material from the website Vine & Fig Tree.)

(The following paragraph is not part of a trial transcript, but is quoted from the website Voices For Evolution)

In 1994, in Peloza v. Capistrano School District, the Ninth Circuit Court of Appeals upheld a district court finding that a teacher's First Amendment right to free exercise of religion is not violated by a school district's requirement that evolution be taught in biology classes. Rejecting plaintiff Peloza's definition of a "religion" of "evolutionism", the Court found that the district had simply and appropriately required a science teacher to teach a scientific theory in biology class. (John E. Peloza v. Capistrano Unified School District, (1994) 917 F. 2d 1004)

A summary of the case follows, taken from the transcript appearing on the website *www.talkorigins.org.*

SUMMARY

High school biology teacher brought action against school district, its board of trustees, and various personnel at high school, challenging school district's requirement that he teach evolutionism, as well as school district order barring him from discussing his religious beliefs with students. The United States District Court, Central District of California, David W. Williams, J., 782 F.Supp. 1412, dismissed and awarded attorney fees to school district. Teacher appealed. The Court of Appeals held that: (1) teacher failed to state claim for violation of establishment clause of First Amendment in connection with school district's requiring him to teach evolution, i.e., that higher life forms evolved from lower ones; (2) school district's restriction on teacher's right of free speech in prohibiting teacher from talking with students about religion during school day, including times when he was not actually teaching class, was justified by school district's interest in avoiding establishment clause violation; (3) teacher's allegations of injury to his reputation as result of allegedly defamatory statements made to and about him were insufficient to support claim for deprivation of liberty interest under § 1983; but (4) teacher's complaint was not entirely frivolous, precluding award of costs and attorney fees under Rule 11 and § 1988.

The case disposition almost entirely ruled against every point the teacher Peloza brought up. One judge, Pole, offered a partial dissenting opinion, of which an excerpt follows.

I am in agreement with the majority's resolution of John Peloza's Establishment Clause and Due Process Clause claims. However, because I believe we can dismiss Peloza's free speech claims only by turning a deaf ear to the procedural posture of this case, I respectfully dissent from parts I. B and II of the majority opinion.

I

Schoolteacher John Peloza seeks a declaratory judgment permitting him to "respond to student-initiated inquiries ... regarding religion" during contract time. The majority opinion concludes that if Peloza's discussions would constitute an establishment of religion, the District may permissibly limit those discussions, even though such limitations restrict Peloza's free speech. With this I have no quarrel. But the majority's premise is that any discussions Peloza might have do constitute such an establishment, and I am unpersuaded that we may reach such a conclusion in the case's present posture.

This is an appeal from the granting of a Rule 12(b)(6) motion. As such, we are not permitted to affirm dismissal of the complaint "unless it appears beyond doubt that plaintiff can prove no set of facts in support of his claim which would entitle him to relief." Love V. United States, 915 F.2d 1242, 1245 (9th Cir.1989). At this stage, we know almost nothing about what past or future discussions might involve. I can imagine a wide range of circumstances and questions "regarding religion" which Peloza could permissibly answer without violating the Establishment Clause. For example, a student might come to a teacher during lunch and ask about Malcolm X or Martin Luther King's religious beliefs, and how and why they evolved, or about the origins of Islam, or what the seven great religions of the world were. Such questions would certainly be "regarding religion," student-initiated, and during contract time. As such, they fall within the class of discussions Peloza seeks to be permitted, yet it is hard to see how the descriptive role a teacher would have in responding to these questions would work any violation of the Establishment Clause.

The majority holding only makes sense if we presume that we know what kinds of questions are being asked and what kinds of answers Peloza would give. In the posture of this case, where we must reverse if there are any facts Peloza could conceivably prove which would entitle him to relief, this is a presumption we are forbidden from making. As a result, the majority holding means that any response to a student-initiated inquiry "regarding religion" during contract time, other than "Ask someone else," works a violation of the Establishment Clause. I cannot join in such a broad legal holding, and indeed the case law forbids it:

In each case, the inquiry calls for line-drawing; no fixed, per se rule can be framed. The Establishment Clause like the Due Process Clauses is not a precise, detailed provision in a legal code capable of ready application.... The line between permissible relationships and those barred by the Clause can no more be straight and unwavering than due process can be defined in a single stroke or phrase or test. The Clause erects a "blurred, indistinct, and variable barrier depending on all the circumstances of a particular relationship." Lemon V. Kurtzman, 403 U.S. [602, 614, 91 S.Ct. 2105, 2112, 29 L.Ed.2d 745 (1971)]. Lynch V. Donnelly, 465 U.S. 668, 678-79, 104 S.Ct. 1355,1362, 79 L.Ed.2d 604 (1984).

Roberts V. Madigan, 921 F.2d 1047 (10th Cir.1990), upon which the majority relies, is not to the contrary. There, the court had before it a host of particulars: the conduct at issue involved a teacher displaying religious books and a poster reading "You have only to open your eyes to see the hand of God" in the classroom. Id. at 1049. That court also had the benefit of a district court factual determination that the conduct "created the appearance that [the teacher] was seeking to advance his religious views." Id. As this case stands, we know far less.

The majority impermissibly attempts to narrow the scope of Peloza's complaint by relying on a written warning from the school district which Peloza has incorporated into the complaint. The letter forbids Peloza from "attempt[ing] to convert students to Christianity or initiating conversations about your religious beliefs." Complaint at 45. Were this all that the complaint said, I would have little trouble joining the majority. But the complaint alleges more; it contends that "the school district ... has directed Plaintiff not to discuss any religious matters during any of this 'instructional time,' including student-initiated conversations regarding religion during lunch, class breaks, and before and after school hours." Complaint at 3. This allegation we must take as true. If all that lies behind it is the far narrower warning the majority cites, then Peloza's case will not be long for this world. But we may not presume that this is so.

I believe that, in a broad range of cases, the majority and I could agree about what would or would not constitute a violation of the Establishment Clause. But the majority errs in presuming to know that what is at stake here is Peloza's right to "discuss his religious beliefs" with students. In doing so, it ignores the fact that this is a Rule 12(b)(6) case. More generally, it gives short shrift to the possibility that we may well be limiting free speech more broadly than the state's compelling interest in avoiding an establishment of religion would warrant.

II

I join in the majority's part II insofar as it dismisses Peloza's § 1985(3) due process and Establishment Clause claims based on his failure to properly allege a violation of these rights. However, because I conclude that Peloza's free speech claim should not have been dismissed, I would also remand, rather than dismiss, his 1985(3) claim based on alleged free speech violations.

III

Religion has been used to justify the suppression of speech for centuries. See Everson V. Board of Ed,, 330 U.S. 1, 8-10, 67 S.Ct. 504, 5074)9, 91 L.Ed. 711 (1947). With the development of a vigorous First Amendment jurisprudence, we have quelled some of the worst abuses. But points of tension remain. We must thus remain vigilant to ensure that in our rush to preserve certain fundamental rights, we do not trample others. Caution is of the essence; only through a methodical and fact-specific jurisprudence can we hope to achieve a proper accommodation.

For the reasons stated above, I respectfully dissent.

1. On appeal, Peloza abandoned his equal protection argument.

2. The Establishment Clause of the First Amendment provides that "Congress shall make no law respecting an establishment of religion..." The Fourteenth Amendment incorporates the Establishment Clause's prohibitions against offending state action as well. Board of Education v. Pico, 457 U.S. 853, 864, 102 S.Ct.2799, 2806-07, 73 L.Ed.2d 435 (1982).

3. See Webster's Third New Int'l Dictionary (G. & C. Merriam Co. Springfield, MA. 1969). p.789 ("evolutionism: 1: a theory of evolution (as in philosophy, biology, or sociology) - See Darwinism 2: adherence to or belief in evolution esp. of living beings").

4. According to Webster's, religion is the "belief in and reverence for a supernatural power accepted as the creator and governor of the universe." Webster's II New Riverside University Dictionary 993.

5. See Smith v. Board of School Com'rs of Mobile County, 827 F.2d 684, 690-95 (11th Cir.1987) (refusing to adopt district court's holding that "secular humanism" is a religion for Establishment Clause purposes; deciding case on other grounds); United States v. Allen, 760 F.2d 447, 450-51 (2d Cir.1985) (quoting Tribe, American Constitutional Law 827-28 (1987), for the proposition that, while "religion" should be broadly interpreted for Free Exercise Clause purposes, "anything 'arguably non-religious' should not be considered religious in applying the establishment clause").

6. The dissent claims this interpretation impermissibly narrows the scope of Peloza's complaint. However, the very sentence quoted by

the dissent, Dissent at p.12064, focuses not on the definition of "religious matters," but on the definition of "instructional time." We agree with the dissent that a complaint must be read charitably at the Rule 12(b)(6) stage. However, a reviewing court need not go so far as to invent claims not within the reasonable intendment of the complaint.

7. As with his equal protection claim under section 1983, Peloza appears to have dropped his equal protection claim from his appeal to this court.

8. See United Brotherhood of Carpenters & Joiners of America, Local 610, AFL-CIO v. Scott, 463 U.S. 825, 830, 103 S.Ct. 3352,3357, 77 L.Ed.2d 1049 (1983) (hate speech rights protected by section 1985 so long as the State is involved in the conspiracy alleged). As to due process rights, there appears to be some confusion within this circuit. Older cases have stated that section 1985(3) provides no remedy for violation of due process rights, Cohen V. Norris, 300 F.2d 24, 28 (9th Cir. 1962) (dicta); Mitchell V. Greenough, 100 F.2d 184, 187 (9th Cir.1938) (holding), cert. denied. 306 U.S. 659, 59 S.Ct. 788, 83 L.Ed. 1056 (1939). In some more recent cases, we have allowed claims of due process violations to proceed under section 1985(3) without comment. See Judie V. Hamilton. 872 F.2d 919,924 (9th Cir.1989); Padway V. Palches. 665 F.2d 965, 969 (9th Cir. 1982). See Taylor V. Gilmartin, 686 F.2d 1346, 1358 (10th Cir.1982) (First Amendment freedom of religion protected by section 1985(3)). cert. denied, 459 U.S. 1147, 103 S.Ct. 788,74 L.Ed.2d 994 and cert. denied, 463 U.S. 1229, 103 S.Ct. 3570, 77 L.Ed.2d 1411 (1983); Action V. Gannon. 450 F.2d 1227,

1234 (8th Cir.1971) (satne); Cooper V. Molko, 512 F.Supp. 563, 570 (N.D.Cal.1981) (same); but see Africa V. Anderson, 510 F.Supp. 28, 30 (E.D.Penn.1980) (freedom of religion not protected by section 1985(3)).

The dissenting judge touches on the key point of the whole argument all of these evolution-related court case have shared. Opposition to the teaching of Evolution can only be on religious grounds and all religious talk must be stifled. Only in that way can Evolution opposition be stifled.

The judge properly questioned how a school district could make a blanket order forbidding the teacher such a wide range of activities. First, they prohibited any discussion of religion at all. Second, they forbade conversations outside the classroom and class time. Third, they forbade even student-initiated conversations.

With the development of a vigorous First Amendment jurisprudence, we have quelled some of the worst abuses. But points of tension remain. We must thus remain vigilant to ensure that in our rush to preserve certain fundamental rights, we do not trample others. Caution is of the essence; only through a methodical and fact-specific jurisprudence can we hope to achieve a proper accommodation.

This is a well-spoken statement, but it is too little, too late. The damage is done. The fundamental right to teach truth and reject error has been trampled repeatedly by court decisions designed solely to protect the State religion of Secular Humanism and its Bible of Evolution Dogma. For a judge to stop now and think of how the judicial system might have gone too far is sad. To date, judges have fervently served as the High Priests of Humanism and defended the dogma against all comers.

In an earlier court case Justice Black was quoted as having brought up Thomas Jefferson's "wall of separation" concept. That non-constitutional statement has since been solidly welded into place and given rise to a host of misinterpretations and abuses of intent and power.

A later case chose to quote Robert Frost's "Mending Wall," as if that were proof of the need for separation when its point is really the opposite. Is it possible that judges do not at all understand the intention of the founding fathers in the Constitution and documents of the same time period? And is it possible that even the United States Supreme Court had a different interpretation of the "separation principle" long after the days of the founding (see the 1844 quotation below) but before Secular Humanism became the law of the land?

The following comes from the website Vine & Fig Tree, which describes itself as Supporting: love, joy, peace, patience, gentleness, goodness, faith, meekness, sobriety [and] Opposing: Secularism, Humanism, Anti-Family Sex, Hedonism, Autonomy, Totalitarianism, and Mass Death.

In stark contrast to the myth of separation, the Founders believed that schools should positively and affirmatively teach religion. Every single person who signed the Constitution believed that religious and moral inculcation was the purpose of schools. Peloza is light-years away from the original intent of the Constitution. Consider Samuel Adams:

As piety, religion, and morality have a happy influence on the minds of men, in their public as well as private transactions, you will not think it unseasonable, although I have frequently done it, to bring to your remembrance the great importance of encouraging our University, town schools, and other seminaries of education, that our children and youth while they are engaged in the pursuit of useful science, may have their minds impressed with a strong sense of the duties they owe to God. If we continue to be a happy people, that happiness must be assured by the enacting and executing of the reasonable and wise laws expressed in the plainest language and by establishing such modes of education as tend to inculcate in the minds of youth the feelings and habits of "piety, religion and morality." (Addressing the Legislature of Mass., 1/16/1795)

Let divines and philosophers, statesmen and patriots, unite their endeavors to renovate the age, by impressing the minds of men with the importance of educating their little boys and girls, of inculcating in the minds of youth the fear and love of the Deity. . . and, in subordination to these great principles, the love of their country. . . . In short, of leading them in the study and practice of the exalted virtues of the Christian system. Letter to John Adams, 1790, who wrote back: "You and I agree." Four Letters: Being an Interesting Correspondence Between Those Eminently Distinguished Characters, John Adams, Late President of the United States; and Samuel Adams, Late Governor of Massachusetts. On the

Important Subject of Government (Boston: Adams and Rhoades, 1802) pp. 9-10

It has been observed that "education has a greater influence on manners than human laws can have." [A] virtuous education is calculated to reach and influence the heart and to prevent crimes. . . . Such an education, which leads the youth beyond mere outside show, will impress their minds with a profound reverence of the Deity [and] . . . will excite in them a just regard to Divine revelation. The Life and Public Services of Samuel Adams, Wm.Wells., ed. (Boston: Little, Brown, & Co., 1865) Vol.III, p. 327.

Art. 3. Religion, morality, and knowledge, being necessary to good government and the happiness of mankind, schools and the means of education shall forever be encouraged. Northwest Ordinance, 1787

In my view, the Christian religion is the most important and one of the first things in which all children, under a free government, ought to be instructed. . . . No truth is more evident to my mind than that the Christian religion must be the basis of any government intended to secure the rights and privileges of a free people. The opinion that human reason left without the constant control of Divine laws and commands will preserve a just administration, secure freedom and other rights, restrain men from violations of laws and constitutions, and give duration to a popular government is as chimerical as the most extravagant ideas that enter the head of a maniac . . . . Where will you find any code of laws among civilized men in which the commands and prohibitions are not founded on Christian principles? I need not specify the prohibition of murder, robbery, theft [and] trespass. Noah Webster, Letters, Harry A Warfel, ed., (NY: Library Publishers, 1953) pp. 453-454, to David McClure, Oct. 25, 1836.

Thomas Jefferson's good friend Benjamin Rush, after he signed the Declaration of Independence, was the first Founding Father to call for free public schools. He said:

[T]he only foundation for a useful education in a republic is to be laid in religion. Without this there can be no virtue, and without virtue there can be no liberty, and liberty is the object and life of all republican governments. Without religion, I believe that learning does real mischief to the morals and principles of mankind.(Benjamin Rush, Essays, Literary, Moral, and Philosophical, 1798, p.6 ["On the Mode of Education Proper in a Republic"])

Rush was clearly a Christian, but no "fundamentalist nut." In his paper entitled, "A Defense of the Use of the Bible as a Schoolbook," Rush argued,

[T]he only means of establishing and perpetuating our republican forms of government . . . is the universal education of our youth in the principles of Christianity by means of the Bible. For this Divine book, above all others, favors that equality among mankind, that respect for just laws, and those sober and frugal virtues, which constitute the soul of republicanism.

Daniel Webster reflected the views of every single Signer of the Constitution:

We regard it [public instruction] as a wise and liberal system of police by which property and life and the peace of society are secured. We seek to prevent in some measure the extension of the penal code by inspiring a salutary and conservative principle of virtue and of knowledge. [1]

[However, t]he attainment of knowledge does not comprise all which is contained in the larger term of education. The feelings are to be disciplined; the passions are to be restrained; true and worthy motives are to be inspired; a profound religious feeling is to be instilled, and pure morality inculcated. [Four years later, the U.S. Supreme Court would agree that this could only be done by having the government teach the Bible.] [2]

The cultivation of the religious sentiment represses licentiousness . . . inspires respect for law and order, and gives strength to the whole social fabric.[3]

[1] Works of Daniel Webster (Boston: Little, Brown, and Co., 1853) vol I, pp 41-42, Dec 22., 1820.[2] vol II, pp 107-108, Oct 5: 1840[3] vol II, p 615, July 4, 1851

The Father of his Country warned:

And let us with caution indulge the supposition that morality can be maintained without religion. Whatever may be conceded to the influence of refined education on minds of peculiar structure, reason and experience both forbid us to expect that national morality can prevail in exclusion of religious principle And secularists would be quick to point out that Washington was less Biblically-oriented than the most influential educators in the nation, such as Benjamin Rush and Noah Webster.

All the scholars are required to live a religious and blameless life according to the rules of God's Word, diligently reading the holy Scriptures, that fountain of Divine light and truth, and constantly attending all the duties of religion . . . . All the scholars are obliged to attend Divine worship in the College Chapel on the Lord's Day and on Days of Fasting and Thanksgiving appointed by public Authority. The Laws of Yale College in New Haven in Connecticut (New Haven: Josiah Meigs, 1787) p. 5-6, ch II, art. 1,4

William Samuel Johnson, signer of the Constitution, was appointed Columbia's first president. Under him, It is expected that all students attend public worship on Sundays. Columbia Rules (NY: Samuel Loudon, 1785) 5-8

Johnson's views on public education were similar to those of every other signer of the Constitution. In his commencement address, he told the graduates:

You this day, gentlemen, . . . have . . . received a public education, the purpose whereof hath been to qualify you the better to serve your Creator and your country . . . . Your first great duties, you are sensible, are those you owe to Heaven, to your Creator and Redeemer. Let these be ever present to your minds, and exemplified in your lives and conduct. Imprint deep upon your minds the principles of piety towards God and a reverence and fear of His holy name. The fear of God is the beginning of wisdom [Proverbs 9:10]. Remember too, that you are the redeemed of the Lord, that you are bought with a price, even the inestimable price of the precious blood of the Son of God. . . . Love, fear and serve Him as your Creator,

216

Redeemer, and Sanctifier. Acquaint yourselves with Him in His Word and holy ordinances. Make Him your friend and protector and your felicity is secured both here and hereafter.

Early US Supreme Court decisions agreed that in a Christian nation such as America, the Bible must be taught in all government-run schools.

In 1844, the Court was asked, Can the state enforce a will which creates a government-operated school which will not teach the Bible? The Supreme Court said that the very idea of a school which will not teach the Bible is contrary to the legal foundations of this Christian nation.

It is unnecessary for us, however, to consider what would be the legal effect of a devise in Pennsylvania for the establishment of a school or college, for the propagation of . . . Deism, or any other form of infidelity. Such a case is not to be presumed to exist in a Christian country; and therefore it must be made out by clear and indisputable proof.

The government made firm assurances that the Bible would be taught in the school, and the will was approved. (Vidal v. Girard's Executors)

The Vidal Court, as it talks about Christianity and the Bible, sounds more like David Barton than anything one would hear from the post-1947 Court. The Vidal Court said that the government in its school "may, nay must impart to their youthful pupils . . . the Bible, and especially the New Testament," which must "be read and taught as a divine revelation in the college -- its general precepts expounded, its evidences explained, and its glorious principles of morality inculcated." The Court asked rhetorically:

Where can the purest principles of morality be learned so clearly or so perfectly as from the New Testament? Where are benevolence, the love of truth, sobriety, and industry, so powerfully and irresistibly inculcated as in the sacred volume?

The Bible MUST be taught in government schools, the 1844 US Supreme Court declared.

You would NEVER EVER hear language like this from the modern secularist Court. But you ALWAYS heard language like this from the Founding Fathers.

The "separation of church and state" is a myth.

Appendix Four: Recommended Reading Websites

Heritage Foundation *askheritage.org* "To build an America where freedom, opportunity, prosperity and civil society flourish. Public policy research organization "

Cato Institute *www.cato.org* "Increase the understanding of public policies based on the principles of limited government, free markets, individual liberty, and peace. "

Discovery Institute *discovery.org.* "Explore ...technology, science and culture, reform of the law, national defense, the environment and the economy, the future of democratic institutions, transportation, religion and public life, government entitlement spending, foreign affairs "

Answers In Genesis *answersingenesis.org.* "enabling Christians to defend their faith ... answers to questions surrounding the book of Genesis, ... train others to develop a biblical worldview... "

Institute for Creation Research *icr.org.* "Scientific research from a biblical perspective ...graduate-level degree program in science education, graduate-level training in biblical education and apologetics ... Publications, Events, and Media. "

Ayn Rand Center for Individual Rights *aynrandcenter.org* "advance individual rights (the rights of each person to life, liberty, property, and the pursuit of happiness) as the moral basis for a fully free, laissez-faire capitalist society. "

National Rifle Association *nra.org* safety and training programs for military, law enforcement, civilian, female protection and child safety, and "a major political force ... America's foremost defender of Second Amendment rights. "

The Internet Sacred Text Archive *sacred-texts.com* Every kind of public-domain material remotely connected with spiritual, philosophical, and broadly religious subjects.

Creation Research Society *creationresearch.org* Education, research, journal publication, "committed to full belief in the Biblical record of creation and early history. "

World Net Daily *wnd.com* Original news articles and links to outside sources for news, opinion, commentary with a conservative emphasis.

Books
James Hannam, Web site and book *God's Philosophers: How the Medieval World Laid the Foundations of Modern Science.* Icon Books, London, 2009.

Allan Bloom, *The Closing of the American Mind.* Documentation on secular humanist influence from non-Christian but conservative perspective with extensive research and proofs.

Francis Schaeffer *The God Who Is There, The Christian Manifesto, How Should We Then Live, True Spirituality, Escape from Reason, Back to Freedom and Dignity.* Schaeffer is reformed in theology, evangelical rather than fundamentalist, left America for

Switzerland. He was the first evangelical to advocate political activism opposing abortion.

Aleksandr Solzhenitsyn *Gulag Archipelago* (3 volumes) Believer imprisoned under Stalin. collected stories of other prisoners massive, well-documented work on the effects of communism on its own people.

Dr. Don DeYoung, *Thousands, Not Billions: Challenging an Icon of Evolution Questioning the Age of the Earth.* Disproves uniformitarianism by collection of individual scientific studies

George W. Dollar, *A History of Fundamentalism in America.* Church history in America from founding to early 70's emphasis on the 20th century.

David O Beale, *In Pursuit of Purity.* American church history up to 1980's emphasizing conflicts between belief and unbelief, as it affects the church.

William Evans. *The Great Doctrines of the Bible.* Brief easy to read basic Bible doctrines.

John Foxe. Foxe's Book of Martyrs. History of martyrs up to Foxe's time sections added mid-16th century.

Humphreys, D. Russell, Ph.D. *Starlight and Time, Solving the Puzzle of Distant Starlight in a Young Universe.*

Josephus, *Antiquities of the Jews.* Roman General and Jewish historian. Late first century writer from Creation to his lifetime.

Josh MacDowell, *The New Evidence that Demands a Verdict.* Conservative evangelical Christian apologist, evidence in support of the Bible's truth.

G. Campbell Morgan. Commentator Baptist preacher English, lived in America.

Michael Oard. *Frozen in Time: The Wooly Mammoth, The Ice Age and the Bible.* Recent information refuting uniformitarianism.

Antonin Scalia. Supreme Court Justice, Conservative constitutional jurisprudence.

William Warren Sweet. *The Story of Religions in America*. Well-documented, honest but liberal perspective.

J.C Whitcomb and H. M. Morris. *The Genesis Flood.* Classic scientific treatise on Earth geology.

Bibliography for Antidisestablishmentarianism

Scripture references are as follows: The Bible: The King James Version, public domain. A few verses for comparison purposes are from other translations as follows: The New International Version, from the HOLY BIBLE, NEW INTERNATIONAL VERSION Registered. NIV Registered. Copyright 1973, 1978, 1984 by International Bible Society. Used by permission of Zondervan. All rights reserved. The New American Standard Version: Scripture quotations taken from the New American Standard Bible Registered, Copyright 1960, 1962, 1963, 1968, 1971, 1972, 1973, 1975, 1977, 1995 by The Lockman Foundation Used by permission.

Antidisestablishmentarianism references hundreds of authors and works, yet one source needs special mention. The website Sacred Texts by J.B. Hare is the largest collection of public domain material of which we are aware. The entire website of over one thousand books is available for purchase on either CD ROM or DVD ROM. Most of the ancient texts used in this work are public domain books from this collection. A problem with this or any other collection is proving the validity of the primary sources. Though we do not know anything about John B. Hare, except the information posted on his website, we believe that he faithfully and accurately scanned the texts. The problem is, are the texts reliable? Since they are public domain, they are older and sometimes not the latest translations. We are confident, however, that they are acceptable. Some sources we use are books where Westerners lived among a tribe and wrote down oral traditions. Though we trust that the authors accurately recorded the oral traditions, how much 'contamination' with outside influences shaped these oral traditions? The Lore of the Whare-Wananga, a New Zealand tribe, is well documented by the translator S. Percy Smith to be older than outside influences and free of 'contamination.' Myths of the Cherokee by James Mooney, however, was published in 1900 after more than 250 years of wars and close contact with outsiders. The level of outside influence on the oral traditions of the North American Indians is impossible to measure or deny.

It should also be noted that some of the authors listed here have been accused of being pseudoarchaeologists or pseudoscientists and are largely discounted by many as scholarly sources because of the conclusions they drew from their research or the inability to substantiate some of their claims. Examples of these authors are Graham Hancock, Emmanuel Velikovsky and Thor Heyerdahl. Their conclusions are in some cases not worthy of serious consideration and some of their findings are unverifiable. However, the research they conducted and the discoveries they claim to have made, when verifiable, bear serious consideration. It is necessary to go back to verifiable evidence uncovered by archaeology, exploration and scientific discovery and to draw realistic conclusions from this evidence based on biblical understanding.

Material used from these books includes discoveries verified by repeated similar references in primary sources, documented archaeological sites which beyond question exist and testimony of ancient manuscripts accepted by scholars for hundreds of years. Some evidence cannot be substantiated because it exists in off-limits areas like the interior of China or other countries experiencing dangerous travel conditions. Presenting such claims does not attest to their truth, but in most cases these finds are part of an established pattern repeated throughout the *world*.

_____. *"1549, 1559, 1662 Acts of Uniformity. "* *Hanover Historical Texts Projects.* History Department, Hanover College, Hanover, IN. *history.hanover.edu.*

_____. Access Research Network (*ARN.org*). (A scholarly website containing scientific research articles.)

_____. *The American Heritage® Dictionary of the English Language,* Fourth Edition. ©2000 Houghton Mifflin Company. Updated in 2003.

_____. *americanpresbyterianchurch.org*

_____. "Ancient temple found under Lake Titicaca. " *BBC News.* Wednesday, 23 August, 2000, 11:04 GMT 12:04 UK.

_____. *answersingenesis.org.*

_____. *Assyrian Kings' Lists.* Various translators, various public domain texts with sources including Google Books, Wikipedia, The Internet Ancient History Sourcebook, (http://www.fordham.edu halsall/ ancient/asbook.html), and various universities which have placed public domain works online.

_____. (Atheist poster compilation) From the website *scottklarr.com.*

_____. Bethel Lutheran Church, Cupertino, CA website.

_____. *Biblefacts.org*

_____. The Book of Enoch. Translated by R.H. Charles, 1917. *The Apocrypha and Pseudepigrapha of the Old Testament.* Oxford: The Clarendon Press, 1913.

_____. *BBC online,* updated April 10, 2002.

_____. "Bible Answers. " Like the Master Ministries. (Mathematical calculation from proves that 10,000 people could have been born before Adam and Eve died.) *Never Thirsty.org* website.

_____. "Boat People, a Refugee Crisis. " *cbc.ca digital archives*. Broadcast May 1, 2000.

_____. "PART I THE BUNDAHIS-BAHMAN YAST, AND SHÂYAST LÂ-SHÂYAST. " *Sacred Books of the East, Volume 5*, 1860. Taken from the Internet Sacred Text Archive, www.sacred-texts.com, managed by John Bruno Hare.

_____. "Cave Reveals Southwest's Abrupt Climate Swings During Ice Age. " *Science Daily.com,* January 25, 2010.

_____. Church Community Services, Elkhart, IN website.

_____. *Church of the Holy Trinity v. United States. U.S. Supreme Court:* 143 U.S. 457 (1892). *www.talkorigins.org.*

_____. *CNN.com.*

_____. "Coal, Volcanism and Noah's Flood," *TJ (Technical Journal)* 1(1):11–29, Creation Ministries International, April 1984.

_____. Committee on the Judiciary House of Representatives, Prohibiting Detention Camps, March 18, 1971.

_____. *Corpus Aristotelicum,* collected works of Aristotle preserved by Medieval manuscript transmission. They are studies of philosophy made by Aristotle's school since many of his original works have been lost. Immanuel Bekker's nineteenth-century edition (1831-1836) is based on ancient classifications of these works. *Gutenberg.org*

_____. "The Date of Christ's Birth," Bible Studies at *The Moorings.org*.

_____. "Dinosaur Blood Extracted from Bone. " Posted: April 30, 2009 10:55 pm Eastern © 2009 *worldnetdaily*.

_____. Discovery Institute. *www.discovery.org*. Website section relating to the *PBS* series *Evolution* aired in 2001.

_____. "Disparate Treatment Based on Religion. " *Best Practices for Eradicating Religious Discrimination in the Workplace. The U.S. Equal Employment Opportunity Commission* website. Last modified on July 23, 2008.

_____. *Documents in Law, History and Diplomacy. The Avalon Project*. Yale Law Library. *avalon.law.yale.edu*

_____. *Edwards v. Aguillard, U.S. Supreme Court*, 1987. *www.talkorigins.org*.

_____. "Einstein In Need Of Update? Calculations Show The Speed Of Light Might Change. " *ScienceDaily*. Retrieved May 18, 2009, from Texas A&M University (2001, February 12). sciencedaily.com

_____. *Epperson vs. Arkansas, 1968, United States Supreme Court*. www.bc.edu/ bc_org/avp/cas/comm.

_____. *Executive Order 12919* [President Bill Clinton, June 3, 1994], *disastercenter.com*.

_____. "Expelled Exposed: Why Expelled Flunks. " *National Center for Science Education*. (website)

_____. *Fellowship of Humanity v. County of Alameda*, 1956.

_____. *GeorgiaEncyclopedia.org* Background on Providence Canyon.

_____. *GORP.com* (Great Outdoor Recreation Page.)

_____. *Greek Apocalypse of Baruch iii.* English translations were published from the Slavonic by W. R. Morfill (Apocrpyha Anecdota II, ed. M. R. James [T&S 5.1] Cambridge: CUP, 1987. Pp. 95-102) and from the Slavonic and Greek by H. M. Hughes (APOT 2. Pp. 533-41). The pseudepigraphon was composed in the beginning of the second century A.D., but it is difficult to discover whether it was written in Greek, Hebrew, or Aramaic. (Background note from Charlesworth, James H. The Pseudepigrapha and Modern Research: with a Supplement. SBLCS 7. Chico, Ca.: Scholars Press, 1981.)M. R. James's publication of the Greek text, until then entirely unknown, in "Texts and Studies: Contributions to Biblical and Patristic Literature," edited by J. Armitage Robinson, v., No. i., pp. 84-94, Cambridge, 1897.

_____. *gulaghistory.org.*

_____. "How Old are Kimberlites and Diamonds?" *American Museum of Natural History* website.

_____. "Judge Says UC (University of California) Can Deny Religious Course Credit. "*Answers in Genesis News to Note.* From the *San Francisco Chronicle,* Aug 16, 2008.

_____. "Kim Jong Il. " *BBC news online.* Asia/Pacific Profile: Page last updated at 11:14 GMT, Friday, 16 January 2009.

_____. "Letter of Oct. 7, 1801 from Danbury (CT) Baptist Assoc. to Thomas Jefferson," *Thomas*

Jefferson Papers, Manuscript Division, Library of Congress, Wash. D.C.

_____. Library of Congress website.

_____. *McLean v. Arkansas Board of Education*, 1982. www.talkorigins. org/faqs/mclean-v-arkansas.

_____. *Magna Carta*, 1215 AD, from *The Avalon Project. Documents in Law, History and Diplomacy.* Yale Law Library. *avalon.law.yale.edu.*

_____. The Mahabharata. "Santiparva," cclx.20, 21, 23 and cxxiv.67, translated by Friedrich Max Müller and others *in Sacred Books of the East* (50 volumes), Oxford University Press, 1879-1910.

_____. *Mayflower* 1620.com (website).

_____. The National Archives. *archives.gov.*

_____. *National Geographic,* photo caption, March 1, 2010.

_____. National Park Services Website.

_____. National Park Service report on Wall Arch collapse August 4-5, 2008.

_____. *The New York Times.* News item published September 14, 1999.

_____. "NC State Paleontologist Discovers Soft Tissue in Dinosaur Bones. " North Carolina State University News Release from *www.ncsu.edu/ news/press* /05-03/05 March 24, 2005.

_____. Novori.com. History and manufacture of synthetic diamonds.

_____. "Parents Fuming as Texas Schools Let Gideons Provide Bibles to Students. " *Foxnews.com,* Tuesday, May 19, 2009.

_____. *Peloza v. Capistrano School District,* 1994. *www.talkorigins.org.*

_____. "Prohibiting Detention Camps. " U. S. House of Representatives, Committee on the Judiciary, March 18, 1971.

_____. "Superbridge. " *NOVA. PBS.* November 12, 1997.

_____. Public Information Office, Jet Propulsion Laboratory, California Institute of Technology, NASA, press release, July 21, 1994.

_____. "Question and Answer with Dr. Mary Schweitzer. " *Nova* online. July 31, 2007.

_____. *Ramayana.* [Charvaka teachings (ancient Indian skeptic philosophy) quoted in, the Ramayana, approximately 600 BC. (Most original source material of the Charvaka beliefs were destroyed, and fragments are preserved in Hindu texts, where they are denounced as heresy.)] Ravi Prakash Arya, (ed.). *Ramayana of Valmiki: Sanskrit Text and English Translation.* (English translation according to M. N. Dutt, introduction by Dr. Ramashraya Sharma, 4-volume set) Parimal Publications: Delhi, 1998.

_____. Reports on the Antarctic research stations at *Antarctic Connection.com.*

_____. Review of the book *Mayflower: A Story of Courage Community and War* by Nathaniel Philbrick, 2007, Penguin. Bookmarks Magazine, Phillips & Nelson Media, Inc., from *Amazon.com.*

_____. *"THE SAMOAN STORY OF CREATION-A 'Tala.' " JOURNAL OF THE POLYNESIAN SOCIETY CONTAINING THE*

TRANSACTIONS AND PROCEEDINGS OF THE SOCIETY. VOL. I. [WELLINGTON, 1892] {Reduced to HTML by Christopher M. Weimer, November 2002} Taken from the Internet Sacred Text Archive, www.sacred-texts.com, managed by John Bruno Hare.

_____. *Segraves vs. State of California,* 1981. *geocities.com/Athens/1618.*

_____. *The Separationist.* Newsletter of the "Secular Humanists of the Lowcountry," May 2002 issue.

_____. Sills, David L. and Robert K. Merton, Editors. *The International Encyclopedia of Social Sciences.* First published in 1968.

_____. *State v. Scopes, Scopes v. State, 152 Tenn. 424, 278 S.W. 57. Scopes vs. The State of Tennessee* (1926).

_____. "Thanksgiving Ain't No Holiday for Wimps. " *Pickens County Progress,* Staff Review of the book *Mayflower: A Story of Courage Community and War* by Nathaniel Philbrick, 2007, Penguin. November 27, 2008.

_____. "Tiny Fossils reveal Warm Antarctic Past. " *National Geographic.* July 26, 2008.

_____. "Titanic" article. *New World Encyclopedia.org.*

_____. *Torcaso v. Watkins. U.S. Supreme Court.*1961. *vftonline.org/* TestOath/Torcaso.htm

_____. University of Oxford, Bodleian Philosophy Faculty Library, Manuscripts and Rare Books "Medieval Manuscript Sources and Incunabula. " *ox.ac.uk.*

_____. Utah Geological Survey, *Utah.gov.*

_____. *varchive.org.* A scholarly archive of Immanuel Velikovsky's unpublished works.

_____. *Voices for Evolution* (website).

_____. *Washington Ethical Society v. District of Columbia,* 249 F.2d 127 (D.C. Cir. 1957).

_____. *Web of Science* (Formerly Science Citation Index). Guillermo Gonzalez - publication record at ISU.

_____. *Webster v. New Lenox School District,* 1990, the Seventh Circuit Court of Appeals. *geocities.com/Athens/618/Webster_vs._New_Le nox.html*

_____. *Wikipedia.org*

_____. The *Wisconsin University website,* overview of the Laramide/ Yellowstone mountain ranges with aerial maps designating geologic ages.

_____. World Net Daily. *wnd.com.*

_____. Youth Ministry Entertainment (or Y-ME ministries). *y-ment.com.*

_____. Abbott, Frank Frost and Alan Chester Johnson (authors, translators and editors). *Municipal Administration in the Roman Empire [concerning the The Law of the Twelve Tables (Duodecim Tabulae), the ancient foundation of Roman law].* Princeton University Press, Princeton, NJ, 1926.

Adams, John. "Argument in defence of the soldiers in the Boston Massacre trial. " December 1770.

_____. "Letter to Abigail Adams. " July 7, 1775.

_____. "Letter to the 1st Brigade of the 3rd Division of the Militia of Massachusetts. " October 11, 1798.

_____. "Letter to a friend. " 1805.

_____. "Letter to Benjamin Waterhouse," 29
     October 1805.

Adams, Samuel. "Letter to John Pitts. " 21 January
     1776.

_____. "The Report of the Committee of
     Correspondence to the Boston Town Meeting "
     Nov. 20, 1772. *history.hanover.*
     edu/texts/adamss.html.

Ahlstrom. Sydney F. *A Religious History of the*
     American People. New Haven: Yale University
     Press, 1972.

Aquinas, Thomas. *Summa Theologica* 1265-1274 AD
     Sixth Article [I-II, Q. 94, Art. 6] Objection 3.
     Translated by Fathers of the English Dominican
     Province. Benziger Brothers, New York. 1947.

Archer, Gleason Leonard, Jr. *A Survey of Old*
     Testament Introduction. Chicago: Moody, c. 1974.
     Updated and revised ed., c1994.

Arndt, William F. and F. Wilbur Gingrich, trans. Bauer,
     Walter. *A Greek-English Lexicon of the New*
     Testament and Other Early Christian Literature.
     University of Chicago Press: Chicago, 1967.

Asimov, Isaac. *The Roving Mind.* Prometheus Books,
     1997.

Athenagoras of Athens. *Legatio pro Christianis* [
     "Supplication for the Christians "]. (Letter to
     Marcus Aurelius), 177 A.D. Translated by B. P.
     Pratten in "Athenagoras." *The Ante-Nicene*
     Fathers, vol. 2, Wm. B. Eerdmans, Grand Rapids:
     Michigan, 1954.

Augustine of Hippo. *City of God.* Selections. series 1,
     vol. 2 of the Nicene and Post-Nicene Fathers.
     Translated Henry Bettenson. Pelican Books,
     England, Clay's LTD, St. Ives Place, 1972.

Austin, Steven. Citing Hamilton Hicks. "Mineralized sodium silicate solutions for artificial petrification of wood," United States Patent Number 4,612,050, September 16, 1986, pp. 1-3. *CatastroRef*--'Catastrophe Reference Database: Catastrophes in Earth History, Geologic Evidence, Speculation and Theory', Institute for Creation Research, San Diego. Entry no. 267.

Austin, S.A. (editor). *Grand Canyon: Monument to Catastrophe*. Institute for Creation Research, Santee, California, 1994.

Ayer. A.J. (editor) *The Humanist Outlook*. Rationalist Press Association, Ltd. 1968.

Bakunin Mikhail. *God and the State*. written 1871. First published 1882 (Discovered posthumously by Carlo Cafiero and Elisée Reclus). Translated by Benjamin R. Tucker. Published by Mother Earth Publishing Association, New York, 1916.

Baldwin, James. *The Fire Next Time*. 1963 by the Dial Press. Copyright renewed 1990, 1991 by Gloria Baldwin Karefa-Smart. Published in the United States by Vintage Books, a division of Random House, first Vintage International Edition, February 1993.

Baldwin, Roger Nash. "Thirty Years Later. " *Harvard Class Book of 1935*. "Baldwin's Class of 1905 on its thirtieth anniversary," Insight on the News 1997.

Balmer, Randall and John R. Fitzmier. *The Presbyterians*. Westport, CT: Praeger, 1994.

Balter, Michael. "How Human Intelligence Evolved—Is It Science or 'Paleofantasy'?" *Science* magazine, 2008.

Barnett, Randy E. "The Case for a Federalism Amendment. " *Wall Street Journal*, April 23, 2009.

Bates, Mike. "Aleksandr Solzhenitsyn: The Power of One," *The National Ledger, an Eclectic Mix.* August 7, 2008. The article quotes from Aleksandr Solzhenitsyn's *The Gulag Archipelago,* 1918-1956, Volume 1, English translation by Thomas P. Whitney and Harry Willetts, Harper & Row, New York, NY, 1973.

Beale, David O. *In Pursuit of Purity.* Bob Jones University Press: Greenville, SC, 1986.

Beckford, Martin, Antony Flew, Richard Dawkins. "Flew Speaks Out: Professor Antony Flew reviews The God Delusion. " (Flew's review is copyrighted as follows) Antony Flew, 2008, *bethinking.org. www.telegraph.co.uk/ science/science-news,* 9:30 PM BST 02 Aug 2008.

Bentham, Jeremy. *The Works of Jeremy Bentham,* vol. 4, Edinburgh: William Tait. 1838-1843. 11 vols, 1843.

Bhartruhari, Neeti Shatakan (spelling varies; a work of Sanskrit philosophical verse). The empire in which he lived lasted from 185 B.C. to 135 A.D. Sahu Dharanidhar published *An English Verse Translation of Three Shatakas of Bhartruhari* in 2003.

Bierce, Ambrose. *The Enlarged Devil's Dictionary.* 1906.

Billington, Ray Allen. *Westward Expansion: A History of the American Frontier,* Macmillan, New York, NY, 1974.

Blackburn, Simon. "Independent on Sunday." *National Secular Society Newsline,* 12 May 2002.

Blackstone, William. Commentaries on the Law of England, 1765–1769.

Bonomi, Patricia U. "Religious Pluralism in the Middle Colonies. " *Divining America: Religion in*

American History, New York University, National
Humanities Center. *nationalhumanitiescenter.org*
accessed May 6, 2010.

Bowden, Thomas A. "Your Child Is Not State Property,"
FrontPage Magazine, April 4, 2008. Reproduced
at Ayn Rand Center for Individual Rights Website.
(Thomas A. Bowden is an analyst at the Ayn Rand
Institute, focusing on legal issues.)

Bradford, William. *History of Plymouth Plantation.*
Bradford's History of 'Plimoth Plantation' From
the Original Manuscript. With a Report of the
Proceedings Incident to the Return of the
Manuscript to Massachusetts. c. 1650.
Gutenberg.org

Breasted, James Henry. *Ancient Records of Egypt:*
Historical Documents from the Earliest Times to
the Persian Conquest, collected, edited, and
translated, with Commentary. Chicago: University
of Chicago Press, 1906–1907.

Brian, Denis. Adapted from *Einstein, A Life.* John
Wiley and Sons, New York, 1996.

Briggs, Charles Augustus. *American Presbyterianism.*
New York, NY: Charles Scribner's Sons, 1885

Brown, Brian. *The Wisdom of the Egyptians* (1923).
Taken from the Internet Sacred Text Archive,
www.sacred-texts.com, managed by John Bruno
Hare.

Budge, E. A. Wallis. "Legends of the Gods. THE
HISTORY OF CREATION. " *The Egyptian Texts,*
edited with Translation. (Brit. Mus. Papyrus No
10,188). [1912] Taken from the Internet Sacred
Text Archive, *www.sacred-texts.com,* managed by
John Bruno Hare.

Butt, Kyle, M.A. "'So We Make Up Stories' About
Human Evolution. " Apologetics' Press. 2008.
www.apologeticspress.org.

Byrnes, Ryan. "Private Sector Jobs Decline, Government Jobs Increase." Quoting Bill Beach, director of the Center for Data Analysis at the Heritage Foundation. *CNS News,* Monday, March 09, 2009.

Calvin, John. Commentary on Luke 24:45. *Commentary On A Harmony of the Evangelists, Matthew, Mark, and Luke.* Translator from Latin and collator with the French version Rev. William Pringle. Edinburgh, Calvin Translation Society, 1847-1850. Calvin's Commentaries, Vol. 33: Matthew, Mark and Luke, Part III, translated by John King, 1847-50.

_____. *Institutes of the Christian Religion.* Thomas Norton, Translator. 1581.

Calabresi, Guido. *A Common Law for the Age of Statutes.* Copyright by the President and Fellows of Harvard College, 1982.

Callaway, Henry. *The Religious System of the Amazulu.* Springville, Natal, 1870.

Carson, Jonathan David. "Science's Sins of the Eyes. " *New Oxford Review,* November 2001.

Castillo, Bernal Diaz Del. *The Discovery And Conquest Of Mexico* 1517-1521. Edited by Genaro Garcia, Translated with an Introduction and Notes, A. P. Maudslay. first pub 1928. Taken from the Internet Sacred Text Archive, *www.sacred-texts.com,* managed by John Bruno Hare.

Catullus, Gaius Valerius (c. 84 – c. 54 BC). *Carmina.* Translated by Leonard C. Smithers. 1894.

Chamberlain, B.H. translator. [1882] *THE KOJIKI PART I.- THE BIRTH OF THE DEITIES. THE BEGINNING OF HEAVEN AND EARTH* Taken from the Internet Sacred Text Archive, www.sacred-texts.com, managed by John Bruno Hare.

Charron Pierre. *De la sagesse* ("Of Wisdom," In Three Parts). French version, 1601. Translated by Samson Lennard, Eliot's Court Press for Edward Blount and Will, Aspley, London, c.1615.

Chaucer, Geoffrey. "Prologue." *The Canterbury Tales.* 14th century. (Description of the Poor Parson). *msgr.ca/msgr-3/church_of_england.htm and the subsite msgr.ca/msgr-3/canterbury_tales_parson.htm.*

Clarke, Arthur C. *90th Birthday Reflections,* 2007.

_____. *Greetings, Carbon-Based Bipeds! : Collected Essays,* 1934-1998 including "Credo " (1991). St. Martin's Press, New York, NY, 1999

Cline, Aaron. Agnosticism/atheism columnist for ten years. *About.com.*

Clinton, Hillary. Speech. Global Business Coalition on HIV/AIDS Annual Awards for Business Excellence Gala at the Kennedy Center in Washington, D.C. Wednesday, Sept. 28, 2005.

_____. Speech in San Francisco, CA. June 28th, 2004.

Coe, R.S. and M. Prevot. "Evidence suggesting extremely rapid field variation during a geomagnetic reversal. " *Earth and Planetary Science Letters,* Elsevier, Amsterdam, Netherlands. Vol. 92, pp. 296-297, 1989.

Coomaraswamy, Rama. "The Conflict Between Science and Faith," from his online archives, 2001.

Covey, Stephen. *Principle-Centered Leadership.* Fireside, Simon and Schuster, Rockefeller Center, New York, NY, 1992.

Cunningham, G., Fluckiger-Hawker, E, Robson, E., and Zólyomi, G.,*The Epic of Gilgamesh, The Electronic Text Corpus of Sumerian Literature,* Oxford 1998-
.

Curtis, Adrian. *Oxford Bible Atlas*, Fourth Edition. Oxford University Press: London, 2009.

Custer, Stewart. *A Treasury of New Testament Synonyms*. Bob Jones Univ. Press: Greenville, SC, 1975.

Cyprian of Carthage (3rd century AD). Letter LXXII, *Ad Jubajanum de haereticis baptizandis*. Translated by Robert Ernest Wallis. From *Ante-Nicene Fathers, Vol. 5*. Edited by Alexander Roberts, James Donaldson, and A. Cleveland Coxe. (Buffalo, NY: Christian Literature Publishing Co., 1886.)

Dalrymple, G. Brent. *The Age of the Earth*. Stanford University Press: Stanford, CA, 1991.

Darwin, Charles. *The Correspondence of Charles Darwin. 1821-1860. Vol. 8* Cambridge University Press, 1993.

_____. *The Descent of Man*. Princeton University Press, Princeton NJ, 1981.

_____. "Charles Darwin's Natural Selection," Being the Second Part of his *Big Species Book* Written from 1856 to 1858, ed. R.C. Stauffer Cambridge, 1975.

Davidson, J. P., W. E. Reed, and P. M. Davis. "The Rise and Fall of Mountain Ranges. " *Exploring Earth: An Introduction to Physical Geology*, Upper Saddle River, New Jersey, Prentice Hall, 1997.

Davies, A. Powell. *America's Real Religion*. Boston: Beacon Press, 1965.

Dawkins, Richard. *The Ancestor's Tale: A Pilgrimage to the Dawn of Evolution*. (Editorial research by Yan Wong) Boston, N.Y.: A Mariner Book, Houghton Mifflin, 2004.

_____. quoted in "The Evolutionary Future of Man. " *The Economist*. 1993-09-11, vol. 328.

_____. The Extended Phenotype: The Long Reach of the Gene. London: Oxford University Press, 1982, 1999.

_____. quoted in "The Flying Spaghetti Monster. " Steve Paulson. *Salon.com*, October 13, 2006.

_____. *The Greatest Show on Earth*. Free Press, Simon and Schuster, New York, NY, also by Bantam Press Transworld Publishers in Great Britain, 2009.

_____. *River Out of Eden*. Basic Books, the Perseus Book Group, New York, NY, 1995.

_____. *The Root of All Evil*. Television documentary, January 2006.

_____. "Science, Delusion and the Appetite for Wonder. " *The Richard Dimbleby Lecture*. BBC1 Television, November 12,1996.

_____. *The Selfish Gene*. London: Oxford University Press, 30th Edition, 2006.

_____. "Slaves to Superstition," *The Enemies of Reason*. [1.01], timecode 00:46:47ff, aired 13 August 2007.

_____. "From Tail to Tale On the Path of Pilgrims In Life. " *The Scotsman*. April 9, 2005.

_____. Speech at the Edinburgh International Science Festival, April 15, 1992.

_____. Speech following the 9/11/2001 Islamic-led terrorist attacks on targets in the United States.

_____. *Unweaving the Rainbow: Science, Delusion and the Appetite for Wonder*. Houghton-Mifflin, New York, NY, 1998.

DeYoung, Dr. Don. *Thousands, Not Billions: Challenging an Icon of Evolution Questioning the*

Age of the Earth. Green Forest, AR: Master Books, Inc., 2005.

Dickens, Charles. *Bleak House.* originally published serially from March 1852 to September 1853.

_____. *A Tale of Two Cities.* 1859.

Dickinson, Emily. "The Bible Is an Antique Volume," poem # 1545, Johnson, Thomas H., editor. *Complete Poems.* Boston: Little, Brown, 1960.

Dillard, Annie. *Pilgrim at Tinker Creek.* Harper's Magazine Press, New York, NY, 1974.

Disney, Walt. Quoted on *justDisney.com.*

Dollar, George W. *A History of Fundamentalism in America.* Greenville, SC: Bob Jones University Press, 1973.

Douglass, Frederick. "What, to the Slave, is the Fourth of July?" address given to a women's anti-slavery society in Rochester, New York. July 4, 1852.

DuBois, W.E.B. essay on birth control in Margaret Sanger's *Birth Control Review.* 1932.

Dunphy, John J. Quoted in *Humanist Magazine,* January-February 1983.

Dyer, B.D. and R.A. Obar. *Tracing the History of Eukaryotic Cells.* Columbia University Press, 1994.

Edison, Thomas A. "The Philosophy of Paine," a June 7, 1925 essay from the book, *The Diary and Sundry Observations,* edited by Dagobert D. Runes (1948).

Edwards, Chris. "Federal Pay Continues Rapid Ascent. " *The Cato Institute Website. Cato At Liberty.org.* The Bureau of Economic Analysis annual data on compensation levels by industry. August 24, 2009 11:57 am.

Edwards, Jonathan. "Sinners in the Hands of an Angry God. " Enfield, Connecticut, July 8, 1741.

Eisenhower, Dwight David. Speech when installed as president of Columbia University in 1948.

Epicurus, from the *40 Sovran Maxims* (or "Sovereign Maxims "), 341-270 BC, as translated by Robert Drew Hicks, 1925.

_____. *Orestes.* Translated by E. P. Coleridge, 1910. Taken from the Internet Sacred Text Archive, www.sacred-texts.com, managed by John Bruno Hare.

_____. Recorded by Seneca the Younger in his *Epistle XX. From Lucius Annaeus Seneca. Moral Essays.* Translated by John W. Basore. The Loeb Classical Library. London: W. Heinemann, 1928-1935. 3 vols.

Epictetus. *The Encheiridion.* Transcribed by Flavius Arrianus. Translated by Sanderson Beck, 1911.

Eskridge, William Jr. *Dynamic Statutory Interpretation.* Copyright by the President and Fellows of Harvard College, 1994.

Eusebius of Caesarea. *Church History or Ecclesiastical History* (Hist. Ecc viii 2.) written by in the 4th century. Translated by Arthur Cushman McGiffert, From Nicene and Post-Nicene Fathers, Second Series, Vol. 1. Edited by Philip Schaff and Henry Wace. Christian Literature Publishing Co., Buffalo, NY, 1890.

Evans, William. *The Great Doctrines of the Bible.* Moody Publishers: Chicago, IL, 1995.

Fa-Hien (or Fa-Xien)). *A Record of Buddhistic Kingdoms, Being an Account by the Chinese Monk Fa-Hien of his Travels in India and Ceylon in Search of the Buddhist Books of Discipline.* Written between A.D. 399 and 412. Translated by James Legge, 1886.

Fange, Erich A. Von. "Time Upside Down. " *Creation Research Quarterly*. June 1974.

Farabee, M.J. *The Online Biology Book*. Estrella Mountain Community College, Avondale, Arizona. emc.maricopa.edu.1992-2002.

Faure, G. *Principles of Isotope Geology*. 2nd. edition. John Wiley and Sons: New York, NY, 1986.

Fowler, Regi (Church/ Community Vice President). "Tolerating Thoughts On Tolerance," *Texas Sings,* Volume 13, number 2, Fall 1997.

Foxe, John. *Foxe's Book of Martyrs*. Written ca. 1560, revised in the 1700s edited by William Byron Forbush. Taken from the Internet Sacred Text Archive, www.sacred-texts.com, managed by John Bruno Hare.

Franklin, Benjamin. *Autobiography*. First English version published London, 1793. (Please see the Great Awakening Appendix for publication history.)

_____. From his speech at the Constitutional Convention Philadelphia, PA. June 28, 1787.

Freud, Sigmund. *The Future of an Illusion*. 1927. Translated by W.D Robson-Scott. English translation published by Horace Liveright and the Institute of Psychoanalysis. 1928.

Gibbs, Phil (original writer, 1996) and Sugihara Hiroshi (1997 update). "Occam's (or Ockham's) razor." University of California, Riverside, *Math.ucr.edu.*

Gibson, Rebecca. "Canyon Creation. " *Answers in Genesis,* September 2000.

Gilley,Gary E. *This Little Church Went to Market–Is the Modern Church Reaching Out of Selling Out?* Evangelical Press, Carlisle, PA, July 2005.

Gish, Duane T. "A Decade of Creationist Research " (Part I). *Creation Research Society Quarterly.* 12 (1): 34-46 June, 1975.

Goetz, Delia, and Sylvanus Griswold Morley. *The Book of the People: POPOL VUH.* from Adrián Recino's translation from Quiché into Spanish. 1954. Taken from the Internet Sacred Text Archive, *www.sacred-texts.com,* managed by John Bruno Hare.

Goldberg, Justice Arthur J. The Supreme Court of the United States No. 02-1574 UNITED STATES OF AMERICA, PETITIONER v. MICHAEL A. NEWDOW, ET AL. ON PETITION FOR A WRIT OF CERTIORARI TO THE UNITED STATES COURT OF APPEALS FOR THE NINTH CIRCUIT REPLY BRIEF FOR THE UNITED STATES. June 26. 2003.

Grant, Peter R. and B. Rosemary Grant. "Genetics and the origin of bird species. " *The National Academy of Sciences of the USA Colloquium Paper,* 1997.

Green, Joey, editor. *Philosophy on the Go.* Joey Green and Alan Corcoran, Running Press, Philadelphia, PA, 2007.

Green, Nathan, Dr. *Course overview for GEO.101,"Introduction to Geology,"* University of Alabama. Spring 2006.

Grinspoon, Lester. *Marihuana Reconsidered.* Quick American Archives. Quick Trading Company, Oakland, CA, 1971.

Hall, Edward T. *Beyond Culture.* Anchor Books, Random House, New York, NY, 1976.

Hall, Fred. "Ice Cores Not All That Simple. " *AEON II:* 1, 1989:199.

Haeckel, Ernst. *The History of Creation.* Vol. 1, 6-9. 1876. Translated by Joseph McCabe, Watts & Company, London, 1912.

Hamilton, Alexander. Letter to James Bayard. 1802.

Hamilton, Alexander and James Madison. *The Federalist Papers.* Signet Classics, Penguin, Putnam: New York, NY, 2003.

Hammond, James Henry (Senator of South Carolina) "Reply to Senator William H. Seward of New York. " 1858.

Hancock, Graham. *Fingerprints of the Gods.* Three Rivers Press, New York, NY: Crown Publishing Group, Random House, 1995.

_____. *Underworld: The Mysterious Origins of Civilization,* Three Rivers Publishing, Crown, Random House, New York, NY, 2003.

Han Fei. c 200 BC. *The Five Vermin.* W. K. Liao (translator and annotator), The Complete Works of Han Fei Tzu. 2 vols, London, 1939-59.

Hannam, James. "Medieval Science and Philosophy" and "Science and Church in the Middle Ages." (From his Web site for the book.) *God's Philosophers: How the Medieval World Laid the Foundations of Modern Science.* Icon Books, London, 2009.

Hapgood, Charles H., J.B. Delair and E.F. Oppe. *The Path of the Pole.* Chilton Books, Philadelphia, PA, 1970.

Harris, Sam. *The End of Faith.* W.W. Norton & Company New York, NY, 2004.

Haught, James A. *2000 Years of Disbelief: Famous People with the Courage to Doubt.* Prometheus Books, Amherst, NY, 1998.

Hawking, Stephen. *The Illustrated A Brief History of Time.* New York, NY: Bantam Dell, a division of Random House, 1996.

Heinlein, Robert A. *The Notebooks of Lazarus Long,* 1978, Pomegranate Publications, Inc., 1999.

Herndon, William and Jesse W. Weik. *Herndon's Lincoln: The True Story of a Great Life,* a three volume edition published by Belford, Clarke & Company beginning in 1889.

Herodotus (484-ca. 425 BC). *Histories.* English translation G. C. Macaulay. Macmillan, London and NY, 1890.

Hesiod. *Theogeny.* Translated by Hugh G. Evelyn-White. 1914. Taken from the Internet Sacred Text Archive, www.sacred-texts.com, managed by John Bruno Hare.

Heyerdahl, Thor. *Kon-Tiki: Across the Pacific in a Raft* (The Kon-Tiki Expedition: By Raft Across the South Seas) F.H. Lyon, Translator. Rand McNally & Company: Skokie, IL, 1950.

_____. *Aku-Aku: The Secret of Easter Island.* 1958.

Hitler, Adolph. Speech given May 1, 1937.

_____. Speech given at Elbing, Germany. November 6, 1939.

Hoagland, Peter. American lawyer and congressman (US House of Representatives, Democrat, Nebraska), in a radio speech with Pastor Everett Silevan, 1983, documented in Bill Clinton: Friend or Foe? Ann Wilson, J. W. Publishing Company, 1993.

Hodges, Charles. *Systematic Theology.* 3 Volumes. Hendrickson Publishers: Peabody, MA, 1999.

Holmes, Oliver Wendell. "The Theory of Legal Interpretation. " 12 Harvard Law Review. 417, 419 (1899).

Homer. *The Iliad*. C. 850 BC Translated by Samuel Butler, 1900. Gutenberg.org.

——————. *The Odyssey.*

Hornberger, Jacob G. "Your Children Are the Property of the State," *The Future of Freedom Foundation Website*. April 2000.

Howorth, H.H. *The Mammoth and the Flood: An Attempt to Confront the Theory of Uniformitarianism with the Facts of Recent Geology*. London: Sampson Low, Marston, Searle & Livingston. 1887. Reproduced by the Sourcebook Project, Glen Arm, Maryland.

Humphreys, D. Russell, Steven A. Austin, John R. Baumgardner, and Andrew A. Snelling. "Helium Diffusion Age of 6,000 Years Supports Accelerated Nuclear Decay. " *Creation Research Society Quarterly Journal*. (CRSQ) Vol 41 No 1 June 2004. Creation Research.org, Copyright © 2004 by Creation Research Society.

Humphreys, D. Russell, Ph.D. *Starlight and Time, Solving the Puzzle of Distant Starlight in a Young Universe*. Green Forest, AR: Master Books, Inc., 2004, Ninth Printing.

Huxley, Aldous. "Confessions of a Professed Atheist," Report: *Perspective on the News,* Vol. 3, June 1966, p. 19.

Huxley, Julian. "At Random," a television preview on Nov. 21, 1959.

Huxley,Thomas Henry. Letter to Charles Kingsley (23 September 1860).

Ingersoll, Robert G. *Thomas Paine*. 1892. Thomas Paine National Historical Association website,

http://www.thomaspaine.org/
bio/ingersoll1892.html.

Iype, George. First press conference of Indian Prime
Minister Manmohan Singh. *Rediff, India Abroad,*
May 20, 2004.

Jay, William. "Charge to the Grand Jury of Ulster
County " on Sept. 9, 1777. from *The Life of John
Jay.* J. & J. Harper, New York, NY, 1833.

Jefferson, Thomas. *Autobiography.* 1821.

_____. "Draft for a Bill for Establishing
Religious Freedom. Proposed to the Virginia
Assembly," 1779. odur.let.rug.nl
~usa/P/tj3/writings/draft1779.htm

_____. "Letter to the Secretary of the Treasury,
Albert Gallatin," 1802.

_____. *The Writings of Thomas Jefferson,*
Albert E. Bergh, ed. (Washington, D. C.: The
Thomas Jefferson Memorial Association of the
United States, 1904), Vol. XVI, pp. 281-282.

_____. University of Virginia Library
Collection of the letters and papers of Thomas
Jefferson.

Jensen, Carl,
*http://web.archive.org/web/20050831053419
/www.pbnnews.*reposted on the website
D.program.net October 1, 2008,

Johnson, Allen H. "James Dale, the Supreme Court and
fond memories of Troop 148," *News and Record I,*
July 30, 2000. *Gay Straight Advocates for
Education Website (gsafe.org).*

Johnson, Samuel. *The History of Rasselas, Prince of
Abissinia.* 1759.

Josephus, Flavius. *Against Apion.* William Whiston,
Translator, 1737. Taken from the Internet Sacred

Text Archive, www.sacred-texts.com, managed by John Bruno Hare.

_____. *Antiquities of the Jews.*

_____. *Autobiography.*

_____. *Hades.*

_____. *Wars of the Jews.*

Justin Martyr. *First Apology.* Translated by Alexander Roberts and James Donaldson. 1867.

Keil, C. F. and F. Delitzsch. *Commentary on the Old Testament. 10 Volumes* Hendrickson Publishers: Peabody, MA, Updated Edition 1996.

King, Coretta Scott. Speech at the Palmer House Hilton in Chicago April 1, 1998.

King, Leonard William, translator. *ENUMA ELISH: THE EPIC OF CREATION (from The Seven Tablets of Creation,* London 1902) Public Domain. Taken from the Internet Sacred Text Archive, www.sacred-texts.com, managed by John Bruno Hare.

Kipling, Rudyard. *The Jungle Book.* originally published serially, 1893-1894.

Kurtz, Paul, Editor. *A Secular Humanist Declaration,* issued by The Council for Democratic and Secular Humanism (now the Council for Secular Humanism). Published in Free Inquiry Magazine, 1980.

LaBahn, Jeri. "Education and Parental Involvement in Secondary Schools: Problems, Solutions, and Effects," *Educational Psychology Interactive.* Valdosta, GA: Valdosta State University, 1995.

Landor, Walter Savage. "Melanchthon and Calvin," *Imaginary Conversations.* 1824-29.

Lee, Harper. *To Kill A Mocking-Bird*. Harper and Row, New York, NY, 1961 (copyright 1960 by the author, renewed 1988).

Lee, Robert E. (General Lee's son). *Recollections and Letters of General Robert E. Lee*. Rod and Black Publishers, St. Petersburg, Fl, 1904.

Leeuw, Nick De. Posting by contributor Monday, Nov. 10, 2008 on the *Right Michigan.com website*, email by Mount Hope Church in Lansing, Michigan attendee who witnessed the infiltration and actions of Bash Back (A Michigan-based pro-gay and lesbian organization) at the church November 9, 2008.

Lenin, Vladimir Ilyich. *Two Tactics of Social-Democracy in the Democratic Revolution*. Written June-July 1905, first published as a pamphlet in Geneva, July 1905, translated by Abraham Fineburg and Julius Katzer, published in Lenin's Collected Works, Volume 9, 1962, Moscow. Taken from Marxist Internet archive.

Lennon, John. "Imagine." Title song from the *Imagine album*. Ascot Sound Studios Tittenhurst Park and The Record Plant, New York, NY. Apple/EMI Label. 1971.

Lerner Lawrence S. *Good Science, Bad Science: Teaching Evolution in the States,* Thomas B. Fordham Foundation, Washington, DC, 2000.

Lewis, Charles. "Gay Altar Server Contests Firing Human Rights Tribunal asked to intervene." *National Post* (Canada). Tuesday, July 14, 2009.

Lewis, C.S. *The Abolition of Man or Reflections on education with special reference to the teaching of English in the upper forms of schools.* 1943. Available online at *www.columbia.edu/cu/augustine/arch/lewis/abolition1.htm*.

Lewis, Joseph. *Ingersoll the Magnificent*, a compilation of Ingersoll's quotations, dedicated at a memorial address in 1954, published American Atheist Press, Austin TX, 1983.

Lewontin, Richard. Quoted in a review,"Billions and Billions of Demons," *The New York Review*, p. 31, January 9, 1997.

Lial, Margaret L., Charles David Miller and E. John Hornsby. *Beginning Algebra*, Harper-Collins College Division, New York, NY, 1992.

Liddell, H.G. and R. Scott, eds. *A Greek-English Lexicon*. Oxford University Press: London, 1982.

Lincoln, Abraham. "Response to Horace Greeley's abolitionist editorial. " *New York Tribune*, August 22, 1862.

Linder, Douglas O. "Speech on the Occasion of the 25th Anniversary of the Scopes Trial," July 10, 2000. "State v. John Scopes" ("The Monkey Trial") *http://www.law.umkc.edu/faculty/projects/ftrial s/scopes/evolut.htm.*

Lisle, Jason, Ph.D. "God and Natural Law." *Answers in Genesis*, August 28, 2006.

Livingston, Dr. David P. "Nimrod: Who Was He? Was He Godly or Evil?" *Associates for Biblical Research*. Originally published in *ABR's BIBLE AND SPADE*, 2001.

Lowder, Jeffery Jay, ed. Farrell Till et. al. "The Jury Is In: The Ruling on McDowell's 'Evidence.' " 1997-2001. *www.infidels.org.*

Lubicz, Isha Schwaller, de. *Her-Bak: The Living Face of Ancient Egypt and Her-Bak: Egyptian Initiate.* Inner Traditions, Santa Fe, New Mexico, 1978.

Lucian of Samosata. c. A.D. 125 – after A.D. 180. An Assyrian rhetorician, and satirist who wrote in the

Greek language, translated by A. M. Harmon, 1936.

Lucretius (Titus Lucretius Carus). *Of The Nature of Things.* (c 95-55 BC) Translator: William Ellery Leonard, 1916. Gutenberg.org.

Lundstrom, Laurel. "Students Free to Thank Anybody Except God. " *Fox News.com.* Monday, November 22, 2004,

MacAuliffe, Max Arthur (Author and translator of Sikh texts). *The Sikh Religion, DIVINE SERVICES BY GURU NANAK AND OTHER GURUS THE JAPJI, Volume 1.* Oxford University Press: London, 1909. Taken from the Internet Sacred Text Archive, www.sacred-texts.com, managed by John Bruno Hare.

McCafferty, Phil. "Instant petrified wood?" *Popular Science.* October 1992.

MacDowell, Josh. *The New Evidence that Demands a Verdict.* Thomas Nelson: Nashville, TN, 1999.

MacRae, Andrew. *Radiometric Dating and the Geological Time Scale Circular Reasoning or Reliable Tools?* Copyright 1997-2004 [Text last updated: October 2, 1998] *Talk Origins.org.*

Madison, James. *Federalist No. 47,* quoting Montesquieu (Charles de Secondat, Baron de Montesquieu, 1689-1755), *The Spirit of the Laws, vol. 1,* trans. Thomas Nugent (London: J. Nourse, 1777).

_____. "Letter to Robert Walsh. " March 2, 1819. *http://www.stephenjaygould. org/ ctrl/church-state.html.*

Malthus, Thomas Robert. *An Essay on the Principle of Population.* 1798.

Manning, Richard and Hans Beimler, writers. Directed By: Robert Wiemer. Executive Producer: Rick

Berman. Created by Gene Roddenberry,"Who Watches the Watchers?" *Star Trek the Next Generation,* Season Three, Episode Four, first aired October 16, 1989.

Marcus Aurelius. *Meditations.* 167 AD. Translated by George Long. 1862.

Marx, Karl and Friedrich Engles. "Address of the Central Committee to the Communist League. " London, 1850. Translated from German in the Soviet Union, individual translators not given. Foreign Languages Publishing House, Moscow, 1951.

_____. "Contribution to the Critique of Hegel's Philosophy of Right," 1843. Published Cambridge University 1970, editor Joseph O'Malley, translators Annette Jolin and Joseph O'Malley.

Matson, Dave E. "How Good Are Those Young-Earth Arguments?" copyright 1995.on *Infidels.org.*

Maududi, Sayeed Abdul A'la. From an address given on April 13, 1939, translation on the site *IslamistWatch.org,* no translator credited.

Merrill, Eugene H. *An Historical Survey of the Old Testament.* Baker Books: Grand Rapids, MI, 1991.

Maxwell, Bill. "Intolerance as policy. " *St. Petersburg Times.* August 9, 1998.

Mill, John Stuart. *Autobiography.* 1873.

Miller, Kevin and Ben Stein, writers. *Expelled: No Intelligence Allowed.* Prod. Logan Craft, Walt Ruloff and John Sullivan. Dir. Nathan Frankowski. Assoc. Prod. Mark Mathis. Ed. Simon Tondeur. © 2008 Premise Media Corporation, Rampart Films Production.

Morgan, G. Campbell. *Acts of the Apostles.* 1924.

Morton, G.R. "Young-Earth Arguments: A Second Look," 1998. *home.entouch.net.*

Montgomery, Peter. Article on *AlterNet.org*. Feb. 10, 2010.

Mooney, Chris. "Survival of the Slickest: How Anti-Evolutionists are Mutating Their Message. " *The American Prospect, Liberal Intelligence.* December 2, 2002.

Mooney, James. *MYTHS OF THE CHEROKEE. From Nineteenth Annual Report of the Bureau of American Ethnology 1897-98, Part I. COSMOGONIC MYTHS.* Taken from the Internet Sacred Text Archive, www.sacred-texts.com, managed by John Bruno Hare.

Morris, Henry M. *The Genesis Record: a Scientific and Devotional Commentary on the Book of Beginnings.* Grand Rapids, MI. Baker Book House, 1976.

Mulsow, Martin and Jan Rohls. *Socinianism And Arminianism : Antitrinitarians, Calvinists, And Cultural Exchange in Seventeenth-Century Europe,* part of the series *Brills Studies of Intellectual History,* edited by A.J. Vanderjagt, University of Gronigen, Netherlands, 2005.

Newton, Isaac. Unpublished notes for the *Preface to Opticks* (1704) quoted in *Never at Rest: A Biography of Isaac Newton* by Richard S. Westfall, Cambridge Paperback Library, 1983.

Nicholls, David. *Atheist Foundation of Australia,* undated article on the Foundation's website.

Nietzsche, Friedrich. Human, *All-Too-Human, A Book for Free Spirits.* German version 1878. Translated by Marion Faber and Stephen Lehmann. English version published by Lincoln: University of Nebraska Press, 1984.

Oard, Michael. *Frozen in Time: The Wooly Mammoth, The Ice Age and the Bible.* Green Forest, AR: Master Books, Inc., 2004.

Ovid (Publius Ovidius Naso). *Metamorphoses.* Completed in AD 8.Translated by Henry Thomas Riley, 1851.

Paine. Thomas. *The Age of Reason,* in 3 parts, 1794, 1795, 1807. *Gutenberg.org*

_____. *Agrarian Justice,* printed in English by W. Adlard in Paris, and in London for T. Williams, No. 8 Little Turnstile, Holborn, 1797.

_____. "Answer to the Bishop of Lladaff. " (Concerning The Age of Reason) published in the *Theophilanthropist,* New York, NY, 1810. [Submitted posthumously by the widow of Elihu Palmer, who attended Paine during his illness in 1806, in the house of William Carver.]

_____. *Common Sense. Gutenberg.org*

_____. "Essay on Dream. " Published New York, 1807. [Full title: "An Examination of the Passages in the New Testament, quoted from the Old and called Prophecies concerning Jesus Christ. To which is prefixed an Essay on Dream, showing by what operation of the mind a Dream is produced in sleep, and applying the same to the account of Dreams in the New Testament. With an Appendix containing my private thoughts of a Future State. And Remarks on the Contradictory Doctrine in the Books of Matthew and Mark. "].

_____. *Examination of the Prophecies,* pamphlet published in 1807.

_____. *First Principles of Government,* 1795.

_____. "Letter to Andrew Dean," New York, August 15, 1806.

_____. "A letter to the Hon. Thomas Erskine, on the Prosecution of Thomas Williams for publishing the Age of Reason. By Thomas Paine, Author of *Common Sense, Rights of Man,* etc. With his *discourse at the Society of the Theophilanthropists.* Paris: Printed for the Author. " This pamphlet was carried through Barrois' English press in Paris, September, 1797.

_____. Memorial to James Monroe, 10 Sept. 1794.

_____. "Of The Books Of The New Testament: Address To The Believers In The Book Called The Scriptures," *Prospect Papers* Magazine (also titled "A View of the Moral World,"), 1804, published monthly by Elihu Palmer in New York.

_____. *The Rights of Man.* Gutenberg.org. 1791.

Palin, Sarah. *Going Rogue: An American Life.* Harper Collins, New York: NY, 2009.

Parsons, Thomas J., et. al. "A high observed substitution rate in the human mitochondrial DNA control region. " *Nature Genetics* 15, 363 - 368 (1997).

Pasteur, Louis. Correspondence I, p. 382-383,"To the Rector of the Academia de Douai," 15 Nov. 1855. Cuny, H., *Louis Pasteur, The Man and his Theories,* Translated P. Evans, London, The Souvenir Press, 1965.

Patten, Donald W. and Samuel R. Windsor. "Catastrophic Theory of Mountain Uplifts (A Crustal Deformation Theory). " *Catastrophism and Ancient History Vol. XIII Part 1* January 1991.

Pell, George, Cardinal. "Varieties of Intolerance: Religious and Secular," Thomas More Lecture on Religion in the Public Square, hosted by the Oxford

University Newman Society, *LifesiteNews*, published March 12, 2009.

Penn, William. *THE TRYAL of WILLIAM PENN and WILLIAM MEAD*, at the Sessions held at the Old Baily in London, the 1st, 3rd, 4th, and 5th of September, 1670. *Gutenberg.org.*

Pierce, Chester M. Address at Childhood International Education Seminar, 1973.

Pitman, Sean, M.D. "Ancient Ice " (a PowerPoint presentation) created in Jan 2006. Includes testimony from a telephone interview with Bob Cardin, project manager to recover "Glacier Girl. "

Plato. *The Republic*. Translated by Benjamin Jowett over a period of 30 years until his death in 1893, completed by Lewis Campbell. *Gutenberg.org.*

_____. *Critias.*

_____. *Phaedrus.*

_____. *Timmaus.*

Plutarch. *Lives*. Translated by John Dryden, 1683. Gutenberg.org.

Poincaré, Henri. "Science et méthode. " ("Science and Method "), 1908, English translation in *The Foundations of Science: Science and Hypothesis, The Value of Science, Science and Method,* The Science Press, translated by George Bruce Halstead, 1913.

Polo, Marco and Rustichello of Pisa, *The Travels of Marco Polo, Volume 1, THE COMPLETE YULE-CORDIER EDITION Including the unabridged third edition* (1903) of Henry Yule's annotated translation, as revised by Henri Cordier; together with Cordier's later volume of notes and addenda. 1920. Chapter XVII. Gutenberg.org.

Porter, Janet. "Forced Vaccines: Ready For Yours?" *Faith2action,* posted: August 18, 2009 1:00 am Eastern 2010 *World Net Daily. wnd.com.*

Prager, Dennis. "Breastfeeding as a Religion. " *World Net Daily. wnd.com.* posted November 11, 2003 1:00 am Eastern.

Protagoras of Abdera (ca. 490-ca. 420 BC) Greek philosopher, agnostic, logician, believed to be from his lost work *On the Gods.* Included in the following work: *Aristophanes. Clouds.* Intro. and trans. by Carol Poster. In Aristophanes 3, ed. David Slavitt and Palmer Bovie. Philadelphia PA: University of Pennsylvania Press, 1999.

Radest, Howard B. "Are We Religious?" By Algernon David Black. Collected in *Understanding Ethical Religion.* Produced for the American Ethical Union Library, 1975.

Rand, Ayn. *Atlas Shrugged,* author's copyright 1957. Signet, New American Library, Penguin Group, New York, NY 1996.

Randerson, James. "We Know Nothing About Brain Evolution. " *Guardian* (UK). Report on a 2008 Lewontin speech titled, "Why We Know Nothing About the Evolution of Cognition. "

Rantoul, Robert. Fourth-of-July address. Scituate, Massachusetts, 1836.

Reese, Lizette. 1856-1935. From the poem "Truth. " *American Women Poets of the Nineteenth Century.* Anthology edited by Cheryl Walker. Rutgers University, New Jersey, 1992.

Regnerus, Mark. "Sex and the Evangelical Teen. " *Forbidden Fruit: Sex & Religion in the Lives of American Teenagers.* Oxford University Press, New York, NY, 2007). THOUGHTS, "Minority report," World magazine, Vol. 22, No. 29, August 11, 2007.

Rickman, Thomas Clio. *Life of Thomas Paine,* 1819.

Robertson, A.T. *Word Pictures of the New Testament.* Broadman Press: Nashville, TN: 1932, 33, Renewal 1960.

Rolston, Bruce. "Speed Of Light May Not Be Constant, Physicist Suggests. " Report on an article co-authored by University of Toronto Physics professor John Moffat and former U of T researcher Michael Clayton and published in *Physics Letters* in 1999. *ScienceDaily,* October 6, 1999.

Rooney, Andy. *Sincerely, Andy Rooney.* Essay Productions, Public Affairs, by the Perseus Group, New York, NY, 1999.

Rosenhouse, Jason. *EvolutionBlog*, Posted March 5, 2010.

Roys, Ralph L, translator. *THE BOOK OF CHILAM BALAM OF CHUMAYEL* 1933. Taken from the Internet Sacred Text Archive, www.sacred-texts.com, managed by John Bruno Hare.

Rummel, R.J. STATISTICS OF DEMOCIDE Chapter 4 "Statistics Of Cambodian Democide Estimates, Calculations, And Sources. " Prepublication excerpt 1997, *Hawaii.edu.*

Rushdoony, Rousas. *The Mythology of Science.* Nutley, NJ: Craig Press, 1967.

Rushdie, Salman. A 1996 speech.

Russell, Bertrand. "Why I am Not a Christian. " Lecture March 6, 1927, delivered to the National Secular Society.

Sagan, Carl. *Contact.* Pocket Books, Simon and Schuster, NY: NY, 1985.

_____. *Cosmos* television series. PBS, 1980.

_____. *Cosmos: A Personal Voyage* (Updated), television series, PBS, 1989.

_____. Interview with Charlie Rose, late-night PBS talk show host, 1996.

_____. *The Demon-Haunted World: Science as a Candle in the Dark,* Ballantine Book, Random House, New York, NY, 1996.

Sand, George (Amantine Aurore Lucile Dupin). 1804-1876 Letter to Gustave Flaubert, 14 September, 1871. Translated by A.L. MacKenzie, 1921.

Sanderson, Terry. Address as president of the National Secular Society of the UK, Dec 17, 2009.

Sanger, Margaret. *Pivot of Civilization,* 1932.

_____. *The Woman Rebel, Volume I, Number 1.* Reprinted in *Woman and the New Race.* New York: Brentanos Publishers, 1922.

Sarfati, Jonathan. "Who's Really Pushing Bad Science?" *Creation.com,* Creation Ministries International, 26 September 2000.

Saxe, John Godfrey. (1816-1887). "The Blind Men and the Elephant."

Sayers, Dorothy L. "The Other Six Deadly Sins." *Creed or Chaos,* Harcourt, Brace and Company, New York: NY, 1994.

Scalia, Antonin. *Common-Law Courts in a Civil-Law System: The Role of United States Federal Courts in Interpreting the Constitution and Laws.* THE TANNER LECTURES ON HUMAN VALUES. Delivered at Princeton University, March 8 and 9, 1995.

Schaff, Phillip. *History of the Christian Church, Volumes 5, 6 and 7.* Charles Scribner's Sons, New York, 1910.

Schaeffer, Francis A. "A Christian Manifesto." An address delivered by Dr. Schaeffer in 1982 at the Coral Ridge Presbyterian Church, Fort Lauderdale, Florida. It is based on the book of the same title.

_____. *The God Who Is There*. InterVarsity Press: Downer's Grove, IL, 1998.

Schmid, Randolph E. (Associated Press). "Skull Suggests Interbreeding of Neanderthal and Modern Man. " *The Denver Post*, January 15, 2007.

Schweitzer, Mary H. and Jennifer L. Wittmeyer, North Carolina State University; John R. Horner, Montana State University; Jan B. Toporski, Carnegie Institution of Washington Geophysical Laboratory. "Soft-Tissue Vessels and Cellular Preservation in Tyrannosaurus rex. " *Science*, March 25, 2005. NC State, the N.C. Museum of Natural Sciences and the National Science Foundation funded the research.

_____. "Soft tissue and cellular preservation in vertebrate skeletal elements from the Cretaceous to the present. " *Proceedings of the Royal Society of Biological Sciences*. vol. 274 no. 1607 183-197, 22 January 2007.

Schleiermacher, Friedrich. Letter to his father. January 1787. Martin Redeker, translator, *Schleiermacher: Life and Thought*. Fortress Press. 1973.

Sedgwick, Adam (Woodwardian Professor of Geology at Cambridge). "Letter to Charles Darwin. " November 24, 1859.

Sellars, Roy Wood and Raymond Bragg. *Humanist Manifesto I draft*, 1933.

Semken, Steven, et. al. "Trail of Time" Exhibit, Grand Canyon National Park. Associate Professor of Geoscience Education and Geological Sciences, School of Earth and Space Exploration at Arizona

State University. From the *Arizona State University website*. 2008.

Seneca, Lucius Annaeus (Seneca the Younger. 4 BC to AD 65). "A letter to Serenus," as translated in *Tranquillity of Mind and Providence* by William Bell Langsdorf, 1900.

Serling, Rod. Last interview before his death, with Linda Brevelle, March 4, 1975.

Shakespeare, William. *Hamlet,* Act I Scene iii, Polonius to his son Laertes.

Shallit, Jeffrey. "Pamela Winnick's Science Envy. " *Blogspot*. Monday, July 10, 2006.

Shaw, George Bernard. *Androcles and the Lion*. 1913.

Shelley, Mary Wollstonecraft. *A Vindication of the Rights of Woman With Strictures on Political and Moral Subjects*, 1792.

Shelley, Percy Bysshe. *The Necessity of Atheism* (1811), to serve as a note to the line in Queen Mab, "There is no God" (1813).

Shepherd. Jessica. "Children educated at home twice as likely to be known to social services, select committee told" and "Home pupils more likely to be known by social services and be out of work, education or training. " *guardian.co.uk*. Tuesday, 13 October 2009.

Shermer, Michael. "The Fossil Fallacy: Creationists' demand for fossils that represent 'missing links' reveals a deep misunderstanding of science. " *Scientific American*. 21 February 2005.

Simon, Sidney. *Values Clarification*. Originally published 1972, Warner Books. Revised edition by Grand Central Publishing, September 1, 1995.

Simpson, George Gaylord. *The Meaning of Evolution.* Revised edition. New Haven: Yale University Press, 1967.

Smith, S. Percy, trans. *The Lore of the Whare-wananga; or Teachings of the Maori College On Religion, Cosmogony, and History.* Written down by H. T. Whatahoro from the teachings of Te Matorohanga and Nepia Pohuhu, priests of the Whare-wananga of the East Coast, New Zealand. (Smith was the F.R.G.S. President of the Polynesian Society.) Part I.-Te Kauwae-runga,Or 'Things Celestial.' New Plymouth, N.Z. Printed for the Society by Thomas Avery. -- 1913. {Reduced to HTML by Christopher M. Weimer, February 2003} Taken from the Internet Sacred Text Archive, www.sacred-texts.com, managed by John Bruno Hare.

Snelling, Andrew. "Radiocarbon in Diamonds Confirmed. " *Answers in Genesis,* November 7, 2007. (This study was conducted during the RATE (Radioisotopes and the Age of The Earth) research project at the Institute for Creation Research.)

_____. "The Earth's magnetic field and the age of the Earth," first published: *Creation* (Creation Ministries International), 13(4):44-48 September 1991.

_____. "The Recent Origin of Bass Strait Oil and Gas. " *Creation,* 5 (2):43–46 March 1982.

Sparks, Muriel. *The Prime of Miss Jean Brodie.* Harper Collins, New York, NY, 1961.

Spence, Lewis. Excerpt from: *The Popol Vuh The Mythic and Heroic Sagas of the Kichés of Central America.* Published by David Nutt, at the Sign of the Phoenix, Long Acre, London [1908]. Taken from the Internet Sacred Text Archive, www.sacred-texts.com, managed by John Bruno Hare.

_____. *The Myths of Mexico and Peru.* (1913). Taken from the Internet Sacred Text Archive, www.sacred-texts.com, managed by John Bruno Hare.

Spurgeon, Charles Haddon. "Our Reply to Sundry Critics and Enquirers," *The Sword and Trowel,* Metropolitan Tabernacle, Elephant and Castle, London, Sept. 1887.

Steinem, Gloria. "Address to the Women of America," at the founding of the National Women's Political Caucus, 1971.

Sternberg, Dr. Richard. *RichardSternberg.org.*

Strong, James. *Strong's Exhaustive Concordance of the Bible.* Hendrickson Publishers: Peabody, MA, Updated Edition, 2007.

Suetonius (Gaius Suetonius Tranquillus). *The Twelve Caesars.* c. 117 138 AD. translation J. C. Rolfe, 1913-1914.

Sun Tzu, *The Art of War.* Estimated to have been written between 476-221 BC. Translated by Lionel Guiles, 1910. Gutenberg.org.

Swatt, Barbara (Preparer, Reference Intern). Adapted from, "Themis, Goddess of Justice," *Marian Gould Gallagher Law Library, University of Washington School of Law.* Updated Oct. 31, 2007.

Sweet, William Warren. *The Story of Religions in America.* Harper & Brothers, New York, N.Y., 1930.

Sykes, Bryan. *The Seven Daughters of Eve: The Science That Reveals Our Genetic Ancestry.* W.W. Norton: New York, N.Y., 2001.

Syrett, Harold C. editor. *The Papers of Alexander Hamilton.* NY: Columbia University Press, 1979. Vol. XXI, pp. 402-404.

Tacitus. *The Annals of Imperial Rome.* 109 AD, XIII. 32. Translated by Alfred John Church and William Jackson Brodribb, 1876.

_____. *The Histories,* 109 AD. Translated by Alfred John Church and William Jackson Brodribb, 1876.

Tamny, John. "Where Are the Supply-Side Democrats?" *National Review Online.* November 18, 2005.

Taylor, Paul (Series Editor) and Elizabeth Deane (Program Executive Producer). *American Experience, Ulysses S. Grant. PBS,* WGBH Educational Foundation, 2002.

Alfred, Lord Tennyson. *In Memoriam, AAH.* 1849. http://www.online-literature.com tennyson/718/.

Tenzin Gyatzo, 14th Dalai Lama, leader of Tibetan Buddhism, "Compassion and the Individual: the Purpose of Life. " From the *Dalai Lama website.*

Thapar, Prof. Romila. *Frontline* magazine. Volume 18 - Issue 19, Sep. 15 - 28, 2001.

Thayer, Joseph Henry. *Thayer's Greek-English Lexicon of the New Testament.* Zondervan: Grand Rapids, MI, 1970.

Thiele, Edwin. *The Mysterious Numbers of the Hebrew Kings.* Zondervan Publishing House, Grand Rapids, MI, 1983.

Thiessen, Henry Clarence. *Lectures in Systematic Theology.* Wm. B. Eerdmans: Grand Rapids, MI, Revised ed., 2006.

Traufetter, Gerald. "Europe's 'Human Zoos' -- Remains of Indigenous Abductees Back Home after 130 Years. " *International: Zeitgeist. Archive Der Spiegel,* 1/13/2010.

Trudeau, G.B. *Doonesbury.* Strip published in November, 1995. Universal Press Syndicate. *Doonesbury* was launched October 26, 1970.

Unruh, Bob. "Homeschooler flees state custody: Melissa Busekros surprises parents at 3 a.m. " Posted: April 23, 2007 12:33 pm Eastern. *World Net Daily.*

_____. "Homeschoolers on run win U.S. asylum Judge: Teaching children 'basic right no country has right to violate.'" January 26, 2010 11:02 pm Eastern. *World Net Daily.*

Ussher, James. *Annales veteris testamenti, a prima mundi origine deducti* ("Annals of the Old Testament, deduced from the first origins of the world"), 1650.

Ustinov, Peter. Interview with Mike Wallace. March 29, 1958.

Virgil. *The Aeneid.* c. 29 BC. Translated by John Dryden 1697. *Gutenberg.org.*

_____. *Georgics,* Book Two, published c. 29 BC. Poetic translation by John Dryden, 1697. Gutenberg.org

Vega, Garcilaso de la ("El Inca," real name Gómez Suárez de Figueroa). *Comentarios Reales de los Incas.* Lisbon, 1609. Translated by Harold V. Livermore. 1965.

Velikovsky, Emmanuel. *Ages in Chaos.* Doubleday, New York: New York, 1952.

Voltaire (François-Marie Arouet). "Of Modern Atheists, Reasons of the Worshipers of God. " *Atheism I, Section I. C.* 1764. Selected and Translated by H.I. Woolf, Knopf, New York, NY, 1924.

Wald, George. "The Origin of Life," *Scientific American,* 191:48, May 1954.

Walvoord, John and Roy B. Zuck. *The Bible Knowledge Commentary, Old and New Testaments*. Cook Communications: Colorado Springs, CO, 1989.

Watts, Charles. "The Secularist's Catechism. " complied in an undated book published by Watts & Co. entitled: *Pamphlets by Charles Watts Vol. I*. 1896.

Weinberg, Steve. "A Designer Universe?" *Address at the Conference on Cosmic Design, American Association for the Advancement of Science*, Washington, D.C. April 1999.

West, E. W., translator. 1880. *PAHLAVI TEXTS*. (Persian language works from c. 180 to 880 AD) Taken from the Internet Sacred Text Archive, *www.sacred-texts.com*, managed by John Bruno Hare.

Willebrands, Johannes Cardinal. *Response to the Boy Scouts of America official position on the admission of homosexual members and leaders*, 2000.

Willette (Site User). *Askville.Amazon.com*. posted late 2009 or early 2010.

Williams, Roger. "Mr. Cotton's Letter Lately Printed, Examined and Answered," (1644), and "The Hireling Ministry, None of Christ's. " *The Complete Writings of Roger Williams*. The Narragansett Club (1652).

Wilson, Edward Osborne. *On Human Nature*. Harvard University Press, 1979.

Winthrop, John. From "A Model of Christian Charity," 1630. *The Avalon Project. Documents in Law, History and Diplomacy*. Yale Law Library. avalon.law.yale.edu.

Whedon, Joseph Hill "Joss." Commentary on *Buffy the Vampire Slayer* series DVD, episode 5.16 ("The Body ") (Season 5, released December 9, 2003), and an interview by Tasha Robinson for *The Onion,* (an online satirical magazine) September 5, 2001.

Wheeler, Charles N. Interview with Henry Ford. *Chicago Tribune*, May 25, 1916.

Whitcomb, J.C. and H. M. Morris. *The Genesis Flood.* Grand Rapids, MI: Baker Book House, 1961.

Whitman, Walt. "Song of Myself." From *Leaves of Grass*, first published 1855. Revised and republished many times until the "deathbed" edition finished in 1892. "Definitive version " published in 1900.

Wysong, Pippa. "Dinosaur Remains Yield Soft Tissue. " *Access Excellence.* Raleigh, NC April 29, 2005. (Access Excellence is an online publication of The National Health Museum, Atlanta GA.)

Xenophanes, pre-Socratic philosopher (570-475 BC). Diels, Hermann. *Die Fragmente der Vorsokratiker* ("Pre-Socratic Fragments "). Translated by Rev. Walther Kranz. Berlin: Weidmann, 1972-1973.

Xenophon. "On Hunting." (430-354 BC). *Xenophon in Seven Volumes.* 7. Translated by E. C. Marchant, G. W. Bowersock. Constitution of the Athenians. Harvard University Press, Cambridge, MA; William Heinemann, Ltd., London. 1925.

Zahn, Drew. "Pastor waits for final word in Bible study citation: Couple ordered to get permit to host friends not out of woods yet. " *WorldNetDaily* Posted: June 01, 2009 10:07 pm Eastern.

_____. "State moves to restrict Catholics in politics. Official contends church must register as 'lobbyist' to speak out." *Faith Under Fire,* Posted: June 01, 2009 9:30 pm Eastern, *World Net Daily.*

Christian Books in Multiple Genres. Join Christian Indie Author ~ Readers Group on Facebook.
https://www.facebook.com/groups/291215317668431/

*Integrity without knowledge is weak and useless,
and knowledge without integrity is dangerous
and dreadful.*
Samuel Johnson

Christians, unfortunately, believe that science is an enemy. There is good reason, since most who use the word "science" have completely abandoned Johnson's demand that integrity go hand in hand with knowledge, replacing truth with selective evidence which supports preconceived conclusions. Christians should not develop either an antagonism toward true science or ignore the very real contributions of true science. Neither should true scientists ignore the very real foundation of science in Christianity. Dennis Prager, anthropologist and historian, laments the unthinking reliance on pseudo-science in today's society.

> "In much of the West, the well-educated have been taught to believe they can know nothing and they can draw no independent conclusions about truth, unless they cite a study and 'experts' have affirmed it. 'Studies show' is to the modern secular college graduate what 'Scripture says' is to the religious fundamentalist."

Empire Saga by Michael J. Findley (Also available as five separates short stories and novellas, including the *Space Empire Trilogy*)

Look at the future of persecution. One day soon the only refuge for the faithful may be Space. Follow a desperate couple fighting isolation and equipment malfunction to pilot a gas-collecting balloon ship to the outer planets. Michael, crown prince of the Space Empire hopes to save his people from external attack with an internal rebellion and a battle cruiser like no other. His plans are shaken by a forbidden romance, political turmoil, and the discovery of Earth's Fourth Empire. Michael and his best friend Randolph might save or shatter the Space Empire's last hope for the future.

Michael's crystals had their fire change from red to blue to green and back to red again. With each change the fire grew weaker.

"Discovery to Earthpost Q."

"Earthpost Q."

"Your father's quit waiting on the Lord. The Occidental outpost has twelve SSTs assembling a particle beam gun. It's Imperial, Michael. Your father set us up. I don't have a chance."

"Is it operational?"

"Yes, but it's not fully charged yet."

"Destroy it."

"I'm by myself. The only way I can fly and fire at the same time is to route the fire control through the forward directional sensors."

"Do it."

"I'll kill everyone down there. There's over a thousand people there, mostly women and children."

Nehemiah, LLC (This book takes place between *Sojourner* and *Empire One: Humiliation* in the Space Empire Universe.)

Why doesn't Tony know what a paper cup is? What is it about a "Glop Drop" that kids can't resist? How can Joan keep the goats where they belong? And, most important of all, can Tony and Joan make the launch window to see the Sojourner on its way to the outer planets?

No light sabres. No warp drive. It's more like the real thing -- an Apollo mission plus floating farms plus Martian underground parks. "It won't fail because of me" takes on a whole new meaning.

from *Chapter Nine: The Task*

"So we can move people in three or four days?" asked Anthony.

"Well, after we finish sandblasting..." said Joan.

"So this is sandblasting?" asked Anthony.

"Well, he can say something besides 'How long will this take?'" said Joan. "You spend your entire life dreaming up ways to give other people work. Stick around and do some of the work yourself. Let me give you a list. We could do more sandblasting. There are at least a hundred projects that need enlargement. If that's not to your taste, we could fill with foam insulation, finish rooms, weld, install furniture, work on making the roof of the production area open to the surface, enlarge the life support systems to cover the new area, synthesize more air and water, transport materials..."

"I really like one thing you said," interrupted Anthony. "That's the 'we could' part."

The Baron's Ring by Mary C. Findley

Prince Tristan tumbles a hundred miles downriver and a world away from his kingdom. How does cloak bartering get him a place in impoverished Larcondale? Why does his best student suddenly disappear from the tiny school?

Disaster might blot out his last hope for love and a future. Will he survive his confrontation with a Witch Queen in the King's Hole?

For wickedness burneth as the fire: it shall devour the briers and thorns, and shall kindle in the thickets of the forest, and they shall mount up like the lifting up of smoke.
Isaiah 9:18

"Do you mind if I continue on a little way?" Tristan asked casually. "I thought I heard voices up ahead, and there's that cursed smell of smoke again."

"All the more reason you should come back with us," Alex said firmly. "None of your men are out here at this time of day. I can't pretend to hear what you're talking about, or smell it either, but if there is someone out there I don't want you here alone."

Tristan drew the sword he always carried when he left the estate, again, in spite of Mayra's protests. "Alex, men are coming this way. I have no idea how many, but it sounds like at least twenty. They're still a mile or two off. As you say, they aren't ours, but I do hear sounds like armor and swords clashing. I need you to take the Lady Mayra back to the house and bring some of our men as quickly as you can."

"I can't leave you here!" Alex cried.

"I can't run," Tristan said desperately. "I can try to hide, and I will, but I have to know that you're taking Mayra to safety."

Benny and the Bank Robber by Mary C. Findley

Benny Richardson and his widowed mother have to move to his uncle's Missouri farm. John Clancy saves them from a sinking barge and when his mother is injured agrees to get Benny to Missouri. But a bag of disguises, a long, sharp knife, and too many secrets to make him anything but a safe traveling companion.

A fleeing bank robber, a savage black stallion, and a "cougar evangelist" all play a part in Benny's journey to accept of God's will when it isn't at all humanly sensible or safe. Benny faces an implacable bully and finds a long-lost treasure from his dead father.

from *Chapter Three – "He'll Go Far!"*

"How come you stopped the barge if you already had a good horse? And why were you hiding that black bag under your saddle?" Benny kept talking, so fast that Mr. Clancy couldn't have answered his questions if he had wanted to. And he certainly didn't seem to want to.

"It looked just like the bag Mr. Carlisle put on the train -- and the one that man in the black suit was carrying. What was in all those bags? Or -- was that you pretending to be somebody else again? Were you the one that killed that man at the bank and stole the money?"

Mr. Clancy had been staring at him all this time without moving. Suddenly he jumped forward and grabbed Benny. He covered Benny's mouth with one hand and with the other pulled out a big, long knife. Holding Benny so tight it hurt, he laid the knife up against his throat and whispered in his ear.

"I guess you do get to go along with me, after all, Benny my boy," he hissed. "But somehow I don't think we'll make it to Uncle Tom's. The chickens'll be so disappointed."

Benny and the Bank Robber 2: Doctor Dad

A new marriage for Benny's mother should be a time of rejoicing. But why is Uncle Tom so angry? While substitute teaching for his mother Benny meets twin girls who turn his world upside down.

A terrifying mystery at a private boys' school in Detroit includes gambling, extortion and attempted murder. Benny makes the mistake of trying to impress members of a secret society, discovers he may have a double, and hopes to survive a meeting with someone who may already have murdered to enforce his will.

from *Chapter Fifteen -- "An Ultimatum"*

That night Benny took one more look through his footlocker. Suddenly he noticed a slip of paper tucked into his winter boots. He pulled it out and opened it.

"The box is the key. Use it to unlock the door to the cat." At the end was a symbol Benny recognized as the Greek letter Omega. Like lightning, Jason leaped across the room and slammed Joseph down on the floor.

"You're the one who stole it!" Jason snarled. "I knew it all the time. We want it back right now!"

"Make him get off of me, or you'll be sorry!" Joseph squealed to Benny.

"Let him up, Jason," Benny ordered. "Joseph, I guess you don't want to be expelled, do you? I just want my cougar skin back. I don't want any trouble."

"You can't prove I had anything to do with that note or your -- cougar skin," Joseph said with an oath. "You can tell me now what's in the box. Then they'll let you know what they want next."

Benny and the Bank Robber 3: The Oregon Sentinel

Ben Carlisle's longtime dream has been to travel west with his family. When he is offered a newspaper job in Detroit, he is forced to question whether moving west is really God's will for him. Can he leave behind his grandfather, the girl he thought he loved, and an opportunity few writers could even dream about? Can he risk the life of one of his best friends, or face an old enemy head-on? What price will he have to pay just to make his writing live?

from Chapter Two -- A New Partner and an Old Enemy

A giant man on a huge buckskin gelding suddenly clambered up out of the gully behind the bush. He pulled up sharply and scooped Sarah up with his long, powerfully-muscled arm. Ben's mother gratefully took Sarah from the newcomer. Sarah giggled delightedly and reached up as if she wanted to ride up into the air again.

"Thanks, Mister," Jeremy said as the man lifted his wide-brimmed tan hat. "I'm Jeremy Carlisle, and this is — "

He broke off sharply and Ben came up beside him as Caleb Sutter looked slowly around at them.

"I guess I know who you are." His blond hair trailed long as an Indian's down his broad back. His shirt hung open and an intricate beaded choker clung to his corded neck. Caleb turned his head slightly and Ben saw a jagged scar running from where his left earlobe should have been halfway down his massive chest.

"I saw your names on the roster, so this wasn't exactly a surprise for me," Caleb went on as the family remained speechless. "Bet it was for you, though. Let me try to make this trip easier for all of us. I'll do my job, and you'll take care of your family, Doc. I don't want to dig up any stuff that's been buried. I sure don't want any trouble. Boss Tibbs relies on me, and what was between Ben an' me — well — Just do me the favor of keeping out of my way as much as is humanly possible so I can keep out of yours."

Hope and the Knight of the Black Lion by Mary C. Findley

(Also available in the "Illuminated Version," echoing the style of a medieval manuscript. "Home to My Father: A Knight's Tale," is a stand-alone excerpt from this novel.)

Seventeen-year-old-Hope rebels against arranged marriage in medieval England. The earl's handsome son Robert tempts her to defiance. A mysterious knight appears to help Hope find her missing family. Does Hugo Brun de March truly travel on a Holy Quest?

What is the a strange diary the Arab Sadaquah gives Hope? When her protector is captured she discovers a plot to subvert English law and justice.

from *Chapter Eleven*

"Sir Knight. I hear that thou wilt not say thy name nor thy true business to anyone."

"It is a vow I have made, that Baron Cloyes must be the first in England to know of these things. "

"Man, thy story might turn my heart completely to thy cause," Lord Godwin said.

"It matters little now, my lord. " Sir Chris coughed several times. "The earl has said I am to be made to confess to the burning of the manor house. To that I cannot confess, and so ... Lady Hope?"

"Yes, Sir Chris?"

"I am sorry I could not help you," he said in a voice I could scarcely hear. "I am sorry, too, that you were not persuaded to know Christ."

Chasing the Texas Wind by Mary C. Findley

Hamilton Jessup agrees a sham marriage with socialite singer Maeve Collinswood. This beautiful spinster needs a handsome wounded war hero husband to show off at Texas fundraisers. Ham has no choice, but they both have secrets to keep from each other.

Ham was supposed to ignore her frequent disappearances. Falling in love with her changed all that. His discovery that their secrets are connected plunges both of them into a race to outwit whoever is supplying arms to Mexico as the countdown ticks away toward the Battle of Monterrey.

from *Part One, between June, 1844 and March, 1845*

"Hamilton?" Maeve said suddenly.

"Yes, Ma'am?" Ham asked.

"The story you told about Goliad," Maeve said, looking pained, "Was it some sort of alcoholic raving or did you tell a true tale?"

Ham looked away. "A true tale, Ma'am," he said. "I could never be intoxicated enough to show so much disrespect to the memory of that event as to fabricate a tale about it."

"Thank you," Maeve said.

Send a White Rose by Mary C. Findley

Leah Masters came to the New Mexico Territory hoping to make a "mail order match" with handsome Judge Bartholomew Durant. She fainted at his feet and when she woke up discovered she had stepped into an assassination plot with her hot-tempered brother as the prime suspect.

Who does Bart Durant trust when facing revolution theology and a still-unknown assassin? How can he ignore the sudden realization that his heart might already belong to someone else besides the woman he still thinks is a stuck-up weakling?

from *Chapter Two*

Bartholomew caught sight of a half-wild rose climber in the chapel garden. *White roses.*

"You -- you know *la Señorita* Alethia at the Orphanage? I am sure ... she would give you a sweet ... if you ... pick the prettiest white rose on that bush over there and take it to her."

"It is a good thing I have my *burro,* or I would not go. It is a long way. I will be back later, but I will not have any more time to waste on you, dead man. I hope you will be quiet, like the other one is."

Bartholomew did not answer, and the footsteps shuffled away.

Carrie's Hired Hand by Mary C. Findley (Novella)

Carrie Wilkes is the Northern widow of a Southern soldier in the middle of the Civil War. Robert Salinger may be handsome but his promise to take care of Ben's family rings hollow as she struggles alone with the farm work. She is grateful to give a deaf and dumb stranger work for food and a place to stay. Southern soldiers come with accusations of spying. Robbie's "secret code" might spell terror for Carrie and her children.

"God bless you ... for all you've done, Rob," Ben whispered, half-opening his eyes and gripping Robert's shoulder. The handsome young man continued his work, but he stared at Ben with the same look of intensity he had given Carrie. "You're ...that friend that ... sticketh closer than a brother ... the Scriptures ...talk about."

Robert produced a canteen and Carrie gave Ben a drink. He choked and groaned. "Carrie, I don't ... want to leave you ... alone like this," Ben said when he could speak again. "All alone."

"I'll look after them, Ben," Robert said suddenly, gripping the dying man's shoulder. "As God is my witness. This was my doing, and I will take care of your family."

"The work's got to get done ... " Ben said faintly.

"It will," Robert promised. Carrie couldn't help wondering how this slight young man, dapper in spite of the filth around them, was going to help get the farm work done.

"You give me the Lord, Rob," Ben said. "Try to give Him to my Carrie, an' my babies too."

Carrie strained to hear. What Ben had just said didn't make any sense. Robert nodded.

"I will try," he said softly.

Biblical Studies Curriculum by Michael J. and Mary C. Findley

(Student and Teacher Editions) Bible Study aids for children, homeschoolers, and adults. Commentary, Review Questions, Free Videos on YouTube. Bible Doctrines, children's whole book studies of Jonah and Ruth with 3D puppet commentary, Proverbs, Adult studies in the New Testament and Major Prophets background, featuring more than 30 videos in the Revelation study alone, Old Testament and New Testament Manuscript History

The Conflict of the Ages Series

Newly revised and expanded homeschool books. Combined teacher manual for books 1-3 covering

Creation to the Flood and Ice Age plus three separate student manuals. *I: The Scientific History of Origins, II: The Origin of Evil in the World That Was, and III: They Deliberately Forgot: The Flood and the Ice Age.* by Michael J. and Mary C. Findley

Science, History, Literature reunited. Eyewitness testimony and the real scientific method. Read ancient manuscripts, search the world, and discover truth instead of buying into preconceptions. When did time begin? Who are the Sons of God? Did ancient Establishments of Religion construct cultural controls and make man a god? Rediscover the Worldwide Flood and the truth about the Ice Age.

It's tough, but you need this exhaustive worldwide study of evidence, investigation, and exalting the Scriptures as the ultimate authority. There was one eyewitness to the beginning of the universe. It might surprise you to know how much of His truth has been preserved, and how many struggle today to put that truth in the hands of teachers and students.

A Dodge, a Twist, and a Tobacconist, The Alexander Legacy Book One: by Sophronia Belle Lyon

The Alexander Legacy Company is on the track of a ruthless enslaver of souls. Prowl the foggy London streets. Encounter a nightmare from the Indian jungles.

Travel the Thames in Sluefoot Sue's Giant Catfish. Soar on a stealth glider with a Bohemian prince. When Oliver Twist unwraps the Algerian mummy at Charley Bates' funeral, will he discover his real enemy? Or is it all just another "dodge"?

"He's going to ram Twist's ship," Kera breathed. "They'll both crash into the house and Mrs. Rose just might have her bomb going off."

I ran along the edge of the roof as if I were looking for a shot. But I already knew my pistol was empty, useless, and the guard was trying to get around another gable to get a clear shot while staying behind cover. I had come to a conclusion a moment earlier that I dared not say out loud lest I be grabbed and thrown down on the roof by both women, but I knew what I had to do.

Just as the spy craft hove around the corner of the house, only a few feet away from the airship, I launched myself off the roof. The smaller ship disappeared and my heart leaped in panic at the thought of being sliced into quarters by the tail rotor. But my fingertips caught hold of a solid object. I found the fuselage of the spy ship and wrapped my legs around it. The thing slewed and spun and began to fall tail-first toward the green lawn.

The Alexander Legacy Book Two: The Pinocchio Factor, by Sophronia Belle Lyon

Can Oliver Twist trust Spring-heeled Jack when he offers to "bodyguard the little'un"? Do costume balls conceal more than the faces of the wealthy and powerful? Trevor Newsome disappears just days before the election but the Legacy Company can't search for him from the London Lockup. When the trip to Switzerland finally becomes a reality, it's for a funeral, not for a wedding.

Quests for immortality meld with the worship of powerful men, with terrifying and tragic consequences. When Long John Silver arrives, Oliver has to think fast to protect more than just his own life from the pirate who says he only cares about rescuing his daughter.

"Twist! Look out!" I spun and swung wildly as the crack of a Colt revolver split the air. Sluefoot Sue had both her firearms out and was shooting at something below me. To my astonishment tentacles rose out of the Thames and wrapped themselves around the Catfish. Each time one of Sue's bullets struck them they disappeared under the water again, but when she paused to reload they re-emerged and began to reach for me, climbing the Catfish sub. I hastily winched myself over toward the dock but a tentacle grabbed hold of my leg just as I started to set myself down. It flung me down on the dock and started dragging me to the edge.

"Hey, boss lady!" Dobbs, Sue's assistant, hollered out from inside the workshop. I was just able to see a pump-action shotgun cartwheel through the air and land in Sue's gloved hands. Just before it began to blast me deaf, I realized that it was in fact no ordinary shotgun, rather had some sort of gattling action, and a bit more. I hoped I would get a better look at it rather than end up 20,000 leagues under in some sea monster's maw.

Write for the King of Glory

Share the fruits of my first five years of publishing. Learn about blogging, writing, cover design, editing, marketing, and find a bunch of great resources to help you in your publishing journey, many of them free. I'm not the be-all and end all of Christian publishing, but I'm here to help, and so are a bunch of other Christian writers and service providers.

I'm living proof that you can get your book published. It doesn't have to stay in those pre-publication versions, or be taken out of your hands and changed to the point where you hardly recognize it. God educated me through some amazing preparation and hard times to the point where I realized that it's up to me to make my books. Nobody's going to do it for me. At least not so that I can control it from start to finish, or within my mostly nonexistent budget, or on my timetable.

So, I have learned to be a cover designer, an editor, an ebook formatter, and everything else I need to create my own books. I have also learned some things about online marketing, to the point where we have regular monthly sales that continue to grow.

Sample our longer works with free excerpts of full-length titles. All our publications are linked on our blogs.

Elk Jerky for the Soul includes posts on current issues, excerpts from our fiction and nonfiction works, Bible teaching, travel and everyday observations, and more. http://elkjerkyforthesoul.wordpress.com/

Visit our tiny but mighty website, which features basic information about Findley Family Video Publications and changing special features at http://findleyfamilyvideopublications.com

Visit our YouTube Channel http://www.youtube.com/user/ffvp5657. Watch Jonah and Ruth as well as "Sojourner," part of the Space Empire Saga, in full 3D animation, book teasers, and upcoming projects related to biblical study and the Conflict of the Ages.

Science, History, Literature, and biblical worldview studies are the focus of our book and video projects.

www.ingramcontent.com/pod-product-compliance
Lightning Source LLC
Chambersburg PA
CBHW070105290526
45789CB00005B/1927

* 9 7 8 1 4 9 9 7 2 6 0 2 2 *